D1480491

296.73 Horowitz, Roger
HOR

Kosher USA

DATE DUE   MAY 2 1 2016

**PLEASE
DO NOT REMOVE
CARD
FROM POCKET**

HUDSON PUBLIC LIBRARY
3 WASHINGTON STREET
HUDSON MA 01749

KOSHER
USA

ARTS AND TRADITIONS OF THE TABLE
PERSPECTIVES ON CULINARY HISTORY

ARTS AND TRADITIONS OF THE TABLE

PERSPECTIVES ON CULINARY HISTORY

ALBERT SONNENFELD, SERIES EDITOR

For a list of titles in this series see page 305

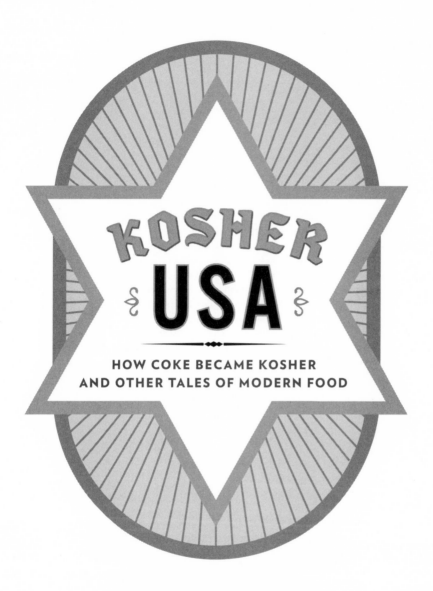

KOSHER USA

HOW COKE BECAME KOSHER
AND OTHER TALES OF MODERN FOOD

ROGER HOROWITZ

Columbia University Press New York

Columbia University Press
Publishers Since 1893
New York   Chichester, West Sussex
cup.columbia.edu
Copyright © 2016 Roger Horowitz
All rights reserved

Library of Congress Cataloging-in-Publication Data
Horowitz, Roger, author.
Kosher USA : how Coke became Kosher and other tales of modern food /
Roger Horowitz.
pages cm. — (Arts and traditions of the table: perspectives in culinary history)
Includes bibliographical references and index.
Summary: "The history of how a set of ancient laws and
regulations adapted to modern practices of American food production
and foodways"—Provided by publisher.
ISBN 978-0-231-15832-9 (cloth : alk. paper) — ISBN 978-0-231-54093-3 (e-book)
1. Jews—Dietary laws. 2. Kosher food—United States.
3. Jewish cooking. I. Title.
BM710.H675 2016
296.7'30973—dc23
2015026798

Columbia University Press books are printed on permanent
and durable acid-free paper.
This book is printed on paper with recycled content.
Printed in the United States of America
c 10 9 8 7 6 5 4 3 2 1

Cover design: Jim Tierney

References to websites (URLs) were accurate at the time of writing.
Neither the author nor Columbia University Press is responsible for URLs
that may have expired or changed since the manuscript was prepared.

TO MY UNCLE STUART SCHWARTZ,
WHO MADE ALL OF THIS POSSIBLE.

CONTENTS

KOSHER
USA

PROLOGUE

UNCLE STU'S QUESTION

UNCLE STUART, my mother's oldest brother, religiously attended the holiday parties at her Manhattan apartment with his wife, Doris—on Christmas Day (brisket, not ham, was on the table) and for the Passover Seder. As they aged, it became harder and harder for them to participate, but, because of Stu's stubborn perseverance, they came nonetheless. Aunt Doris went through a long struggle with Parkinson's disease that progressively deprived her of control over her body—and eventually the ability to speak. Stu went to great lengths to bring her, even after he developed incurable bone cancer, and could no longer lift Doris into a taxi as he once had. The last time I saw Stu, at the 2005 Christmas Day party to which my mother invited friends, business associates, and family, the visit was especially difficult. Without the aide who was spending the day with her family, Stu had pushed Doris's wheel chair a mile in a bone-chilling December rain (draping it with clothes and large garbage bags to protect her) from his Upper West Side apartment to my mother's place on 72nd Street.

When they arrived, Stu was only good cheer—not a word of complaint. We pulled out my mother's slivovitz (a powerful plum liquor popular among our Romanian ancestors) and drank several shots; he asked after my son and talked about the Spanish lessons he was taking. I told stories and didn't ask after his health or Doris, knowing the answers already and not wanting to dent his upbeat mood. It got late, and Stu's younger brother Ernest offered to drive him and Doris home; Stu tried to demur, but, we insisted, the rain had not stopped. As Doris could not stand, and

Stu no longer could lift her, I was enlisted to help. So we went downstairs, and I carried Doris from her wheelchair into Ernie's SUV and then helped Stuart get in before returning upstairs to collect the raingear he had used earlier. On an impulse, I grabbed the one advance copy I had received of my new book, *Putting Meat on the American Table* and gave it to Stu in the car. I rode back to his apartment so I could help move Doris inside; we had a chance to talk about the book for a short time before I walked back to my mother's place. I think we both sensed that this might be the last time we would see each other.

A day or two later, he called my mother about the book; she rang a few days later to relate the conversation. He had read it, said he liked it, but wanted to know why I didn't write about kosher meat. After all, it was part of our heritage and should have been part of the story that I was seeking to tell—and he would like to talk with me about it.

We never had that conversation—Stu died a few days later. But his question stayed in my mind, even if the opportunity to talk with him again was gone. It was a profound question (befitting a person whom my father once called "the smartest man he ever knew") that stirred my mental energies—Stu was asking, in essence, was it possible to write about the modern food system and ignore kosher food? Did kosher food fit into the industrial methods that now delivered so much food to our society? Or was it in some way marginal, excluded, unimportant in modern secular society? What did that answer say about the place of Jewish traditions in American culture? His question also pointed to how I might bring something unusual to an answer—personal experience growing up in a kosher household, and the scholarship to conduct the necessary research. Much as this Christmas evening left a riveting impression on me, it was Stu's intellect and insight that put me on to this project for almost a decade—not sentimental obligation; and I think that was what Stu would have wanted.

Shortly afterward, I related these thoughts to my colleague and friend Arwen Mohun, who caught the edge of the issue when she blurted out that Stu's question fundamentally was about religion and modernity. How could a set of practices and beliefs rooted in antiquity persist, and in some ways flourish, but at the same time also struggle to survive in a society ineluctably shaped by different religions and belief systems? Her insight only reinforced to me the value of answering Stu's question.

FIGURE 0.1 Stuart Schwartz and the author, Passover 2005. Personal collection of Roger Horowitz.

But as I started my research, I found a simple, uplifting narrative largely in place, a celebration of kosher food's increasing acceptance among food manufacturers and appeal to a largely non-Jewish population. Relentlessly promoted by Lubicom, the public relations firm behind the Kosherfest food trade show, and then given extended form in several books and articles in major media outlets, the story was that of kosher food's success and incorporation into the American supermarket. And, indeed, there was a great deal of truth to this narrative, as the first half of *Kosher USA* will detail.

Yet as a historian I was suspicious of just how tightly this success story worked, how all roads seemed to lead to its fulfillment. By their nature, historians are wary of Whiggish stories in which events of the past inevitably lead to a singular outcome. And quiet alarm bells start to go off when the sources used to document these processes had a stake in the conclusions of the books and articles that relied on their recollections. I began to suspect that rather than the previous histories of kosher food discovering an outcome, they had been guided to one that was only partially true.

To more fully answer's Uncle Stu's question, then, I had to take readers into unfamiliar territory by closely exploring key historical episodes in the intersections of kosher law and modern food production in the twentieth-century United States, the technology and business arrangements so entailed, and the accommodation—if at all—of kosher requirements with the methods used to make conventional food. The story that emerges in this book therefore focuses on kosher food and its place in the American food system in the industrial era of mass production and distribution; its encroachment, conquests, and exclusions. It explores how in many places kosher requirements could be internalized by food manufacturers, especially after post-1980 regulatory requirements and production control technologies increased incentives and reduced costs for doing so. But it also traces the regions where kosher food could not be assimilated into mainstream food production, instead relegated to its margins and rendered virtually invisible to non-Jewish consumers.

Chapter 1 draws out the implications of a family argument over sturgeon to explain the development of Jewish law as it pertained to food, and defining what was "fit and proper"—the proper translation for *kosher*—for Jews to eat. Chapters 2 through 5 chart the expansion of kosher food in twentieth-century America, and with that the remarkable success of the Orthodox (a small minority among Jews) to insert a particular interpretation of kosher requirements into the practices of a secular food system. Chapters 6 through 8 strike a more troubling tone, containing as they do tales of turbulence and decline with the far more attenuated relationship between our food system and the kosher requirements for wine and meat, especially the controversies over *shechita*, the Jewish requirements for slaughter of animals. The conclusion details the countervailing pressures on kosher food by modernist notions of ethics—and, correspondingly, Jewish practices—as we head into the twenty-first century.

Creating this account required a research strategy that departed from the focus of previous books on a set of usual suspects, largely contemporary kosher food industry leaders and insiders. Instead I went looking for the silences and the stories that the kosher food's "success" narrative squelched by its very cohesiveness. I found pieces of a fuller, more complex, and at times more disturbing history by combing through archival collections, reading obscure trade journals, interviewing people once influential but now forgotten—and through the memories of my family.

Historians usually abjure their personal family history as a source; in my case such an approach simply was not possible. Inspired by Uncle Stu's question, family memories bubbled out of conversations with my mother and father as my research proceeded. Stories of their own experiences, their parents, and even grandparents surfaced as I recounted to them what I had found in the archives. These conversations deepened in intensity as my parents' health began to fail, and, much as in my last encounter with Stu, the charged question "how are you feeling" unleashed unpleasant emotions. We knew what was happening; so, rather than dwell on that pain, my mother and father talked about the past and encounters with kosher food in their younger days in that process of life review so common among the elderly coming to the end of their lives. My grandparents, many years gone, came alive again in those stories; and I had to think of them in a different light than I had as a child, seeing them instead as subjects in the historical account that I was writing. And, of course, we talked about my book, which gave them so much pride, especially after Columbia University Press offered a publishing contract in September 2010.

Shortly afterward the end finally came. A month after I signed the contact, my father informed me that cancer had spread into his lymph nodes; two months later he was dead. At the same time, my mother began to lose her long fight with chronic obstructive pulmonary disease; she died exactly a month after my father. It was uncanny that my parents, divorced for forty years and living two thousand miles apart, came to their ends so close together. They also each made me executor of their complex estates, duties for which I put aside this book for over two years.

My parents' deaths in the middle of writing this book did not change it into a personal account; it remains a work of history. But it was impossible for the searing experiences of our conversations amidst their decline to not affect my writing profoundly. The many stories that passed between us conveyed so much and allowed me to bring in the experiences of my family at many points. Told often over meals, and later sitting next to a sick bed, these family stories forced themselves into my research and then into this account by their very relevance. Most of these experiences were prosaic, unexceptional, if not "typical," certainly representative of some sections of the Jewish population. Indeed, their mundane features were their great value: everyday experiences of some Jews with kosher food. And, as I reflected on my parents in the aftermath of their passing, many of my own childhood memories of our kosher home seemed more vibrant, more pointed, and, as Stu so keenly realized, assets that I could draw on to write this book.

The very differences among my family—some Orthodox, some Conservative, some nondenominational—taught me something essential about kosher food and modern Jewish history. My family often did not agree about kosher food; their experiences with it differed markedly, and their stories showed how kosher food could be a source of conflict as well as community. While kosher food may be central to Jewish experience, disagreement over what it was and what it meant is vital to its history. Arguments mattered as much as shared meals. But still, much as my family squabbled about what was kosher (and if keeping kosher mattered), kosher food nonetheless remained at the center of our identity as Jews, a touchstone of our relationship to Judaism, an indelible marker of the space between our pasts and our futures.

1

MY FAMILY'S STURGEON

FOR MANY years my mother's family traditionally broke the Yom Kippur fast with a lavish meal at her parents' home. Her father Charlie had done very well as an attorney active in the movie business and, along with his wife Bertie, enjoyed hosting large events at their capacious Central Park West apartment. A few years before I was born, my mother's new husband brought his parents Abraham (we called him Abe) and Florence (whom we did *not* call Flo) to join the Schwartz clan's meal. After the usual round of early 1950s cocktails, the group moved to the dining table, only to see a sturgeon laid out for the fish course. As Orthodox Jews, Abe and Florence were horrified. There was no question among the rabbis they followed that sturgeon was forbidden for Jews to eat. End the Jewish High Holy days by sharing a table with a *treif* animal? Unacceptable!

The result was a family confrontation, which I learned about over fifty years later from my father and mother. In his firm voice, Abe announced that he was not going to sit down at the table with a *treif* fish. Charlie, an articulate adherent of Conservative Judaism, vigorously defended sturgeon as kosher. References to Jewish law and fish anatomy flew back and forth across the room in front of anxious—and quite hungry—children and relatives. To preserve family peace (but also not conceding the point), Charlie had the sturgeon removed so that his in-laws would sit down and the meal could begin. After all, sturgeon had been a source of disagreement among Jews for one thousand years, and an answer was not to be found on an empty stomach.

FIGURE 1.1 Author's family, Waldorf Astoria Hotel, June 1955, on the occasion of his parent's fourth wedding anniversary. From left to right: Louise Horowitz, David Horowitz, Stuart Schwartz, Doris Schwartz, Ernest Schwartz, Florence Horowitz, Charles Schwartz, Bertie Schwartz, and Abraham Horowitz. Personal collection of Roger Horowitz.

The case of my family's sturgeon offers a starting point to appreciating kosher law's complexity and its place in the Jewish faith. "Judaism is fundamentally a way of life," Bertie and Charlie astutely observed in their 1947 book, *Faith Through Reason*.[1] Defining what food is fit and proper for Jews to eat reflects Judaism's concern with practice and how its rules seek to embed observance in seemingly mundane routines. However, among a people scattered throughout the Western world, periodically uprooted by eruptions of anti-Semitism, ever encountering new climates, animals, plants, and foods, "daily life" was not a stable category. Judaism's very concern with the practical and ordinary made kosher law engage with the endlessly complex profane world, in many places and in many cultures, repeatedly generating debates in which the rabbis of the past were interrogated to understand the complexities of a highly varied present.

Kosher law begins with the Jewish Torah, the five books of Moses—Genesis, Exodus, Leviticus, Numbers, and Deuteronomy. As the foundation of Judaism, the spare phrases in these books were the source for all future definitions—and disputation—over kosher food's boundaries. Distinguishing clean from unclean in the animal kingdom is first explained in Leviticus 11:3 through 11:47 and then repeated in Deuteronomy 14:4 through 14:20. Understanding sturgeon started here, with the requirement in Deuteronomy 14:10 for acceptable animals "that live in water" to have "fins and scales."[2] Sturgeon seemed to have both—but determining its kosher status turned out to be a lot more complicated.

What complicated matters was the forced transformation of Jewish society with the Roman destruction of the Second Temple in 70 c.e. and the deportation of most Jews from what had been their homeland. A religion constituted around devotion and sacrifices at a central temple survived by becoming the Rabbinic Judaism that holds sway today, a religion defined by widely decentralized forms of observance adjudicated by an ecclesiastical caste. New rules elaborating acceptable behaviors and practices, promulgated orally, were redacted (written down) into two collections over the next five hundred years, one developed by the rabbis who remained in the historical lands of the Jews and the second cataloged by the thriving Jewish society in Baghdad, where many had taken refuge. Of these, the latter Babylonian Talmud would become the enlarged foundation of Jewish law for a civilization bound by a set of beliefs and practices. Composed of the Mishnah, a set of concise rules, and the Gemara, a record of rabbinic debates over those rules, the Talmud runs over five million words and forms the principal basis for the *halacha*—Jewish law.

From this watershed two different types of requirements would enter the *halacha*—biblical commandments, based directly on the Torah and rabbinic elaborations of those commandments deemed necessary to buttress observance. Rabbis became judges, with the authority to *pasken* (rule) on whether a particular practice was acceptable under Jewish law—such as whether it was permissible to eat sturgeon. Not all Jews accepted this profound change in their religion; the most durable dissenters, the

Karaite sect, rejected rabbinic authority and with it the Talmud. But the vast majority of Jews followed the rabbis, and the consolidation of Judaism into a religion defined, above all, by the everyday practices expected of its adherents, rather than the exceptional obeisance performed at a central shrine.

With the concern over everyday practices came a necessary elaboration of many terse statements in Leviticus and Deuteronomy. To return to my family's sturgeon: as Jews dipped their nets into new rivers and seas far from their original lands, what were their rabbis to make of the fish they caught? Pulling unfamiliar fish out of nets made the biblical rule hard to interpret—what was a fin and what did it mean to have scales? The Mishnah, reflecting rabbinic opinions of the second-century C.E., clarified the aquatic anatomical requirement by defining fins as appendages that helped fish swim and scales as flat material attached to the fish's exterior. The Gemara's commentaries on the Mishnah, redacted in the sixth century, had more to say because of questions raised about new varieties of fish caught by Jews, probably mackerels and sardines. Fish without scales when young were acceptable if they grew them later, as were fish that shed scales once caught. Scales also received a more exacting definition, as equivalent to *kaskasim*, from 1 Samuel 17:5, which described the Philistine champion Goliath wearing "a breastplate of scale armor"—also translated as a "coat of mail."

Sturgeon still seemed to fit. They had fins in abundance, along with several rows of tough protuberances running up and down their sides. Yet were these *kaskasim*? Scraping them off with conventional fish knives was impossible; the sturgeon's "scales" were so deeply embedded in the flesh that doing so also tore the skin. The biblical analogy—the term *kaskasim*—did not provide a self-evident analogy. Certainly a person could easily doff a coat of mail and keep their skin intact; seen in that light, the sturgeon's protuberances were not scales. But a coat of mail was composed of many individual small metal pieces that could not be removed from the coat without irreparable damage. Could this perhaps also explain the sturgeon's outer layer?

Close arguments over the text's meaning were shadowed by a deeper dilemma for kosher law—the challenge of *minhag*, or local customs. A people who spread through the trading towns of the Mediterranean basin

FIGURE 1.2 Sturgeon. J. G. Woods, *Natural History Picture Book* (London: George Routledge, 1867), 66.

of Europe, North Africa, and the Middle East, often in very small and widely dispersed settlements, naturally experienced wide divergences in dietary practices. With rabbis having authority to approve foods as kosher, so long as those decisions could provide a clear source in the Torah and Talmud, Jews could develop varied customs without feeling they were departing from their faith. Their rabbi approved—how could there be a problem? Local divergences were overlaid with a profound split of Jews into two discreet religious communities—the Sephardi who lived under Muslim rule, and the Ashkenazi in Christian Europe. Determining acceptable foods became bound up with the larger issue of whether to accept local *minhagim* (plural of *minhag*) and, if not, how to eliminate them.

The great problem of standardizing observance among a dispersed people motivated Rabbi Moshe ben Maimon, the great Jewish thinker known as Maimonides or the Rambam, to compile his remarkable work of Jewish law, the *Mishneh Torah*, in the late twelfth century. Seeking to quiet the cacophony of opinions among rabbis, his controversial work avoided references to past opinions and instead presented a digest of Jewish law—and with the Rambam's spin. Some Ashkenazi were deeply offended at the pretension of a Sephardi living in Egypt determining, without references, the corpus of Jewish law; a few European Jewish communities even burned copies of the *Mishneh Torah* in protest.

The Rambam's restatement of Jewish law on permissible fish varieties added an important requirement, that scales should be removable. Certainly this could be read to strengthen the case against sturgeon, as its protuberances were so tough that typical fish scalers were ineffective. But, in a separate ruling, Maimonides permitted Turkish Jews to consume sterlet, a species of sturgeon found in the Black Sea. An earlier twelfth-century ruling by the French *halachic* authority Rabbeinu Tam (Jacob ben Meir) similarly permitted Turkish Jews to eat sterlet. Sturgeon thus remained ambiguous, generally out of favor among Ashkenazi Jews, but acceptable in some places among the Sephardim.[3]

Despite Maimonides' assertion that, with the *Mishneh Torah*'s publication, "a person will not need another text at all with regard to any Jewish law,"[4] it did not become authoritative. Ignoring other rabbinic opinions and only including his own conclusions in the text offended many contemporaries. His method was fundamentally at odds with that of Ashkenazi rabbis influenced by Rashi, the immensely popular eleventh-century French rabbi Shlomo Yitzchaki, whose commentary on the Torah and Talmud is widely used today. Rashi's school became known as the *Tosafot*, literally the commentators, for their emphasis on extended exploration of the Talmud's texts. Beginning with the early printings of the Talmud, publishers would place Rashi's commentary on one side of the main text and the combined observations of the Tosafot rabbis on the other. By seeking to avoid a discussion with other texts, Maimonides became just one voice among many—a powerful voice to be sure, but not the last word on Jewish law.

A far more influential effort to standardize Jewish law came from within the commentary tradition. Rabbi Joseph Caro, one of the great Jewish thinkers of the Middle Ages and a Sephardic Jew (like Maimonides), had both an encyclopedic mind and a systematizing temperament. Caro followed the model of an earlier effort to summarize

Jewish law, the *Arba'ah Turim* (often referred to simply as the *Tur*) completed in the fourteenth-century by Rabbi Jacob ben Asher (known as Rabbeinu Asher) whose father was part of the Tosafot school. The *Tur* restructured summaries of Jewish law into four "rows"—daily life, dietary laws, marriage, and civil and criminal law—rather than follow the Talmud's organization. Caro first wrote a massive review of the *Tur* called the *Beit Yosef* before publishing a far shorter summary in 1542 that he called the "set table"—the *Shulchan Aruch*. Benefiting from the arrival of the printing press, it circulated widely within the Jewish world over the next few decades.

Caro consolidated much of current Jewish law regarding food into the section of the *Shulchan Aruch* called the Yoreh De'ah; henceforth all debates about kosher food in some way trace back to this work. Initially, however, Caro's effort generated a round of new controversies. His principal sources for rabbinic opinions were Rabbi Asher ben Jehiel (father of the *Tur*'s author and known as the Rosh), Maimonides, and Rabbi Isaac Alfasi—one Ashkenazi and two Sephardim; when they disagreed, Caro adopted the majority opinion, giving his decisions a decidedly pro-Sephardic cast. Caro also dismissed many Ashkenazi *minhagim*, viewing these local iterations of Jewish law as inconsequential at best and at odds with Jewish traditions at worst.

Polish rabbi Moses Isserles (known as the Rama) was one of Caro's most formidable critics; but his very differences would make the *Shulchan Aruch* widely accepted. Rather than author a separate volume, he wrote a line-by-line commentary called the *Mapah*, or the "tablecloth," which he placed on top of the "set table" of the *Shulchan Aruch*. In so doing, Isserles created a combined volume integrating Sephardic and Ashkenazi views that would have authority throughout the Jewish world. His success also reaffirmed Jewish law as an ongoing debate among authorities. Subsequent volumes of the *Shulchan Aruch* contained the often conflicting opinions of both Caro and Isserles; over several centuries the book grew to accommodate additional rabbinic commentaries, generating ever more expansive editions. (Interestingly, the incomplete English translations of the *Shulchan Aruch* summarize the text without distinguishing between Caro, Isserles, and other commentators.)[5]

FIGURE 1.3 A page from the 1873 edition of the *Shulchan Aruch* published in Vilna, Lithuania, that illustrates how the original text by Rabbi Joseph Caro appeared in dialogue with commentaries by other rabbis. The largest text in the upper center is from Caro; it is interspersed with sentences in fine type that are Rabbi Moses Isserles's comments on Caro. On either side and at bottom in smaller type are later rabbinic commentaries. S. I. Levin and Edward Boyden, *The Kosher Code of the Orthodox Jew* (New York: Hermon, 1975), frontpiece. Courtesy University of Minnesota Press.

Creating the *Shulchan Aruch* as a dialogue also maintained sturgeon's disputed status within the Jewish world. In section 83:1 of the Yoreh De'ah, Caro simply restated Maimonides opinion that scales were the "peels" set into the skin. Isserles extended this argument by specifying that such peels only qualified as scales "if they can be peeled off by hand or with an instrument." In the event they could not be removed, such protuberances were not *kaskasim*, and thus the fish was not kosher.[6] Isserles thus drew from the explicit statements in the Torah and Talmud to indicate more firmly that sturgeon were not kosher. Caro was more cautious, limiting himself to Maimonides, and leaving room for permitting sturgeon.

Consequently, the seemingly authoritative *Shulchan Aruch* did not finally settle the matter of whether my family could sit down and eat sturgeon to break their fast. The ambiguity resurfaced vigorously in Jewish law two hundred years later when Rabbi Hirsch Segal sent an actual sturgeon to the widely respected chief rabbi of Prague, Ezekiel Landau, asking him to *pasken* whether it was kosher. Residents in his town of Temesvar, Romania, had asked Rabbi Segal to determine if this fish, which they consumed regularly, was kosher—and he wasn't sure. Siegal specifically asked Landau if the Atlantic sturgeon was equivalent to the sterlet permitted by the Rambam and thus acceptable for Jews to eat.

In his responsum, Landau explained that the fish had *kaskasim* that could be cut off by a knife and pulled off by hand after soaking in a lye solution. Going back into kosher law, he noted that the Talmud did not specify that scales needed to be removable to qualify as *kaskasim*, and this requirement was a *humra* (interpretation) added by the Rambam. In Landau's opinion, it was not necessary to go beyond the Rambam's views and, since he did not specify that it was not permissible to soak a fish before removing the scales, using this method was in accordance with the requirements of the Talmud. Landau also compared the sturgeon with pictures of the sterlet, and determined that with regard to kosher law, these were the same fish. For both reasons, then, sturgeon was once again kosher.[7]

Landau's opinion generated enormous controversy, especially after his death when his students continued to defend his ruling. One opponent, Hungarian rabbi Isaac Girshaber, even resorted to outright fraud.

Determined to suppress the practice of eating sturgeon, Rabbi Girshaber claimed he had received a letter from Rabbi Landau before his death recanting his acceptance of sturgeon and asking Grishaber to forward the letter with his revised views to Rabbi Siegel's congregation in Temesvar. When no such letter could be procured, Rabbi Girshaber claimed it must have been lost in the mail and that the copy he had kept could not be found. The letter's convenient disappearance naturally generated new rounds of accusations; the consensus among those who have explored this incident is that Girshaber simply lied, so determined was he to suppress the great sin of eating sturgeon.[8]

Girshaber's fraud did not end the debate about sturgeon. Two decades before the fish provoked an argument among my grandparents, the rabbinic journal *Ha-Pardes* included sturgeon among its list of kosher fish, citing among other sources Rabbi Landau's late eighteenth-century opinion. Continued debate afterward among Orthodox Jews provoked a powerful intervention from Rabbi Moshe Tendler, who drew on his scientific training to argue that the sturgeon's so-called scales were not in fact scales, as they were composed of animal fibers different than the scales on approved fish. Conservative Jews such as my grandfather were unconvinced; in 1967 the Rabbinical Assembly of the Conservative movement commissioned Rabbi Isaac Klein to prepare a *teshuva* (ruling) that once again affirmed sturgeon to be kosher.[9]

The exchanges over sturgeon generated striking acrimony for disagreements over a fish peripheral to most diets, Jewish or otherwise. In a private letter, Rabbi Tendler condescendingly advised Rabbi Wolf Kelman, executive vice president of the Conservative's Rabbinical Assembly, that it was his ignorance of Jewish law regarding sturgeon that allowed him to adopt positions at odds with the will of God. Kelman, for his part, explained he had recently had some delicious sturgeon during a trip to Eastern Europe and ridiculed Tendler's "piscatorial preoccupation" with the status of a fish. He also lamented his participation in a debate over such a trivial matter at that particular historical moment, thinking perhaps of the assassinations of Martin Luther King Jr. and Robert Kennedy not long before the August 1968 exchange with Tendler.[10]

My mother shared with Rabbi Kelman the view that there was something overwrought about the "sturgeon debate" given the state of the world. Perhaps she had a point, but for the grandparents who argued over whether a sturgeon had scales much more was involved than simply whether it should be on the table. Seeking answers in the Torah, Talmud, *Mishneh Torah*, *Shulchan Aruch*, and the many rabbinic rulings of the past brought Jews of one era into conversation with those who had lived before them. Charlie and Abe, despite their argument, drew from the same sources, ranging back to Jews living in fifth-century Baghdad, twelfth-century Egypt and France, fifteenth-century Poland, and seventeenth-century Prague. The Rambam and Ramo were not merely ancestors, but deeply respected compatriots whose lives and opinions were present in the way Abe and Charlie thought about the world. Those arguments, moreover, forged a powerful intellectual tradition of attention to text, argument—and the world itself.

Kosher food, then, brought Jews together, not only to share a meal but to sustain connections within a group that was a small minority of the world's population and dispersed, for the most part, among many nations for thousands of years. Arguments, however heated, were intrinsic to that lineage; the simple act of arguing over sturgeon among family members affirmed Jewish traditions. And, by removing the fish, Charlie and Bertie avowed that, despite their disagreements with Abe and Florence, we were family, willing to set aside differences to confirm our greater membership in what it meant to be Jewish.

The complications of sturgeon, however, would be dwarfed in the twentieth century by what to make of modern food. At least a fish could be looked at and examined; how to understand products with many ingredients, invisible and unidentified? The Jewish sages of the past would be hard-pressed to offer unambiguous answers to Jews seeking to understand the challenges of the modern era.

2

KOSHER COKE, KOSHER SCIENCE

PASSOVER WAS a very special occasion for me as a child. My big moment, in what often seemed an interminable reading of our Passover Haggadah, was reciting the Four Questions (first in English, then in Hebrew), each of which asked how this night was different from all other nights. To the four answers (this night is different because . . .) I could have offered a fifth—I got to drink Coca-Cola in those ceremonial moments when the adults downed glasses of wine.

In my family of the early 1960s, Coke was only available on special occasions, such as Passover, or at the Sabbath meals held at my mother's parents' house. Otherwise, we drank milk, water, or juice. That was it. But as a child, I of course never wondered how Coke achieved the status of a drink acceptable on this Jewish holiday where observance of kosher rules was so important. Not until I began researching the history of modern kosher food did I understand how this came about.

I quickly learned that other scholars had looked at how Coca-Cola became kosher and began with those sources. The standard account had a comforting narrative and a decisive ending. In 1935 Atlanta Orthodox rabbi Tobias Geffen interceded with Atlanta-based Coca-Cola as a result of inquiries from rabbis in other cities as to the *kashrus* (kosher status) of this popular drink. After careful investigation of its properties, Rabbi Geffen suggested a couple of changes in the drink's composition that were accepted by Coke for a special Passover run of the product. Subsequently, as Marcie Cohen Ferris explains, "Observant Southern Jews breathed a sigh of relief" as they could both be kosher for Passover and still enjoy an "ice cold Coke."[1]

The closer I looked, however, the more holes appeared in this reassuring tale. Documents from the Coca-Cola archives showed that Coke had received rabbinic endorsement in 1931, and from a rabbi based in Chicago. If this was so, then why did Rabbi Geffen get involved at all? Newspaper articles showed that controversy still swirled around Coke's kosher status in the late 1950s, shortly before I began drinking it at my family's annual Passover Seder. These discrepancies pointed to a far more interesting, and profound, process of certifying kosher Coke, one that not only involved this signature beverage but also exposed one of the major challenges for proponents of kosher food in the mid-twentieth century: how to integrate concepts rooted in centuries of Jewish tradition with modern food chemistry. The struggles over Coke's kosher status involved not only the drink itself, but the terms under which modern foods' kosher status should be evaluated, what was necessary to do so, and what kind of knowledge was needed to assess a manufacturer's claim that its products did, indeed, satisfy the requirements of traditional Jewish law. In this, Rabbi Geffen had to overcome the resistance of rabbis for whom such scientific knowledge did not seem necessary to determine if Coke was indeed kosher.

It turned out that Coke, as one of the first iconic American foods to seek kosher certification, was a testing ground for how kosher law could change modern food—and how, in turn, modern food would change the practice of kosher law. The debates sparked by certification of Coke taught Jewish authorities that they needed to assimilate modern food chemistry and understand ever changing manufacturing methods to assess a product's compliance with kosher law. While Rabbi Geffen limited his intervention to Coca-Cola, contemporaneous initiatives by Organized Kashrus Laboratories, and its creator, Abraham Goldstein, generated a broad effort to incorporate scientific knowledge into the kosher certification process. In the end, it was the dynamic engagement of rabbinic authorities and food companies that yielded kosher Coke and opened the door to the widespread expansion of kosher food in America.

OF COCA-COLA AND GLYCERIN

For Rabbi Geffen, the challenge of certifying Coca-Cola was only a small part of his service to preserving Judaism and strengthening observance among Jews. His unpublished memoirs do not mention this episode, instead dwelling on his many personal interventions to help Jews— ensuring the meat provided by local *shochetim* was in fact kosher, developing Hebrew education for local Jews, securing a *get* (religious divorce) for women whose husbands had left them, and aiding a Jew who had been shockingly sentenced to eight years on a Georgia chain gang. Geffen's special role in the case of kosher Coke reflected his location in Atlanta and the wide respect in which he was held among the networks of Orthodox rabbis in the United States.

Born in Kovno, Lithuania, in 1870 (at that time part of Russia), Tobias Geffen came from a deeply religious family that sent him to the yeshiva in Slobodka, Lithuania, a prestigious institution of higher Jewish learning in Europe. After ordination, he studied with several of Lithuania's leading rabbis before marrying and deciding to emigrate to America in 1903 following the Kishinev pogrom and the rise of anti-Semitic violence throughout Russia. After stays in New York City and Canton, Ohio, Geffen settled permanently in Atlanta in 1910. While his main responsibility was care of his congregation, Geffen was one of the few European-trained rabbis in the American South, with both his credentials and activities bringing him to the attention of Orthodox rabbis throughout the United States.

As he was the leading Orthodox rabbi in Atlanta, Coca-Cola's headquarters, letters came to him from rabbis across the United States wanting to know if Coke conformed to Jewish dietary law. While Rabbi Geffen was not solely responsible for Coke's eventual acceptance among observant Jews, he did correctly identify the main challenges. To determine Coke's *kashrus*, he of course needed to learn what it contained—a subject jealously guarded by the company, eager indeed to keep its famed "secret ingredient" a secret. Promising complete confidentiality, Geffen obtained access to Coke's manufacturing operations and had samples tested by impartial chemists.

FIGURE 2.1 Rabbi Tobias Geffen. Louis and Anna Geffen family papers, box OP11, Emory University Manuscript, Archives and Rare Book Library.

The main problems turned out to be alcohol and an odd trace ingredient called glycerin. Coke used alcohol in the manufacturing process, though there was no residue left in the final drink. During most of the year this would not have posed a problem for observant households; but Passover was special. Grain provided the source for the alcohol, thereby violating the Passover rule against eating leavened bread during that special week. Drinking Coke that used grain alcohol in the processing stage was as unacceptable on Passover as placing a loaf of bread on the table. Fortunately it was not difficult for Coke's manufacturers to obtain alcohol from fermented molasses, thereby addressing one of Geffen's objections.

Glycerin posed a much more intractable problem. Essentially an industrial by-product, glycerin assumes independent existence during the processing of fatty oils for soap. It is simply the predominant chemical left in the residue created after the soap is extracted. In Geffen's view, glycerin's kosher status depended on the oil from which it came—and most of the oil used to create it was derived from animal sources, livestock bones, fats, and other parts unacceptable for food consumption. In the late nineteenth century large packinghouses developed rendering operations that boiled inedible parts into a viscous liquid sold to soap manufacturers. Such efficient use of by-products was a source of profit and also reduced the volume of foul refuse extruded from these plants. As kosher-slaughtered animals comprised only a small proportion of animals killed in a plant, it was not economical for the company to separate their bones from the body parts of nonkosher carcasses. Given this industrial practice, Geffen concluded that glycerin was *treif*.

But it was present in Coke in only minute quantities, less than 0.01 percent. Did such a minor ingredient necessarily make Coke *treif*? Kosher law, in fact, contained a permissive set of rules known as *bitul* (nullification) that held out the possibility that the glycerin in Coke could be considered *batul*—nullified—as it was such a small quantity in a large mixture. Under traditional kosher law, *bitul* provides that when a small amount of a nonkosher ingredient accidentally ends up in a mixture its *kashrus* is not affected. As the most prevalent cases of *bitul* apply when the offending ingredient is no more than one-sixtieth of the mixture and does not affect it materially (known as *bitul b'shishim*), its intent was to address simple mistakes in the kitchen. Could such a concept apply to Coke?

With careful reference to traditional Jewish law, Geffen ruled that glycerin did not qualify for the *bitul* exemption. Basing his opinion on a ruling by the twelfth-century French rabbi Samuel ben Meir (known as the Rashbah) and the endorsement of this ruling by Moses Isserles in the sixteenth-century Yoreh De'ah, Geffen held that *bitul* applied only in cases where the mixing of troubling chemicals "was accidental, fortuitous, or unpremeditated." Because the addition of glycerin was "normal procedure" and essential to Coke's manufacture, the resulting mixture was *treif*. For these reasons Geffen held that Coke was not kosher.[2]

Glycerin's widespread use in processed foods and beverages made determination of its status an issue that affected many more products than simply Coke. Since it has never aroused controversy (except among observant Jews!), glycerin's role in our food system is not well known.

Glycerin is hygroscopic, hungry for water or other liquids, and slightly sweet and syrupy at room temperature. With these qualities, glycerin permeates our foods, makes sliced bread stay fresh and cakes remain moist and crumbly—as well as keeping antifreeze and our car windshield washer fluids from freezing! In fact, a 1945 book on glycerin listed over fifteen hundred uses for this amazing chemical. Its kosher status thus posed enormous challenges for food companies using it in a wide array of products.[3]

Coke, it seemed, could not do without glycerin—though glycerin certainly was not its famed secret ingredient. Indeed, as glycerin "finds wide employment in the preparation of base extracts for flavoring purposes,"[4] it is most likely that Coke's secret concoction was dissolved into a glycerin solution so that the taste would diffuse evenly through the syrup shipped to bottling plants. And Coke was not alone in its dilemma: all soft drink manufacturers, indeed all food manufacturers that relied on bottled flavors, had traces of glycerin in their products.

Geffen may have realized that a lot was at stake with his decision on glycerin. At issue were not only the kosher status of Coke and other products containing glycerin, but, even more, the application of *bitul* to all modern processed food. If glycerin could be nullified under the principle of *bitul b'shishim*, what other substances could attain the same exemption? Might this create an avenue for loosening kosher requirements for other ingredients that were present in foods in minuscule quantities? Fundamental questions of kosher law and modern food were at stake.

Geffen's *teshuva* (ruling) reflected a stringent application of kosher law. Plausibly he could have ruled differently, since glycerin did not impart any noticeable taste to Coke and comprised far less than one-sixtieth of its volume. By those measures, Geffen could instead have held that the principle of *bitul b'shishim* did apply and that glycerin's presence was thus irrelevant to Coke's *kashrus*. Instead, Geffen looked at processing methods and deduced that glycerin's importance in processing meant its *kashrus* was in play. By doing so he endorsed the integration of modern scientific knowledge into kosher law—and created a kosher headache for food manufacturers.

Cottonseed oil offered a fortuitous solution for the problem of non-kosher glycerin. Since it was a vegetable product, it could serve as source for kosher glycerin. Cottonseed oil production grew steadily throughout the South in the early twentieth century as a shortening that offered an alternative to butter and lard, with firms such as Procter & Gamble and Lever Brothers developing vegetable oils for home use under the brand names Crisco and Spry. Procter & Gamble already supplied Coke with glycerin, so with Coke's considerable leverage the company agreed to refine a special batch of cottonseed oil–derived glycerin to create kosher Coke. Rabbi Geffen inspected the factory making vegetable glycerin in July 1934; satisfied, he placed his "seal on the drums containing this ingredient." With acceptable glycerin and alcohol secured, the rabbi issued his famous teshuva in time for Passover in 1935. In subsequent years he relied on affidavits from Proctor & Gamble executives to ensure that the glycerin used in Coke "was made from vegetable sources and no animal fat."[5]

This is where our happy story should end, with American Jews reassured by Rabbi Geffen's *hecksher* (endorsement) on Coke bottle caps that they could now drink Coke on Passover. And indeed, when it came to Coke, all seemed fine—at least for the next twenty years. But the extension of Rabbi Geffen's ruling was another matter; Coke was hardly the only processed food attracting the attention of observant Jews. Rabbi Geffen did not become involved further determining the kosher status of other processed products; that initiative fell to a lay Jew whose efforts would provide the underpinnings of American kosher certification organizations.

THE INVISIBLE CHEMIST

Parallel to Geffen's involvement with Coke, a more comprehensive attempt to apply chemical knowledge to kosher certification was taking shape in New York City under the leadership of Abraham Goldstein. A devout Orthodox Jew and a chemist by trade, Goldstein appreciated the complex challenges of certifying kosher food long before many rabbis whose knowledge of kosher law was rooted in foods made in nonindustrial settings. Deeply concerned that Jews would stray from the religious practice of *kashrus* because of modern food's allure, Goldstein devoted his life to strengthening the capacity of Jewish organizations to enforce kosher law. While not alone in his efforts, Goldstein was distinguished by the degree of his devotion to seeing chemical knowledge incorporated into the practice of kosher certification.

Goldstein's activities are utterly absent from the official Orthodox accounts of the origins of kosher certification in America. The documentary evidence makes abundantly clear that he was the principal architect of the Orthodox Congregation's (later the Orthodox Union) kosher certification program in the 1920s and 1930s. A member of its executive committee, he was the first person to bring charges against food vendors who violated New York State's kosher food regulations; OU sources also credit Goldstein with devising its strategy of certifying national firms who sought to sell kosher food. He negotiated the first such agreement with Heinz foods in 1923 and oversaw the creation of the famous *U* within a circle symbol for its use. As he later recalled, the company "thought it impossible to use the insignia of the Union, which had 'Kosher' in Hebrew letters." By 1929 he had cemented agreements with several other firms including the Loose-Wiles Sunshine Biscuit Company, Sheffield's dairy products, Duggan's breads and cakes, and the Jaburg Brothers' vegetable fat company.[6]

Yet his name does not appear anywhere on the Orthodox Union website, nor in accounts of its history. The most egregious erasure of Goldstein's role takes place in the Orthodox Union's official history, published in 1997 by longtime staff member Saul Bernstein. Drawing from the same documents I perused, Bernstein overlooked the references to Goldstein as chair of the OU's Kashrus Committee, the accolades he received in speeches delivered at OU conventions, and his official position as the OU's chemical expert.[7] These silences about Goldstein's role more than fifty years after his death reflect both the controversies he provoked and the deep emotions he aroused in his efforts to integrate scientific knowledge with traditional Jewish law.

It took information supplied by his grandson and great-grandson to fill in important details of his life. Born in 1861, Abraham Goldstein was raised in East Prussia, at the time part of Germany, just south of Lithuania and its great center of Jewish knowledge, Vilna. He was a well-educated man before he joined the enormous wave of Jewish immigration to America in the late nineteenth century. While it is unclear how Goldstein learned chemistry, Germany was the center of this emerging

FIGURE 2.2 Abraham Goldstein (sitting) with daughters (left to right) Clare, Sarah, and Rebecca. Courtesy Ezra and Monica Friedman collection.

scientific field, and there would have been abundant opportunities for him to do so. He arrived in New York in 1891 and, after brief sojourns in Baltimore and New Jersey, settled in the Washington Heights neighborhood of Manhattan where he pursued various opportunities using his training as a chemist. A devout man, he tried to work with the Agudath Harabonim (the Union of Orthodox Rabbis, an association of European-born rabbis) to improve *kashrus* standards in New York and participated in successful efforts to pass legislation in the 1910s that brought kosher food under state regulation.

It was only in the early 1920s, following many years of efforts to improve kosher standards, that Goldstein shifted his considerable energies to the Union of Orthodox Jewish Congregations, a New York–based network of Orthodox synagogues seeking to create a central organization for the Orthodox strand of Judaism throughout America. After a decade of behind-the-scenes efforts with food manufacturers, Goldstein tried to reach out to observant consumers in the early 1930s by starting a "Kashruth Column" in the *Orthodox Union*, the Union of Orthodox Jewish Congregation's monthly magazine. Billed as the Rabbinical Council's "chemical expert," Goldstein provided concrete answers to questions about particular products, and offered to investigate when he did not know the answer.[8] The magazine's small circulation limited the column's effectiveness; usually questions from only six or so letters were addressed in each. Soon Goldstein would find a better vehicle for reaching observant Jewish consumers.

Disagreements between Goldstein and Orthodox rabbis over the role of science in kosher certification simmered throughout the 1920s and early 1930s and came into public view shortly after he founded the Organized Kashrus (OK) Laboratories in 1935. Constituted formally as an organization to advise rabbis on food science, OK's free English-language journal, the *Kosher Food Guide*, gave Goldstein a platform to make his views widely known in Jewish circles. The first sentence in its March 1935 opening editorial was a clarion call for the importance of scientific knowledge in kosher certification. "The rapid changes in the process of manufacturing of new articles of foods," he declared, "made it necessary to investigate the ingredients contained therein as well as the method of fabricating to ascertain if they do not contain trefa [*treif*] substances in itself or come into contact with such during the process of manufacturing." Accompanying his robust appeal was a warning that rabbinic authorities previously had not appreciated this need. He wrote that in the past "such investigations were unfortunately not entrusted to chemists," with the result that rabbis "were misled to state that the article in question conform[ed] to the Jewish Dietary Laws." To the "opposition to our work," he affirmed that in fact the same end was served, the expansion of kosher food options "in a variety equal to non-Kosher food" such as "to strengthen Judaism."[9]

The *Kosher Food Guide* offered comprehensive lists of kosher food products as well as articles on *kashrus* issues Goldstein deemed important. As the most comprehensive source of information on kosher-certified food, the publication was extremely popular among observant Jews; in 1938 Goldstein noted that he received thirty to forty letters daily regarding the *kashrus* of particular products. With its focus on science, and its offer to serve as a chemical laboratory that could test food provided by any rabbi, Goldstein forced the issue of the relationship between modern food science and traditional kosher law. And, with his platform, he aggressively criticized rabbis who, in his opinion, had placed their *hecksher* on food products without making sufficient effort to understand their underlying chemical composition.

WORRIED KOSHER CONSUMERS SPEAK OUT

To establish a dialogue with the observant Jewish public in the pages of the *Kosher Food Guide*, Goldstein started a column called "Questions and Answers" modeled on his "Kashruth Column" in the *Orthodox Union*. Unlike the *Orthodox Union* journal, however, the *Kosher Food Guide* was a widely distributed publication funded principally by advertising whose circulation quickly rose from 50,000 to 150,000 copies of each quarterly issue. The popularity of the guide's "Questions and Answers" column was apparent in the torrent of letters sent to it from all over North America. The January 1937 issue plaintively noted that over twenty pages of questions had to be omitted due to space limitations. In a column published a year later, Goldstein answered forty-six letters sent from Toledo, Baltimore, Detroit, Philadelphia, Tulsa, Burlington (Vermont), Jessup (Pennsylvania), Carlsbad Springs (Ontario), and Atlantic City, as well as New York City. Some correspondents wrote several times, such as Mrs. M. Evans in Corsicana, Texas, who wanted to know if Gold Dust cleanser was kosher (after writing the manufacturer, Goldstein determined that it was not).

The correspondence with Goldstein indicates that concern over Coke's kosher status was part of a larger phenomenon: observant Jews' desire to sample the packaged foods carried by the new retail food chains such as A&P. Jews continued to patronize shops operated by coreligionists, especially for fresh items such as beef, chicken, and bread, but increasingly visited the chain stores to see what new foods were available. Women were not yet replacing home-cooked meals with convenience goods; instead, they were seeking to understand which of the new packaged goods were permissible under kosher law.

FIGURE 2.3 "Refreshing hallah, sponge cake, and cookies for Sukkos." Advertisement for Pillsbury Best XXXX Flour, *Americaner*, October 18, 1919, 20. Collection of Shulamith Z. Berger, courtesy National Library of Israel, Jerusalem.

Worries about popular brands indicate the impact of chain stores on shopping patterns. Mrs. A. D. Simpson of Brooklyn, New York asked whether "White Rose Products canned, in jars, or bottles" were kosher, as did Mrs. R. J. Kalfen of Perth Amboy, New Jersey, the latter also inquiring about Campbell's soups. Many questions concerned Ann Page products, A&P's private label, such as those from Mr. S. Applebaum, who asked about the entire line. "Your question is too general," Goldstein replied to his query "as there are Kosher and trefa products packaged under this trade name."[10] Befitting his care with kosher certification, Goldstein asked for identification of specific products before offering an opinion.

The longer letters indicate what observant Jews were seeing on store shelves and probably including in their families' diets. Mrs. J. Finkelstein from Cleveland wanted to know if Kellogg and Ralston cereals were acceptable (they were), whether Crisco and Spry shortenings could be used for cooking (they could), whether paprika and vanilla could be added to food (under some conditions), if Kraft's Miracle Whip and A&P ketchup could go onto sandwiches (yes), and whether Hershey Chocolate Syrup and A&P fruit cocktails could be included with desert (both were acceptable, though Goldstein warned that some Hershey chocolates contained milk). Mrs. William Packer from Brooklyn worried if the Zwieback crackers, lady fingers, cereal, and canned vegetables that she was feeding her baby were kosher for Passover. Goldstein kindly advised Mrs. Packer that these items were not, recommending using matzoh meal instead and steaming her own vegetables. He admitted that perhaps these would be "tedious" to make, "but what mother minds a little work for her baby."[11]

Goldstein's positive responses to Mrs. Finkelstein were unusual; more often his correspondents were disappointed by what they learned from him about popular products. *Treif* ingredients ruled out Gerber baby food, Kraft Velveeta and American cheese, most white breads including Wonder Bread, and popular crackers such as Ritz, Graham, and Uneeda. Some flours, a few brands of ice cream, and most varieties of peanut butter were acceptable, as was Aunt Jemima pancake mix. Wrigley's chewing gum and Milky Way candy bars were kosher; but Dentyne gum and Baby Ruth bars were not. Goldstein moderated these disappointments by offering alternatives such as Dugan's baked goods (including their white bread), Loose-Wiles Sunshine crackers, Reid's Kosher Ice Cream, and the Heinz line of canned goods (including baby foods), as well as the foods made by Jewish companies such as Rokeach and Manischewitz. To Jews interested in Italian and Chinese foods, he was able to find kosher suppliers, recommending Skinner's macaroni to Mrs. B. Fasman in Oklahoma and Toy Fong Chow Mein noodles to Mrs. D. Coplan in Pennsylvania.

The simple questions contained in these letters communicated the worries and frustrations of observant Jews seeking food for their family to eat at home or to enjoy in a public place. Much as they might want to buy the same food as Christian Americans, observant Jews realized that many appealing products did not comply with the requirements of their religion. They could look, but dared not touch. The emotional conflict between longing for and resentment of these products must have been enormous, especially for the families whose children might want a treat at Coney Island or a soda at a baseball game.

Frequently glycerin was the problematic ingredient, as small amounts appeared in many products. Goldstein warned that flavorings for ice cream and soda drinks often contained glycerin and that vanilla extract and almond paste, commonly used in baked goods, similarly "very often contain glycerine." Glycerin was a huge problem for popular candies; Goldstein advised that "licorice candy very often contains glycerine" and that candies manufactured by Schraft's, Barricini, and Fanny Farmer included many "where glycerine might be used." He also worried that, with the incessant changes in production methods, glycerin was showing up in more and more foods, such as the new artificial sausage casings that were reaching the market in the mid-1930s.[12]

Glycerin's use in nonfood products created challenges as well. Mrs. E. Ackerman in Brooklyn learned that "some lipsticks contain glycerine," and, since glycerin coated many varieties of cellophane, Mr. R. Neuman was advised to "taste the cellophane paper. If it is sweet, glycerine has been used." Even cleaning one's teeth was worrisome. "Most dentrifices are prepared with glycerine," Goldstein informed Mrs. Naomi Klein in Richmond Hills, New York, and he told Mr. A. M. Feier that "most toothpastes contain glycerine." An observant Jew could not get a breakfast muffin, a sandwich, an ice cream cone, a candy snack, or even brush his teeth without encountering glycerin.[13]

Glycerin's importance was such that its *kashrus* was the very first controversy addressed by Goldstein in the *Kosher Food Guide*. In its second issue (published at the same time as Geffen's negotiations with Coke), he critiqued a lengthy memo by an unnamed author that contended glycerin could be kosher even if derived from nonkosher oils. The essay, originating from an unidentified firm that made glycerin, argued that glycerin was not actually in the oil from which it was derived, since it was only formed after a strong "chemical action." Hence the author

concluded that glycerin drawn from either meat or vegetabl[
was kosher.

Goldstein made short work of this argument. His rip[
straightforward: a food's *kashrus* depended on the material from which
it was drawn—the same position as Rabbi Geffen. Glycerin intrinsi-
cally was neither *treif* nor kosher; what mattered was its source. And
he ridiculed the unnamed author, pointing out that with his argument
"lard could be Kosher, because it is not in the pig as lard. Only when
it is subjected to a great heat it separates out as lard." For this reason,
Goldstein viewed all foods that contained glycerin as *treif*, including
Coca-Cola.[14]

Coke's *kashrus* (along with Pepsi's status) was the subject of repeated
queries. The problem, very simply, was that "Coca Cola is made with
glycerine," Goldstein warned Mr. Saul Weberman in April 1937. In 1939
Goldstein repeated this warning to Mr. L. Levy in Baltimore, and in 1942
to Mr. M. Schreiber in Philadelphia. Sounding weary, after responding
to dozens of letters on this topic, in June 1943 Goldstein wrote Miss
Elaine Weiss that "there has been nothing new discovered in regard to
Pepsi-Cola and Coca-Cola. We still maintain that both these products
contain glycerine."[15]

Goldstein was unmoved by Geffen's endorsement of Coke's special
Passover concoction, though he avoided explicit criticism of the rabbi.
He told Dr. Maurice Appel in 1938, "The hechsher given by the Rabbi
you mention in your letter does not alter the facts in this case. As we
ourselves do not drink Coca-Cola during the year, we certainly would
not drink it on Passover." In a longer essay on the continuing challenge
of glycerin in processed food, he indirectly criticized Geffen's method of
relying on Procter & Gamble statements to certify the glycerin used in
Coke. Goldstein declared that "the issuance of affidavits" (a reference to
the documents obtained by Geffen from Procter & Gamble) "stating that
only pure vegetable oils have been used does not deserve any credence."
Goldstein probably was not aware that Rabbi Geffen had personally
inspected the Proctor & Gamble factory in 1934 and thus had satisfied
for himself that there was no improper taste transfer between *treif* and
kosher glycerin during processing.[16]

FIGURE 2.4 Coca-Cola advertised extensively in popular Yiddish newspapers. In this one, Yiddish text on the awning reads, "Drink Coca Cola in Bottles." *Morgen Journal,* July 21, 1922, 3. Collection of Shulamith Z. Berger, courtesy National Library of Israel, Jerusalem.

THE PROBLEM WITH PARDES

The principal target of Goldstein's ire, however, was not Rabbi Geffen, but instead the first rabbi to issue a *hecksher* for Coke, Rabbi Shmuel Aaron Levi Pardes (1887–1956), editor of the influential Hebrew-language rabbinic journal *Ha-Pardes.* What Goldstein did not know is that in private

Geffen had waged a strong campaign against Pardes and the very same practices that Goldstein found objectionable.

In the 1930s Pardes was one of the nation's most prominent Orthodox rabbis. Born and educated in Poland where he established *Ha-Pardes* in 1913, Pardes moved to America in 1924 and settled in Chicago in 1927, where he reestablished the journal. It became the unofficial voice of the Agudath Harabonim. To finance the journal, Pardes accepted advertising from manufacturers whose products he certified as kosher, issuing a *hecksher* for a fee—and thereby generating a rather glaring conflict of interest.

Coca-Cola began advertising in *Ha-Pardes* in 1931. In March Pardes issued a teshuva, an official statement certifying Coke as kosher. In it he explained that he had visited Coke's Atlanta plant, where he learned about the "secret ingredients" in the drink. After investigating Coke's contents "from beginning to end," he declared that "everything is KOSHER according to the Jewish law, and this is a drink which is permissible for all Israel to drink." But, without any training in chemistry, and based on no more information than a visual inspection of the Cola-Cola plant, Pardes was not in a position to make such an authoritative statement.[17]

While Goldstein would become Pardes's most vocal critic, Rabbi Geffen was equally an opponent of Pardes's approach to kosher certification. Indeed, it seems that Geffen's decision to intervene in the certification of Coke was a deliberate effort to curtail Pardes's influence. Geffen had been profoundly concerned with Coke's *kashrus* since at least February 1927, when Abraham Nachman Schwartz wrote him with information supplied by Baltimore butcher David Chertkoff that Coca-Cola used glycerin, a fat "made of the refuse of things that are impure and prohibited." Startled by this disturbing report, Rabbi Geffen asked Georgia's state chemist to analyze Coke's contents. In May he learned, certainly to his dismay, that the allegation was true; the chemist certified that Coca-Cola contained 0.09 percent glycerin. At some point between then and 1932, Rabbi Geffen personally inspected Atlanta's Coca-Cola plant and confirmed that the drink did indeed contain glycerin.[18]

With this information, Rabbi Geffen must have been deeply disturbed by Pardes's unconditional endorsement of Coke along with the news that he had come to Atlanta and inspected the Coke facility without involving Geffen, Atlanta's leading Orthodox rabbi—a profound breach of rabbinic etiquette. Soon Geffen could see advertisements for kosher Coca-Cola in other newspapers, where local rabbis added their endorsement to the drink that was bottled in their area. Rabbi Morris N. Taxon certified Coke in Memphis, as did Rabbi Hersch Kohn in New York City; the national Hebrew-language weekly *HaDoar* carried Pardes endorsement as well as a message, "Rejoice in your festival with Coca Cola." Knowing that this so-called kosher Coke contained glycerin derived at least in part from pig fat, Rabbi Geffen planned carefully how to counter the claims of a far more prominent national rabbinic leader.[19]

Geffen first confronted Pardes privately by writing a series of letters in 1931 challenging Coke's certification. While those letters have not survived, Pardes's angry retorts have, and they illustrate the profound nature of Geffen's challenge. He accused Geffen of being the only rabbi to doubt Coke, as "there are currently rabbis all over the country who say it is kosher." And he asserted there was no glycerin in Coke, based on affidavits from Coke's Chicago chemist and the head of its Chicago operations, the latter promising Pardes "he would give me the whole factory" if Coke did indeed contain this troubling ingredient.[20]

Since Pardes would not budge, Geffen began to correspond with other Orthodox rabbis, expressing his doubts about Coke. In doing so, Rabbi Geffen could draw on the long rabbinic tradition that accorded primacy to the opinion of the rabbi who resided in the place where a questionable product originated. These letters had a dramatic impact. Many wrote to Pardes demanding an explanation, leading him to complain to Geffen that "there are now letters from all of the rabbis who provided kosher certification for Passover." Rabbi Hersch Kohn wrote to Geffen directly, apologizing for his acceptance of Pardes's certification and taking responsibility for his error. "I did not truly know," he explained, "that there was in there, in Atlanta, so great and distinguished rabbi as himself, and if I had known that before, I would have addressed your scholarliness in the first place, because I, for my part, did not go to the boundaries of investigating the opinion." Indeed, the great volume of letters sent to Geffen provoked him to issue his teshuva, as "it was very difficult for me to answer each of these inquiries." Geffen doubtless privately conveyed this furor to the Coca-Cola company and the value of making the changes he requested in Coke's chemistry so that none of this became public and impacted Coke's image.[21]

Rabbi Geffen kept the controversy as quiet as he could, even as he moved decisively—and successfully—against Pardes. But Geffen's intervention stopped here, his principal objective achieved; he was not inclined to extend the dispute into wider Jewish circles. Temperamentally, Abraham Goldstein had none of Geffen's circumspection. In the pages of the *Kosher Food Guide* he alleged publicly that the monthly advertisements from Coke and the fees garnered from issuing the *hecksher* had influenced Pardes's judgment. "Such men undermine the very foundation of our religion," he thundered. "There is no room for such scoundrels in decent company." Goldstein also had no leverage other than public exposure of practices he thought violated Jewish law. Since he was, by his own admission, "neither a rabbi nor the son of a rabbi," Pardes would not deign to debate him. Cloaked in his authority as a rabbi and editor of a leading rabbinic journal, Pardes continued accepting advertisements from companies he certified—and that offered even more controversial products.[22]

THE IMPROBABLE "JUNKET" CONTROVERSY

The heated arguments over glycerin paled next to the vehemence of the exchanges over rennet, an enzyme used in cheese manufacturing that typically came from a calf's fourth stomach. The origins of this explosive debate went back to 1926, when Goldstein (as the OU's representative) met with executives of the Hansen Laboratory to ascertain the kosher status of Junket, a powdery product that, when added to milk, created custardlike deserts. The company offered six flavors and aggressively marketed the product to mothers whose babies resisted drinking milk. The rennet that gave Junket its coagulating quality came from calves that were not kosher slaughtered. Nonetheless, the company claimed the product was kosher—because the offending rennet disappeared when the mixture transformed into a thick custard. Goldstein rejected their claim, taking the same position he would later articulate with regard to glycerin—that anything taken from a *treif* source remained *treif*. Over his objections, the company secured kosher certification from Rabbi Pardes and, similar to Coke, began advertising in *Ha-Pardes* trumpeting the claim that it was "kosher without any fear or doubt." Hansen Laboratories also bought large advertisements in Jewish papers and even launched a radio campaign that featured music sung by an Orthodox cantor.[23]

In 1936, with the *Kosher Food Guide* as his platform, Goldstein opened a withering assault on Pardes's certification of Junket. His adversary responded in kind with articles in his Hebrew language publication and by securing the Orthodox Union's backing for Junket (and leading to Hansen Laboratories placing advertisements in the OU's journal). This *"cause célèbre"* over an obscure product even spilled overseas, as Goldstein and Pardes wrote to influential European rabbis to secure their support.

Goldstein's diatribes on rennet were interspersed with further commentaries on glycerin, because to the chemist they presented the same challenge: how to track modern food production's introduction of *treif* ingredients into supposedly kosher food. Since rennet and glycerin had as their source animals that were not kosher, in his view nothing containing those chemicals could be kosher. With this argument, Goldstein made a critical claim (one that paralleled Rabbi Geffen's opinion): that *bitul* (nullification) could not take place with rennet, glycerin, or indeed any chemical derived from a nonkosher source that played an essential role manufacturing a particular food. His passion and unyielding language on the subject reflected a scientist's view that an essential principle of kosher law was at stake, even as he granted that Junket, in itself, "is of very small importance to the Jewish community."[24]

What worried—and infuriated—Goldstein was the blithe disregard for scientific knowledge in Pardes's and the OU's endorsements. They do not have the "ability to find anything in regard to the question of Junket," he declared, "because they do not know the least thing about the Chemistry of the article." He relied on food science, for example, to refute one of Pardes's defenses that the rennet could become *batul* because the company needed to add salt, sugar, flavors, and muriatic acid to it before it was effective. This was an important claim under kosher law; if indeed the rennet was not an active ingredient, the principal of *bitul b'shishim* would allow it to be nullified, as it comprised far less than one-sixtieth of the final product. And, if this was the case, Junket was kosher. Goldstein ridiculed this argument as one no rabbi would make if he were "acquainted with a chemist familiar with Dairy products." Meat processing companies added salt, muriatic acid, and occasionally boracic acid to the stomach, he explained, as part of a curing process to prevent its deterioration before extracting the rennet; those ingredients did not contribute to rennet's subsequent coagulating effect on milk. Since it was rennet, and rennet alone, that affected the milk, it was essential to the final product, just as glycerin was for Coca-Cola; hence it could not be nullified, and, similar to Coke, the final product was *treif*.[25]

Pardes's endorsement, however, rested as well on another element of kosher law—that the processing of the rennet had eliminated its *treif* origins entirely; thus the product was kosher to begin with! By making this startling claim, Pardes actually was following an accepted method of isolating a concept discussed in rabbinic commentaries and extending it to new situations. In principle, his approach was entirely, well, orthodox; but his conclusions had profound implications for kosher certification.

His source was impeccable—the opinions of the Rama, Rabbi Moses Isserles. Pardes made much of one of the Rama's rulings that when an animal's stomach was dried as hard as wood, milk could be carried in it as no taste or flavor would transfer. The Rama was concerned with a common practice in early modern agricultural communities of placing milk within dried calves' stomachs to create cheese, and whether doing so created the prohibited mixture *b'sar bacholov*, combining meat and milk in violation of the admonition in Deuteronomy 14:21, "You shall not boil a kid in its mother's milk." In considering this issue, the Rama assumed that both the milk and rennet came from kosher animals and that the stomach remained in a dried state throughout the process. Since the stomach used for this practice was dry, the Rama ruled that no flavor would transfer; hence an improper mixture did not result. With this precedent, Pardes contended that the Rama's comments supported his *hecksher*, and his argument that Junket was kosher, since the "taste" of the dried, powdered rennet added to milk did not transfer to the final product.

The notion of "flavor transfer" used by the Rama and Pardes translates roughly as *b'lios* and is a core concept of kosher law. "Under certain circumstances," Rabbi Zushe Yosef Blech explains in his exhaustive volume *Kosher Food Production*, "contact between two foods allows for transfer of flavor between them."[26] As developed over centuries, *b'lios* is a complicated concept whose application varies widely depending on the materials in question. While there were many iterations of rabbinic opinion, there was wide agreement that dry and hard materials posed much less of a problem than warm and wet ones. The core issue remained the transfer of flavor from one to the other, and physical properties largely determined what was likely to take place. Indeed, the Rama was not alone in suggesting that once a material was "dry as wood"—as the operative phrase usually read—it would not affect the *kashrus* of other foods; Pardes thus had reason to believe that he was on firm ground with his ruling.

Pardes rested his claim on European production methods "where rennet powder has been manufactured for the last 50 years." Missing from Pardes's assessment was an awareness of how industrial meatpacking operations in the 1930s bore little resemblance to those he referenced. Twentieth-century processing operations extracted rennet from stomachs that were neither dry nor kosher. An authoritative 1927 account explained that stomachs destined to yield rennet for cheese manufacturing were "held in a dry condition until needed for use, the juices [e.g., rennet] being extracted by placing [the stomachs] in a water solution." Drying thus only preserved the stomach until there was a need to remove the rennet, and which took place through a liquid process. Since the stomach was moist when used to supply rennet, and the rennet came from nonkosher animals, Goldstein argued that the Rama's commentary did not provide support for Pardes's certification. To him, it was yet another example of how traditional Jewish law could only be applied to current *kashrus* issues by incorporating knowledge of contemporary food production methods.[27]

Goldstein's quarrel with Pardes was part of a larger argument over the place of science in kosher certification and, with that, the role of lay Jews in this process. Under Jewish law, rabbis alone had the authority to issue a *hecksher* declaring a product kosher and only other rabbis could dissent from his decision once made. After Goldstein established his own journal, he had his own voice, and his dissenting opinions angered the Orthodox rabbinic hierarchy, which was offended by the presumption of a lay Jew questioning their judgment and, by implication, their authority.

By the late 1930s, leading Orthodox rabbis had lost patience with Goldstein. Pardes doubtless reflected sentiment among his peers when he complained to Hungarian rabbi David Schlussel, "Your honorable

Reverend has thrown his letter to common men who constantly shame learned educated men," after Rabbi Schlussel had responded favorably to Goldstein's query regarding rennet. Asking Pardes in print, "How much money has been paid for this false Hecksher," or the OU if any of its members "participated in the division of this money," did not help the tenor of the debate. The Rabbinical Council of the Orthodox Union backed Pardes and demanded that Goldstein submit *Kosher Food Guide* issues for rabbinic review before publication. When Goldstein refused, the OU went so far as to rewrite the minutes of its March 1936 executive council meeting to imply he had reneged on such an agreement when there was in fact no record of Goldstein accepting this requirement.[28]

Goldstein's claim to superior knowledge, along with his open defiance of rabbinic authorities, led to, in effect, his excommunication from the Orthodox wing of organized Judaism. The sordid episode climaxed when a rabbinic court of Orthodox rabbis issued a proclamation that improbably branded Goldstein "a thorough ignoramus in matters Jewish" and complained that he "has impudently assumed authority to decide in matters of *kashrus*" thereby "assuming the authority of a rabbi." For these transgressions the court pronounced "the unreliability of this individual in relation to kashruth," and directed Jews "to pay no heed to the O.K. pamphlet." Seeking to isolate Goldstein, the declaration went to rabbis and synagogues throughout New York City as well as to manufacturers that had advertised in the *Kosher Food Guide*. To a gentile business owner genuinely seeking to satisfy perplexing kosher requirements for his products, the conflict must have sounded like a bizarre jurisdictional dispute hardly befitting the religious authority claimed by Jewish organizations.[29]

GOLDSTEIN'S POSTHUMOUS VICTORY

Abraham Goldstein passed away at the end of 1944 with his publication and organization intact, but deeply embittered by the ostracism occasioned by the 1939 rabbinic proclamation. There is no evidence that advertisers withdrew from the *Kosher Food Guide*; indeed the listings it contained were far more extensive than in the competing guides published by the Orthodox Union. But during the remaining five years of his life there is also no indication that the Orthodox rabbinic hierarchy softened their stand toward him.

Within a few years, though, Goldstein's views would be vindicated, along with his message to attend to scientific knowledge and the technicalities of food manufacturing systems. In 1952, with the support of many influential rabbis in Israel and the United States, leading Orthodox Rabbi Eliezer Silver proclaimed an *issur* (a ban) that declared Junket *treif*. Even though Silver was a member of the rabbinic court that had denounced Goldstein for his advocacy of the same position, there was no admission of the history behind the issur. Concerned Jews remembered nonetheless; Abraham's son George Goldstein, now editor of the *Kosher Food Guide,* gloried in the decision, writing that "the layman who dared to tell the truth, and was shunted and pushed aside, is now proven to be right." He could also express gratitude toward the hundreds of Jews who wrote to the journal in the decision's aftermath thanking the *Kosher Food Guide* for its stands.[30]

Rabbi Silver's reversal on rennet conceded (without admitting so) that lay knowledge was necessary to correctly define kosher requirements for contemporary foods. Rabbi Geffen had pioneered such a methodological shift in rabbinic circles in the 1920s and 1930s, and Abraham Goldstein had relentlessly argued for such an approach in the 1930s and 1940s. Finally, in the 1950s, the core institutions of Orthodox Judaism accepted the need to understand science and technology so as to effectively enforce kosher law. Ironically, doing so also brought Coke's kosher status back under a close lens.

In 1957 a huge public controversy erupted over Coke's *kashrus*. Glycerin was, yet again, the main issue. It turned out that the allegedly kosher glycerin supplied by Procter & Gamble was manufactured in the same plant, and on the same equipment, used to process nonkosher meat-based glycerin. Procter & Gamble could still provide affidavits certifying that the glycerin supplied for kosher Coke was made only from vegetable sources, and since they were unfamiliar with the concept of *b'lios* probably felt that they were in full compliance with kosher requirements—when in fact they were not. In an adept extension of *b'lios* from the home to the industrial factory, Rabbi Eliezer Silver (who broke the scandal) compared

Procter & Gamble's action to "frying ham in a skillet, and then placing kosher meat in the same skillet." To satisfy the highly publicized complaints, Procter & Gamble constructed a parallel production line for vegetable-based glycerin at a cost of $30,000.[31]

Eighty-seven by this time, Geffen was not actively involved in Coca-Cola's certification and could be forgiven for not clambering over the glycerin manufacturing operations he had inspected in 1934 as a much younger man. For many years he had received annual affidavits from Proctor & Gamble certifying that the glycerin supplied to Coke "was made from vegetable sources and from no animal fat." However, Proctor & Gamble had never informed Geffen that it was now using different technology to refine glycerin, in all likelihood unaware that doing so created a new problem of *b'lios*.

When Geffen had first certified Coke, glycerin producers generally used a batch processing method where they emptied the entire contents of a railroad tank car into processing containers that cooked and filtered the liquids. The "special process" alluded to by Procter & Gamble probably referred to the segregation of cottonseed oil in these processing chambers, from which came the vegetable-based glycerin that went to Coke's Atlanta plant. Fatty oil processors by the 1950s had developed a more efficient continuous-flow system where separate processing stages were connected by pipes, making complete segregation of a vegetable-based glycerin batch far more difficult to achieve. While the vegetable oil may have been processed in a separate tank, the common network of pipes conveying the glycerin output to successive processing stages meant that it came into contact with the meat-based product that had passed through the same pipes.[32] To Procter & Gamble, glycerin production simply had been modernized, but to kosher certifiers the *kashrus* of this ingredient—and with it, all the products it went into—had been irretrievably compromised by the transfer of taste from *treif* materials.

The response by Coca-Cola and Proctor & Gamble was, nonetheless, consistent with their acceptance of kosher strictures two decades earlier. Their chemists probably found the uproar hard to understand; after all, there was absolutely no difference in the chemistry of vegetable-based product intended for kosher Coke and the meat-based glycerin that supposedly contaminated it. Yet they accepted the need to invest tens of thousands of dollars to accommodate Jewish religions requirements. Doubtless Rabbi Geffen and George Goldstein were in the end pleased by the outcome.

A great deal was necessary, therefore, for my family to feel comfortable letting me drink Coke on Passover. While fabrication of a kosher glycerin was critical to developing kosher Coke and kosher versions of processed foods, that accomplishment, however important, was not the most significant outcome of this episode. Even more fundamental was the consensus of rabbinic thought generated by the debate over glycerin's *kashrus* (along with rennet) that modern food science and manufacturing methods needed to be understood to apply traditional kosher law in the modern era. Rabbi Silver's decisive interventions aptly captured such acceptance, as he was one of Goldstein's bitterest opponents but also a revered Orthodox rabbi whose opinions commanded deep respect among the most traditional segments of the Orthodox community.[33]

Glycerin was one of the early ingredients employed by food chemists to facilitate the creation of processed foods, and the agreement among Orthodox authorities on the importance of its origins had profound implications for other ingredients. Accepting as kosher foods containing glycerin under the concept of *bitul* would have established a loose *kashrus* principle applicable in theory to many food ingredients. Rennet's importance was not principally in its effect on Junket's *kashrus* (indeed the product soon faded from the marketplace), but as part of the same conceptual conundrum as glycerin. The eventual accord among Orthodox rabbis for a narrow interpretation of *bitul* and a stringent scientific inspection of *all* ingredients' origins established a critical *kashrus* requirement for many postwar packaged food products. Similarly, enforcement of the principle of *b'lios* in manufacturing operations would have an enormous impact on the requirements for manufacturers wishing to secure kosher status for their goods. Kosher certification of processed food was still in its infancy in 1960, but the process through which Coke had become kosher augured well for the future development of modern food acceptable to observant Jews.[34]

Far greater challenges, however, lay ahead, with the emergence of many packaged foods in whose contents lurked a multitude of ingredients unknown to the sages of Jewish law. Cake mixes, frozen dinners, and

other easy-to-make foods spread in the 1950s and 1960s as food preparation time shrank in American homes. Observant Jewish homemakers
naturally wanted to make use of these new and wonderful products, but
they also had to worry whether they were kosher. Ironically, a critical
battle affecting all these foods erupted around a seemingly innocuous
if ubiquitous dessert—Jell-O—that was one of the first packaged
"convenience" foods.

3

THE GREAT JELL-O CONTROVERSY

WHEN I helped my mother make Jell-O in our kosher home of the early 1960s, I didn't realize that by combining warm water with powdered gelatin and placing the mixture in the refrigerator we were entering into the single most controversial subject in contemporary kosher law. Jell-O was a simple, enjoyable dessert of my childhood, as it was for millions of my generation, but for the rabbis who adjudicated kosher law it was a conundrum whose complicated *kashrus* resisted easy answers.

Jell-O's very presence in our home reflected how our notion of kosher hewed to the interpretation favored by the Conservative branch of Judaism. Much as my mother's father accepted sturgeon as a kosher fish, my parents viewed the various leniencies permitted by Conservative Judaism as consistent with our Jewish faith. The simple act of getting my sister and me to make Jell-O (an activity doubtless used by many mothers to get their children involved in a safe kitchen project) was a statement of the kind of Judaism we observed.

Orthodox Jews did not agree with us. By the early 1960s, the Orthodox wing of Judaism was firmly against declaring Jell-O kosher; a decade later, Conservative Judaism came down equally decisively that it was acceptable. In doing so, Jell-O served as the proverbial tip of the iceberg, functioning to mark the deep divide between Jews about the modern understanding of kosher—and indeed what it meant to be Jewish in contemporary America.

The controversy was over gelatin, the animal-derived material that gave Jell-O its jiggly composition. As with Coke, the problem was how to understand and classify ingredients chemically extracted from other materials, and of which traditional Jewish law could only be drawn on for guidance through inference. Gelatin's *kashrus*, however, was far more complex than that of glycerin, and the guidance offered by the learned Jewish sages of the ancient and early modern world was much more contradictory. Influential rabbis endorsed gelatin as a kosher product in the 1930s, and at least until the 1950s the dominant position among Orthodox Jews was that gelatin products were acceptable to observant Jews. A long and distinguished body of rabbinic commentaries, including some of the leading *poskim* (experts) of Jewish law, could be drawn upon to support the position that Jell-O was kosher. In mid-century America, opponents of this view were definitely a minority, with arguments resting on a much thinner band of rabbinic commentaries that had less purchase among contemporary religious authorities.

The ultimate determination by Orthodox rabbis that Jell-O—and the gelatin it contained—was *treif* thus marked a significant development in kosher law. In so doing, they ruled against one strong body of opinion and favored another that was more stringent in its interpretation of traditional principles. Their action tightened kosher law considerably, eliminating not only the use of gelatin in kosher food but also precluding application to other products of principles articulated in the rabbinic commentaries used to argue Jell-O was kosher. Much as determination of glycerin's *kashrus* had vastly narrowed the margin for food companies to include traces of nonkosher foods in their products, Jell-O's passage into the *treif* category raised the bar for evaluating the *kashrus* of other ingredients that might be added to processed food.

JELL-O FOR JEWS?

Jell-O's widespread use in the homes of American Jews stemmed from its emergence as a cheap dessert in the early twentieth century. While gelatin-based desserts can be traced to the mid-nineteenth century, Jell-O was the first ready-to-eat mass-produced dessert that only needed boiling

FIGURE 3.1 "It's so simple . . . Jell-O . . . America's favorite compote." Jell-O Recipe booklet, rear cover, Genesee Pure Food Company, 1922. Courtesy LeRoy Historical Society.

water to be added to its powder mix. Its first manufacturer, the Genesee Pure Food Company, promoted the product avidly through advertisements in popular magazines and by distributing recipe collections door to door. Immigrants were a target audience, as Jell-O was quite inexpensive; in the 1910s the company published recipe booklets in several languages including Yiddish.[1]

With several million Jews in New York City, the Genesee Pure Food Company turned to the Joseph Jacobs Organization in the 1920s to help promote Jell-O. An advertising agency that promised product manufacturers it knew how to reach "the better classes of the otherwise unreachable

Jewish-speaking people," the Jacobs organization is best known for its efforts to bring Maxwell House coffee into the homes of observant Jews. Through advertisements in Yiddish papers such as the *Jewish Daily Forward, Jewish Morning Journal,* and the *Day,* the agency boasted in 1926 that it had "introduced" mainstream food products such as Post, Ralston, and Kellogg cereals, White Rose white bread, and Aunt Jemima Pancake flour to New York's Jews.[2]

Since the advertisements for Jell-O in the Yiddish press did not include a rabbinic endorsement, observant Jewish readers naturally wondered if the product was kosher. In response to a 1935 query, one paper sent a mimeographed answer (probably written by the Jacobs agency) that clearly had gone to others who had inquired. It claimed that, due to ten years of advertising in the Jewish press, "Jell-O is used in most Jewish homes, and its popularity among our people is constantly increasing." And it vigorously defended Jell-O as kosher, portraying it as "a derived product" that had experienced a "complete chemical change" and did not use "the kind of gelatin found in animal tissues."[3]

Such endorsements were sure to arouse the ire of ever watchful Orthodox Kashrus Laboratories president Abraham Goldstein. Such advertisements "are not only deplorable from a Jewish religious viewpoint," he thundered, but are "an outrageous attempt to smuggle an absolutely trefa article into Jewish homes."[4] Not surprisingly, he took the same position with regard to gelatin as he had with glycerin and rennet—that any product whose origins were *treif* remained *treif.* Invoking a principle known as *kol ha-yotzei min ha-tamei tamei* (whatever issues from an unclean animal is unclean), he argued that gelatin and its product Jell-O were not kosher, since the gelatin came from the bones and skins of *treif* animals.

Consistent with Goldstein's approach to glycerin, his concerns about Jell-O reflected an understanding of the gelatin manufacturing process. As the meatpacking industry churned out more meat and a greater range of products generated from edible parts of the animals that did not yield consumer cuts (such as hot dogs), considerable effort went into making use of the piles of inedible bones, cattle hide trimmings, and pigskins discarded in the production process. Much as animal fats got turned into soap and glycerin, firms developed methods to extract collagen from the bones and hides from which to profitably make glue—and gelatin.

Collagen is one of the basic proteins in animal bodies, humans included, with its fibers acting to help to hold together living tissue and bone. Equivalent substances are not found in plants; hence, unlike glycerin (which can come from plants or even artificial sources), collagen must be extracted from dead animals. Chemically, gelatin is a hydrolysate of collagen, where twisted collagen strands are first separated into individual fibers and then broken into smaller pieces through soaking in acids or alkalis and heating in water. Changed into what we call gelatin, these shortened molecular strands can disseminate widely through a liquid creating three-dimensional structures that trap water, making gelatin a perfect substance to hold tasty yet delicate solutions together.[5]

Any cook of tough meat cuts is familiar with the household process of turning collagen into gelatin. Meat taken from parts of an animal that were heavily used for activities is filigreed with connective tissues that hold well-developed muscle fibers together. Largely consisting of collagen, these tissues can be softened through slow, moist cooking such that they turn into gelatin. The disintegration of the long collagen bands into short gelatin molecules permits a tough brisket to become the tender pot roast that falls apart with the touch of a fork.

Making gelatin by slowly cooking consumer cuts obviously was not an option for industrial producers; their raw materials were the otherwise unusable refuse of the packing industry. Bones were an excellent source of collagen, easy to obtain in large quantities—but complicated and slow to process. They had to be cleaned, crushed, and treated with chemicals for weeks, if not months, to strip them of everything but the collagen they contained. Much softer hide trimmings from cattle and pigs were harder to obtain in sufficient quantities but easier to handle; just a few days of soaking in lime allowed the gelatin to be extracted. Whatever collagen's source, the final processing stage was to cook the residue slowly in large water-filled tanks until it turned into gelatin that could be dried, packaged, and sold for commercial use.[6]

Gelatin offered unique advantages to modern food producers. With the capacity to retain up to ten times its weight in water, gelatin could absorb several distinct ingredients, creating soft gels, or act as an emulsifier, retaining milk fat in an aqueous solution, thus preventing creaming. With these properties, gelatin's most popular use in the early twentieth century was for ice cream and in baked goods. In the mid-1920s, Americans ate about five million pounds of gelatin in their ice cream and consumed additional quantities in cake icings, whipped cream, and marshmallows. The new vitamins that were becoming popular in the twenties all relied on gelatin to hold the nutritious elements in an easy to digest capsule. Gelatin was everywhere—not just in Jell-O.[7]

THE GELATIN CONTAGION

Gelatin's prominence in the food chain made it one of Abraham Goldstein's most all-encompassing campaigns. Repeated inquiries sent to the *Kosher Food Guide* concerning Jell-O's kosher status indicate the widespread use of the product in Jewish homes. "A surprising great number of inquiries about the permissibility of gelatin have reached us lately," he noted in 1939. Indeed, until the early 1940s almost every issue of the *Kosher Food Guide* addressed questions concerning Jell-O or other gelatin-based products.[8]

New York's leading English-language Jewish paper, the *Jewish Examiner*, was one of the first to ask Goldstein about Jell-O's kosher status, receiving an answer in 1936 that both Jell-O and marshmallows containing gelatin were *treif*. The esteemed Orthodox Rabbi Leo Jung, who had worked closely with Goldstein in the Orthodox Union, asked him to answer a letter from Sioux Falls, South Dakota Rabbi Asher Katz concerning Jell-O, a tacit endorsement of Goldstein's hard-line position. A year later, Goldstein fielded a similar question about Jell-O from Mrs. D. Goldman in Ambridge, Pennsylvania, to whom he explained, "Jello is trefa and should not be used in any Jewish home." To Bronx resident Mrs. S. Levine, he elaborated that "Jello is trefa because it consists mainly of gelatine and sugar with flavoring. The gelatine is trefa." Subsequent letters from Mrs. F. Husid in Brooklyn, Rabbi Max Green in Loch Sheldrake, New York, Mr. H. Hochheiser in Richmond Hill, New York, and Mrs. B. H. Kaminitzky in Fayetteville, North Carolina, all received the terse answer "Jell-O is trefa." To Mr. S. Baumgarten in Brooklyn who wanted to obtain kosher animal gelatin, Goldstein advised that by "buy[ing] a calf's foot and by boiling it you will obtain all the gelatine you need for a whole week." Doubtless this suggestion did not motivate observant Jewish homemakers, attracted by Jell-O's convenience, to make gelatin at home.[9]

Questions concerning marshmallows received similar discouraging responses. In October 1936 Goldstein told Mr. Herbert L. Batt of New Haven, Connecticut, that all manufacturers used gelatin to make marshmallows and offered a recipe that he could use to make a gelatin-free version at home instead. Mr. Saul Boyarsky in Burlington, Vermont, and Mrs. S. Novick in the Bronx learned to their chagrin that Campfire Marshmallows were *treif* due to their gelatin content, as did Mrs. M. Lintz in Gardener, Massachusetts, regarding Marshmallow Fluffs. Offering some hope that these confections could be made in a form acceptable to observant Jews, Goldstein promised Mr. J. Budnick in Philadelphia that he would personally visit the manufacturer of Drake Baker's Snowball marshmallows "and try to convince them to make the marshmallow without gelatine which can be done."[10]

Ice cream posed challenges as well, since gelatin helped maintain a smooth appearance and kept ice crystals from developing within the cream. Goldstein warned Miss Rose Moidel in Pittsburgh that "Reich's Dairy Company and other companies in Pittsburgh manufacturing ice cream prepared with animal gelatine should not be used" and delivered gloomy news to Mr. S. Baten in Patterson, New Jersey, regarding his local Country Club Ice Cream as well. Alternatives were available, however, so it was possible for Goldstein to steer observant Jews to acceptable brands. Breyer's seemed the most reliable national firm, for, as he told Mr. Herbert Goodman in Washington, DC, the company did "not use any gelatine in their ice cream." Borden's was more uncertain, as the company used different ingredients at different times in different plants, leading Goldstein to initially recommend the product to Mrs. Joseph Bernstein and Mr. S. Belt in Chicago, only to rescind his approval in 1939 when the company changed production methods in its principal Chicago facility.[11]

Gelatin's use in other food products solicited several wide-ranging queries from cautious observant consumers. Mrs. J. Shapirode in Pittsburgh asked generally about gelatin, eliciting Goldstein's stern warning, "If the manufacturer states that gelatine is used in his products, you can be sure that trefa gelatine has been used and such products should not be eaten." Mrs. J. Harris in Brooklyn learned the gelatin contaminated several desired products, including bulk marmalade as well as Loft's candies and ice cream. Gelatin capsules also held the flavors of popular desserts, prompting warnings to Mrs. L. Cohen in Detroit about the lemon and peppermint flavors of Kre-Mel products and Mrs. B. Mendlowitz in Brooklyn concerning lemon My-T-Fine pudding. Goldstein's message was clear: observant Jews needed to keep their eyes open for any effort to sneak gelatin into processed food products.[12]

With all his efforts to keep gelatin out of kosher kitchens, Goldstein was outraged when a new group of gelatin-based dessert products reached the market in 1941, only this time bearing the *hecksher* of individual rabbis (Jell-O did not then have rabbinic endorsement). Particularly inciting his wrath was the naming of these products with language that would lend credibility to observant Jews, such as Kosher-Gel, produced by Emes Kosher Food Products in Chicago, and Kojel, manufactured by the Kosher Desserts, Inc., and the more modestly titled Gel-Dessert, legitimated by its manufacturer's name, the Carmel Kosher Food Products Company.[13]

Kojel was especially objectionable to Goldstein since it carried the approval of Rabbi Judah Seltzer, a close associate of his arch-nemesis Rabbi Shmuel Aaron Levi Pardes. Housewives who questioned Kojel's kosher status received a mimeographed letter on the stationary of the Union of Orthodox Rabbis (the Agudath Harabonim, Pardes's organization), reassuring them that Rabbi Seltzer "would not give his supervision to a product of which Kashruth he was not absolutely convinced." Granting that "what disturbed you [about Kojel] was reading the food guide" (an indication of Goldstein's influence), the letter sought to place rabbinic endorsement of the product in a positive light as "a service to the Jewish public." Since "many Jews still use Jell-O which is trefah," it noted, Seltzer's *hecksher* would instead steer them to a kosher gelatin desert and thus "prevent many Jews from eating trefah."[14]

Queries began pouring into the *Kosher Food Guide* about "kosher" gelatin as soon as these dessert products became available. Indeed, questions about Jell-O came to a sudden halt at the same time, indicating that observant Jews were turning away from a suspect product in favor of ones that carried rabbinic endorsement. Goldstein's rejection was unequivocal. He wrote Mrs. A. Matkin from Pittsburgh that "Neither Carmel,

Emes, or Kojel gelatines can be used in Orthodox homes. They are trefa gelatines, despite the Rabbinical Heckshers." He delivered a similar message to Mr. Joseph Katz in Chicago, that "the Hechsher printed on the carton of Kosher-Jel does not alter this fact." Goldstein offered the same message, albeit in terse form, to letters from many urban areas, including Chicago, Youngstown, Baltimore, Newark (New Jersey), and of course from the greater New York City area. Abraham's son George maintained his father's policy following his death, writing Mrs. Naomi Myers in 1946 that "the latest defense of these animal products are that they are chemical gelatines and therefore kosher and parve. Our opinion remains absolutely unchanged, that any gelatine produced from trefa animals, skins, tissues, or bones, remains trefa and cannot be made kosher by any Rabbinical endorsement."[15]

The Goldsteins' unequivocal position ignored how the arguments in favor of kosher gelatin could claim deep roots in rabbinic thought and could reference leading authorities stretching back more than a millennia. Indeed, George Goldstein's disparagement of the "defense" of gelatin referred to a decade-long international discussion among rabbinic scholars that drew on an extensive body of sophisticated kosher law.

THE RABBIS SAY IT'S KOSHER!

Acceptance of gelatin in American rabbinic circles can be traced to an early 1930s query from Rabbi Pardes to several leading European *poskim* soliciting their opinion on gelatin's kosher status. His letters received lukewarm responses from two senior rabbis, Isaac Burstein in Ostroleka, Poland, and Yehuda Leib Tzirelson in Kishnev, Romania; but a most expansive and authoritative endorsement came from Rabbi Hayyim Ozer Grodzinski from Vilna, Lithuania. Universally recognized as one of the great authorities on Jewish law in the twentieth century, Grodzinski's ruling formed the basis for all subsequent arguments in favor of gelatin's kosher status.[16]

While it might seem peculiar that devout Orthodox rabbis would countenance declaring a substance kosher that originated in nonkosher animals, traditional Jewish law did in fact contain important exceptions to its general prohibitions. The reasoning began with the concept of *bitul* (nullification) that under some circumstances Jew might eat nonkosher foods in mixtures so long as they comprised a small minority. (Rabbi Tobias Geffen had wrestled with this very same concept when it came to the matter of glycerin in Coca-Cola.) In those mixtures, Jewish law had to consider the bones that might end up in the stew along with the prohibited meat attached to it to determine the acceptable proportions— should the bones count as part of the permitted portion or were they as equally *treif* as the meat, even though they could not be eaten? The Jewish prohibition on insects also had to contemplate the *kashrus* of honey, in which an animal that was not itself kosher created a kosher product that sometimes contained the legs of the bees who made it. The very precision of these commentators on incidents hundreds of years ago—and the disagreements among them—militated against direct application of their insights to problems created through modern forms of food production.

For Grodzinski and his contemporaries to rule on gelatin, they thus had to extrapolate from a wide range of opinions and situations that were quite different from the particulars they faced. They also had to rely on the information concerning gelatin manufacturing that Pardes supplied, a dubious source given his lack of familiarity with science and food manufacturing. So whatever may be said for their knowledge of Jewish law, these European *poskim* were not well-situated to understand industrial gelatin production or the chemistry involved.

Grodzinski's influential teshuva teased out several strands of rabbinic commentaries to accept gelatin. He began by narrowing the biblical prohibition from Leviticus 11:8, "Of their flesh ye shall not eat," to apply to flesh alone; the bones and other inedible parts of nonkosher animals were not covered under this rule. Following from that, he reasoned that since the biblical prohibition did not apply to inedible materials that came from animals, and gelatin was rendered inedible during the manufacturing process, it was exempt. Finally, and most important to later debates, Grodzinski held that the chemical transformations that took place in the process of making gelatin were such as to make it a completely different material than the bones and hides from which it came. Such a change, known as *ponim chadashos* (literally a new face), removed any *issur* on the original materials. *Ponim chadashos* was a particular powerful concept, for it meant that the kosher status of gelatin's source was irrelevant. For all these reasons, Grodzinski endorsed Pardes's view that bones and hides from nonkosher slaughtered cattle could be used to make kosher gelatin.[17]

The path to this remarkable conclusion lay through problems of kosher food in medieval Europe. Exempting bones from the prohibition in Leviticus relied on a chain of reasoning that began with a ruling on twelfth-century honey production. In this case, Rabbeinu Tam (Rabbi Jacob ben Meir) assured nervous French Jews that they need not worry about honey that included bees' legs. Basing his own ruling on a passage in the Mishnah that "the bones of an ass are clean," he ruled that "the legs of a bee, since they are mere bones, are permissible because bones are clean." A century later, Spanish rabbi the Rosh (Rabbi Asher ben Jehiel) endorsed Rabbeinu Tam's decision, as to him, bones were *afra be'alma* or "mere dust." Drawing on these two opinions, *Shulchan Aruch* author Rabbi Joseph Caro concluded that in a mixture of forbidden and permitted foods the bones counted toward the permitted portion that could nullify the forbidden part. Some authorities, mostly notably Maimonides and Rabbi Moses Isserles, dissented, their opinions stressing that bone could contain enough moisture to affect the "flavor" of a mixture, hence limiting this permission to hard, dry bones. This narrow yet long strand of reasoning over many centuries, drawing on the opinions of the leading scholars of Jewish law, was the basis for Grodzinksi's ruling that while the flesh of a nonkosher animal was prohibited, the same animal's dried and chemically treated bones could be used to make a gelatin that was kosher.[18]

The manner in which chemicals used in gelatin manufacturing created an inedible product allowed for an additional chain of reasoning supporting the same conclusion. Grodzinski traced back to the Talmud admonitions that once nonkosher cattle deteriorated to the extent that they were unfit for human consumption the prohibition against their meat lapsed. The measure of this point (befitting the era in which it was written) was "when it is rendered unfit as food for canine consumption."[19] In other words, *treif* meat could become kosher when it was so awful that not even a dog would touch it!

While such an exception would seem unlikely to have much application, the seemingly paradoxical notion that what was once prohibited could become acceptable for people to consume once it was unfit for even a dog to eat was picked up by medieval rabbinic commentators. The thirteenth-century Italian rabbi Zedekiah HaRofeh (author of an influential body of commentaries known as the *Shibbolei Haleket*) and Rabbi Moses Isserles both ruled that once meat became inedible, "mere wood" without moisture, it was no longer prohibited. The sixteenth-century Polish rabbi Sabbatai ben Meir ha Kohen, also called the Schach, similarly authorized Jews to consume saffron, even though it often contained traces of non-kosher dried beef, because the saffron "was as dry as wood."[20]

The sweeping *ponim chadashos* "defense" was, however, the most controversial of Grodzinski's arguments at the same time as it seemed the most plausible. Contending that gelatin was a transformed substance utterly unlike the materials from which it came was an effective popular defense of Jell-O and similar products. To most people, it seemed obvious that this soft and pleasant substance bore nothing in common with the bones and hide that were its source; it appeared self-evident that gelatin had experienced "a complete chemical change." Certainly this argument was far easier to understand than the counterintuitive claim that bones from a nonkosher animal were kosher even if the flesh was not. *Ponim chadashos* also had the value of severing gelatin's *kashrus* from the materials used to make it, permitting hides from nonkosher sources to be used as well. For those same reasons, it also had deeply disturbing implications for the boundaries of kosher certification.

The *ponim chadashos* theory rested principally on the ruling of twelfth-century Catalan Rabbeinu Yonah (Rabbi Yonah ben Abraham Gerondi) in the case of an obscure spice known as musk. Originating from a growth on the neck of an animal whose identity has never been confirmed, musk was a spice whose wide use in Spain came into question because of its source, an animal's congealed blood. Its popularity among Jews was deeply troubling because of the strong biblical prohibition against the consumption of blood. Rabbeinu Yonah ruled that musk was acceptable, as it was *ponim chadoshos*, a new substance entirely, unrelated and dissociated from the prohibited substance (blood) that was its source. Grodzinski ignored the skepticism of many rabbinic authorities at Rabbeinu Yonah's ruling and went on to draw a parallel between the natural process that produced musk (which he wrote as "mosk") and the manufacturing procedures creating gelatin. He concluded that gelatin was "similar to the case of mosk," with its kosher status determined "as if a new substance has appeared."[21]

Drawing on this extensive base of *poskim* opinions, Grodzinski extracted a general principle: "When a forbidden substance is reduced to dust, it ceases to be prohibited by Jewish law." As applied to the case of gelatin, he explained that the original bone and skin "were completely decomposed as a result of the caustic soda and phosphoric acid," thereby eliminating all moisture from the gelatin that emerged from this process. Hence this gelatin did not carry any prohibition that might have applied to the materials from which it came—and so long as the process was, as he understood it, relying on nonkosher beef bones and hides, gelatin was kosher.[22]

THE PIG IN THE ROOM

The *Kosher Food Guide*'s fulmination against gelatin products could make little headway among observant Jews in light of such strong rabbinic endorsement. From the constant protests that appear in the journal in the mid and late 1940s, it seems that sales of the accursed kosher gelatins only grew; indeed, additional products with similar kosher claims entered the marketplace. George Goldstein fumed at the dismissive response he received from Rabbis Pardes, Seltzer, and others in the Agudath Harabonim, who told him that unless he spent several years studying the classic Hebrew texts, "their decisions should not even be open to question." While he deplored how "Rabbis spend their time and delve into every old Mishna, Talmud, and Gemora" to defend how a product could be kosher, he no longer offered his father's response of *kol-ha-yotzei min ha-tamei tamei*. Instead he retreated to an appeal to "good common sense" and the hope that those who read his publication would "be the final judge" on kosher issues.[23]

Without fanfare, the Orthodox Union quietly accepted kosher gelatin. In 1950 Kosher Gelatin Desserts, manufactured by Van Dutch Products, made its first appearance in the OU listings of approved foods. The OU also ignored Goldstein's repeated warnings that Loft candies included

FIGURE 3.2 George Goldstein. Courtesy Goldstein Family collection.

gelatin and carried the company's products as the only permitted candy in its kosher food guide. While not openly endorsing the gelatin desserts certified by Agudath Harabonim rabbis, the OU clearly had accepted Grodzinski's ruling.[24]

The Joseph Jacobs agency certainly found the wider acceptance of gelatin among observant Jews appealing to potential food industry customers who used gelatin in their products. The agency expanded from newspaper-based promotions to advertiser-sponsored programs on WEVD, a Yiddish-language AM station owned by the *Daily Forward*. Popular Jewish radio personalities promoted mainstream products on WEVD; Menasha Skulnik (modestly billed as "America's top-rated Jewish comic") served as a spokesman for Jell-O. In 1951 Goldstein complained that the Jacobs agency had arranged for another unidentified "very large firm" to sponsor a Yiddish radio show that announced its product did not contain *treif* gelatin "and could be used in the most Orthodox Jewish home." The promotion generated dozens of concerned letters complaining that when they obtained the dessert package a gelatin capsule held its flavoring mix.[25]

Kosher endorsement of Jell-O and similar products rested on Grodzinski's interpretation of traditional Jewish law; his ruling, however, was limited to the process that had been explained to him, one that relied on using "dried bones" to make gelatin. But, unbeknownst to most Jews, the materials entering gelatin changed dramatically after World War II. These innovations were hidden from general view, with information about them exchanged in obscure, specialized journals meant for the trade and read by few outsiders, often willfully concealed from consumers for fear of generating adverse publicity. So it is no wonder that Orthodox rabbis, with their internal focus on the Jewish community and limited familiarity with food processing technology, were unaware of the complex transformation affecting gelatin production. What had once depended on beef products, albeit from animals not slaughtered by kosher methods, was increasingly likely to contain collagen originating in pigs. The presence of pork in allegedly kosher gelatin was a ticking time bomb that would explode in Orthodox circles in the early 1950s.

Much of the gelatin that formed the basis of kosher dessert mixes came from Wilson & Company, one of the four large national meatpacking firms. As the slaughterhouse that supplied Wilson's Chicago gelatin works produced beef and pork, it is plausible that for some time the company segregated the bones and hide trimmings from its cattle killing operations from pork products to make gelatin through the process deemed acceptable by Grodzinski.[26]

Shifts in gelatin manufacturing methods following World War II made it increasingly likely that pork products comprised some of the materials that entered the allegedly kosher gelatin. In May 1950 a representative of Wilson's Chemical and Organic Products Division told a conference of food technology experts that the company was making considerable use of pork skins to make gelatin, as "collagen in bone will not readily convert to gelatin after a short acid treatment as do pork skins and requires considerable more treatment." Indeed the skins were sufficiently valuable and produced in such large quantities that they were frozen into hundred-pound molds and shipped to the company's gelatin plant by refrigerated railroad car.[27]

Behind the Wilson & Co. representative's statement were dramatic changes in pork processing that had altered the economics for the use of pig skins. Until World War II, pig skins were largely an annoyance to meat processors, as they were tedious to remove and generally too soft to be used for leather goods outside of their acclaimed place in football. Generally they were thrown into the mix of fat and meat trimmings rendered into lard. Following the war, pig skins became more of a problem as producers shifted from cured to fresh cuts and found that consumers were replacing lard with vegetable shortenings such as Crisco. In response to these market pressures, farmers started to produce small, leaner hogs more useful for the production of consumer cuts. As lard could no longer serve as a destination for pig skins, what then to do with these materials that still had to be removed from the bacon, hams, and chops destined for the household?

A new firm called Townsend Engineering offered an answer—use pig skins to make gelatin! Based in Des Moines, Iowa, the heart of the pork industry, the company developed the first mechanized pork skinner in 1947. Five years later, it could boast that its full line of skinning machines made it profitable for firms to "save those skins for gelatin." Indeed, the meat industry was so excited by the opportunities created by this new technology that its principal trade journal titled one appreciative article "Profits in Pig Skins." The economics were simple—pig skins took but a day before they were ready for gelatin conversion, while bones had to be soaked in lime for at least a month. With these considerable savings, gelatin production changed radically. By the 1970s fully 70 percent of American-produced gelatin came from pork sources.[28]

These changes in gelatin production were not known outside the food industry—that is, until the official kosher certification of Jell-O in 1951. With the widening acceptance of gelatin among observant Jews and the entry of companies that offered Jell-O-like desserts sporting an Orthodox rabbi's *heksher*, the General Foods company decided to secure its own rabbinic endorsement. To great fanfare, the firm announced in July that two leaders of the Agudath Harabonim, Brooklyn rabbis Samuel Baskin and Simon Winograd, had ruled that Jell-O was kosher and could thus be served by observant Jews "without reservation." Through the Jacobs agency, announcements were "broadcast over the radio, publicized in newspapers and published in advertising circulars." A few months later the firm secured a public endorsement from Rabbi Seltzer, at the time honorary president of the same rabbinic organization. In October the widely read Yiddish paper *Jewish Morning Journal* (which the Jacobs organization represented) carried banner articles on this momentous occasion, including a picture of rabbis Baskin and Winograd thoughtfully inspecting General Food's Jell-O manufacturing plant.[29]

Jell-O's kosher certification was based on, as Seltzer himself explained, "the ruling and decision of the late renowned Rabbi Chaim Ezer Grodzinsky." Indeed the Baskin and Winograd teshuva drew on the same rabbinic precedents to stress that bones of nonkosher animals were kosher. Their core argument, though, stressed *ponim chadashos* (chemical transformation) as the most important factor, citing the case of musk. As "the bones and skins undergo a metamorphosis and become like wood and glass," they explained, "and since this gelatin process is extracted from them by chemical means, this new product known as gelatin bears no resemblance to the original skins and bones, but is a new substance entirely, and is kosher beyond doubt." With the emphasis that gelatin was a new product, and the use of elliptical phrase "animals, kosher and non-kosher" to refer to the source for the gelatin used in Jell-O, the rabbis elided the uncomfortable question of whether pigs supplied any of these materials. This issue, however, could not be avoided.[30]

The sensational certification of Jell-O also was extremely controversial. It was a relatively small matter to disagree over the *kashrus* of a few products made specifically for the Jewish market. For a dessert advertised so broadly, endorsed on radio by Jack Benny and a host of other celebrities and occupying such an important place in the American cultural landscape, to receive unequivocal endorsement was quite another. If such a product that openly used nonkosher products in its manufacturing could be kosher, and perhaps even materials from pigs, what other products might be able to secure rabbinic acceptance and a place at the observant Jews' table?

A storm of protest reached the *Kosher Food Guide,* especially after the October 1951 coverage in the Yiddish press. To correspondents who wrote him "from far and wide," Goldstein assured them that he was doing whatever he could do to combat Jell-O's certification. He also urged them to directly contact the Agudath Harabonim. The implication that pork contaminated alleged kosher gelatin generated great urgency to these concerns.

These protests strengthened the hand of Rabbi Eliezer Silver and others within the rabbinic association who objected not only to Jell-O's certification but also to the ominous implications of the interpretive approach that lay behind it. In November, Baskin and Winograd found themselves—and their certification of Jell-O—"brought for judgment before a special meeting of the *Agudath Harabonim*." Constituted in essence as a religious court, the assembled rabbis determined, based on the information supplied to them during the interrogation of the two rabbis, that the gelatin used for Jell-O was not kosher. Baskin and Winograd were then forced into the humiliation of withdrawing their certification and Seltzer had to retract his endorsement. Silver visited the Wilson plant soon thereafter to inspect the so-called Kosher Gelatin Department that supplied Kojel, Kosher-Gel, and other similar products. The inspection determined that this gelatin was not in fact kosher, as pork skins were used in the manufacturing process. The debate then continued in the pages of *Ha-Pardes*, where Seltzer and other rabbis offered sharp disagreements with Silver's action and continued to argue that Jell-O was kosher. Indeed, Baskin and Winograd even retracted their retraction and again endorsed Jell-O. Despite this dissent, Rabbi Silver's action ended the official Orthodox flirtation with kosher Jell-O. In October 1952 Silver, after consulting with other Orthodox rabbis, issued an *issur* against so-called kosher gelatin desserts as well. The Orthodox Union, whose rabbis followed this struggle closely, if quietly, went along with this change of direction and removed both Loft Candies and Kosher Gelatin Desserts from its list of approved products.[31]

The Jacobs organization, however, just went elsewhere for certification. In 1953 they found Rabbi Max Felshin to offer official approval; by the early 1960s Rabbi David Telsner had assumed this role, relying on the same *ponim chadashos* reasoning as Baskin and Winograd. While none of the Orthodox certification organizations would accept Telsner's *hecksher*, Jell-O's manufacturer continued to claim it was kosher. On its own authority, the company placed a prominent *K* on its packages to reassure observant consumers that Jell-O was indeed kosher.[32]

Far from ending the controversy, however, the company's continued insistence that Jell-O was kosher kept the controversy alive—and continued to excite anger among observant Jews. In July 1963, for example, an irate consumer identified only as Mr. O in company documents barged into General Food's test kitchen to contest the kosher designation on Jell-O packages. To company representatives, Mr. O derided the certification by Rabbi David Telsner, as he was a man "in the business of selling kosher certifications." Influenced by the steady drumbeat of criticism in the pages of the *Kosher Food Guide,* Mr. O instead claimed that Jell-O was *treif,* as pork skins comprised the principal source of the gelatin it contained. The lawyer assigned to the case placated Mr. O by assuring him the firm would look into the matter, but to his colleagues he offered an attorney's caution: "I hope that our certification from Rabbi Telsner is not quite as weak as Mr. O says."[33]

As Mr. O's confrontation in General Foods laboratory kitchens indicates, the company's insistence on Jell-O's kosher status did not end the controversy. Pork's presence in "kosher" Jell-O was simply too much for many observant Jews to accept. The manufacturer freely admitted this was the case. Worried Jews who inquired directly of General Foods received a standard press release explaining that the gelatin used in Jell-O came from the "collagen-bearing tissues of food animals, principally beef, calf, and some pork." Permitting a manufacturing process to introduce pork—however transformed—into gelatin threatened a basic rule of separation intrinsic to kosher law.[34]

JELL-O—AND JEWISH IDENTITY?

Since the early 1930s, Abraham and George Goldstein and the OK Laboratories had campaigned against rabbinic acceptance of three ingredients: glycerin, rennet, and gelatin. They contended that in all instances modern food manufacturers threatened to weaken the traditional separation between kosher and *treif,* especially exclusion of all pork products. They only won on glycerin, and that was largely due to the intervention of Rabbi Tobias Geffen. Otherwise the Goldsteins' protestations were ignored by the Orthodox rabbis—until the 1950s, when their positions suddenly were adopted by the major rabbinic organizations, albeit without proper recognition. Such a dramatic change indicates that something more than a rethinking of kosher law was at work, something certainly more fundamental than whether Jell-O was kosher, something that closely touched basic issues of Jewish identity in postwar America. Kosher certification had become one of many areas of observance where the Orthodox were becoming more stringent to ward off the challenge posed by Conservative Judaism.

While Silver's reasoning is not recorded, Goldstein used the pages of the *Kosher Food Guide* to reprint rabbinic arguments that advocated a more critical stance toward products created by modern industry. One such commentary, by Rabbi Chaim Bloch (who described himself as only "a minor scholar" but is better known as author of the classic book, *The Prague Golem*), engaged in the typical citation of rabbinic commentators to rebut, point by point, Jell-O's certification.[35] He went on, though, in an unusual fashion to stress the politics of "such weak Heterim [leniencies]" and to argue, instead, that it was wiser to follow the saying of the nineteenth-century Polish rabbi Shlomo Kruger that "the policy now is to be strict." If rabbis expended such great effort to permit at best marginal practices, he worried "how ordinary persons would react, on seeing orthodox Rabbis acting in this manner." Rather than serving Judaism, he warned that such leniency "breaks the fences of our sages." Such arguments reflected wider sentiments in Orthodox circles for stricter observance of traditional practices in many areas of Jewish law.[36]

Kashrus issues were a prime candidate for more stringent observance; the continued presence of Jell-O packages sporting what many Orthodox felt was a misleading *K* lent primacy to the gelatin issue. In the early 1960s a candy firm (probably Astor Chocolates) under Orthodox Union supervision asked for permission to manufacture a marshmallow-flavored product. The OU supervisor used this request to create a test case for gelatin's kosher status by referring it to three influential *poskim* associated with the OU's rabbinic association, including Rabbi Moshe Feinstein (1895–1986), certainly the leading Orthodox expert on *kashrus* issues in the late twentieth century. To give more authority to their decision, this body (essentially a religious court of three judges) consulted with many leading rabbis in the United States, Europe, and Israel.

The rabbis, unsurprisingly, turned down the company's request to make marshmallow-covered chocolates containing gelatin. Their ruling, however, went far beyond this particular issue and rejected much of the traditional *halachic* argumentation drawn on to support earlier certifications of gelatin. In so doing, they essentially shut the *ponim chadashos* loophole and its potential to justify acceptance of a wide range of modern foods containing chemically transformed *treif* substances.

Grodzinski's decision, and his authoritative rabbinic sources, was a formidable obstacle to this decision. Feinstein and the other rabbis turned to Maimonides (whose more restrictive opinions had been dismissed by Grodzinski) to develop, in essence, a competing strand of rabbinic opinion on which to base their decision. In contradistinction to Grodzinki's conclusion (and those of the rabbis he had referenced), Rabbi Feinstein and his associates ruled the bones and hides of nonkosher animals were prohibited under biblical law and that returning an inedible food to an edible state did not necessarily remove a prohibition against the original material, that is, pig skin. As for *ponim chadashos*, they drastically narrowed its applicability by ruling that the natural transformation that created musk—the underlying basis for the concept—could not be applied to a chemical transformation precipitated by a mechanical process. In so doing, they laid great stress on Maimonides as well as one of his sources, the *Sifra*, redacted in the second century C.E., which served as a guide for the rabbis' interpretation of Leviticus.[37]

Their decision was a dramatic rejection of a body of rabbinic argument with a rich history and distinguished lineage and an affirmation of what had been minority opinion since at least Grodzinski's decision, if not earlier. By doing so, Feinstein and the other rabbis dramatically turned kosher law—at least as defined by the Orthodox—in a more restrictive direction. For gelatin the meaning was clear: in order to be kosher, all the materials had to come from kosher-slaughtered cattle. Hence no kosher Jell-O! But the implications went far beyond Jell-O. Excluding the lenient strand of Jewish thought from application to modern *kashrus* issues created a kosher law that was going to be far more difficult for food manufacturers to satisfy.

Such a shift in rabbinic opinion drew on the scientific revolution in *kashrus* supervision as modern food production methods became better

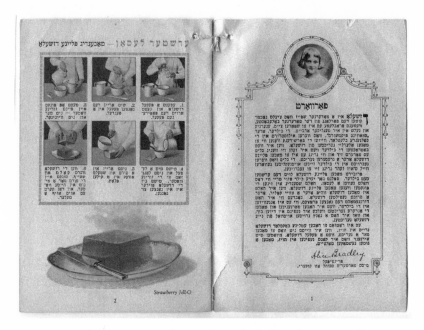

FIGURE 3.3 Yiddish text is a translation of standard Jell-O directions. Jell-O Recipe booklet, inside rear cover, Genesee Pure Food Company, 1922. Courtesy LeRoy Historical Society.

understood. What might have seemed in the 1930s to be an isolated case involving a trivial dessert product now represented a large set of issues defining what it meant to be an observant Jew. Jell-O's importance, and the emotions it aroused, reflected, among the Orthodox, its significance as the opening wedge of assimilation without observance, a signpost for how the pursuit of the good life in America (or at least an easy-to-make dessert) could undermine religious faith and practice. Conservative Judaism's rabbis simply did not agree; hence the Jell-O controversy failed to die. Gelatin became one of the lines of demarcation between the Orthodox and Conservative wings of Judaism as they fought for adherents in the 1950s and 1960s.

During the same years the Orthodox tightened kosher law, they were suffering substantial defections to Conservative Judaism. By the early 1960s, the Orthodox were but a small minority among self-identified

Jews, perhaps as little as 10 to 15 percent. Orthodox leaders attributed these losses to "a heavily-financed campaign of infiltration" from outsiders "penetrating" communities that were "solidly orthodox" such that, before bewildered leaders knew what was happening, the synagogues "were captured outright."[38] With this language, redolent of cold war descriptions of Communist subversion, the rabbis and lay leaders of Orthodoxy proclaimed their readiness for a battle to defend what it meant to be an observant Jew.

Such terminology imputing subversion concealed the attraction of Conservative Judaism's greater flexibility toward patterns of postwar American life, especially in the new suburbs that attracted many affluent Jews. In 1950 the Conservative Rabbinical Assembly decreed that it was acceptable to drive on the Sabbath to attend synagogue (a major if necessary concession to the geography of Jewish suburban life), characterizing such use not "as a violation of the Sabbath but, on the contrary, such attendance shall be deemed an expression of loyalty to our faith." Unspoken was whether, during such a drive, it was permissible to stop at one of the new suburban supermarkets that so often were not open on Sundays! In the same year, the Rabbinical Assembly authorized certain uses of electricity on the Sabbath and even answering the telephone and watching television. And, in a break from traditional practice, Conservative synagogues permitted women and children to sit together with men rather than segregate them to separate areas. Unlike Reform Judaism, the United Synagogue's Rabbinical Assembly claimed it remained in close adherence with Jewish law, but with these decisions the RA opened a greater gap between the Orthodox and Conservative wings of Judaism—with the numbers clearly favoring the latter.[39]

Certainly my own experiences growing up among Jews who followed Conservative principles indicate the conveniences made possible by these leniencies. We never worried about taking a taxi to services on the High Holidays of Yom Kippur and Rosh Hashanah, even if they fell on Saturday, and there was no thought of avoiding television or the movies on the Jewish Sabbath. When my parents got married, my mother's father filmed their extravagant party at the Waldorf-Astoria, which incorporated many elements of a mainstream American "white wedding"—though they also performed the traditional Jewish rituals of saying their vows under a chuppah (wedding canopy) and breaking glasses after the rabbi declared them husband and wife. In the 1950s and 1960s at least, it was a lot easier to be a Conservative Jew than an Orthodox Jew.

Kosher issues naturally entered into the fray—above all, Jell-O and its principal ingredient, gelatin. In the mid-1930s the RA endorsed the stringent position that gelatin, and the products that contained it, were "inadmissible from the standpoint of Jewish dietary law." The softening of the Orthodox position on Jell-O, however, encouraged the Conservative rabbis to take a new look at this issue. In 1953 the RA's Law Committee recommended that the Conservatives adopt the position that "gelatin is kosher" and commissioned a "responsum" to fully explore the issue. This about-face undoubtedly owed a great deal to the furious struggle among the Orthodox as well as the Conservatives' greater willingness to modify—or modernize—Jewish law.[40]

Buffalo rabbi Isaac Klein (1905–1979) became Conservative Judaism's expert on the Jell-O controversy and, indeed, on all *kashrus* issues. He surveyed the *Kosher Food Guide* and the Orthodox Union for their opinions, reviewed what he would later term the "violent" controversy in the pages of *Ha-Pardes*, and engaged in his own scientific review of the Jell-O manufacturing process.

As knowledge of his role spread within Conservative circles, he received letters from many perplexed rabbis asking for direction. Rabbi Robert Hammer, from Congregation Rodef Shalom in Denver, wrote to ask for clarification of kosher law's application to the new foods of modern life, asking in particular whether the *K* on Jell-O boxes actually signified it was kosher. A similar note was struck by Rabbi Sanford D. Shanblatt from Pittsfield, Massachusetts, who admitted that he was quite confused about the issues surrounding Jell-O and other gelatin dessert mixes. Rabbi J. Leonard Asneer asked if it was permissible to serve Jell-O in Temple Anshe Emeth's newly opened Home for the Aged in Youngstown, Ohio; interest in offering after-service Jell-O desserts to the members of Congregation Beth Torah in Orange, New Jersey, prompted its rabbi, Arnold Lasker, to ask Klein a similar question. Since these concerns revolved around the use of Jell-O and other gelatin products at the synagogue itself, the rabbis' worries about transgression of kosher law are understandable. And these letters' typical linkage of Jell-O to other *kashrus* issues indicates the extent to which this seemingly simple dessert had become a touchstone for larger worries about modern food and Jewish dietary law.[41]

In his responses, Klein endorsed Jell-O's kosher status because of Rabbi Telsner's *hecksher*, and the traditional practice of accepting a rabbi's authority to *pasken* matters of kosher law. His support was lukewarm, though, because of Telsner's connection to the Jacobs agency, the OU's opposition to Jell-O, and perhaps augmented by Telsner's diffident rebuff of Klein's repeated requests to inspect the General Foods plants that made Jell-O. Conservatives eagerly awaited Klein's ruling, as the silence left the Orthodox (including dissidents such as Telsner) as the sole authority on kosher issues.[42]

Klein's position, expressed in his long-awaited teshuva "Is Gelatin Kosher?" (endorsed in 1969 by the Rabbinical Assembly), drew on the same fount of rabbinic scholarship as Grodzinski and others who had debated the subject. As such, Klein was demonstrating that Conservatives did indeed pay heed to the wisdom of traditional Jewish law. He sought, however, to define an approach that was as distinctively Conservative as the decisions on driving and use of electricity on the Sabbath. Klein placed particular emphasis for his *halachic* decision not on traditional sources but instead on the impact of modern manufacturing methods. "Our main support for a *heter*," he explained, "comes from the fact that in the manufacture of gelatin the materials used go through chemical changes which make the end product *panim chadashot*, something entirely new." For this reason, he concluded, "Gelatin that is made from bone or from hides is kosher."[43]

To underscore his disagreement with the Orthodox, Klein explicitly reversed Rabbi Feinstein's reasoning that natural and mechanical processes could not be compared. Referring to the lenient opinion of Rabbeinu Yonah that the bee's legs did not affect the kosher status of honey, Klein contended, "It is neither difficult nor incorrect to extend this to chemical change." With a summary statement that could not have been more at odds with Feinstein, Klein concluded, "A substance treated by another substance which transforms it chemically becomes *panim chadashot*." In making this decision, he was indeed enlarging the *ponim chadashos* leniency that the Orthodox wanted to circumscribe.[44]

While his decision clearly indicated that gelatin made from pork skins was acceptable, Klein understandably was nervous about this conclusion. He granted that "there is an emotional reluctance to pronounce as kosher any product coming from a pig," so he initially advised against endorsement of gelatin that included pork products. After many letters asked him to explain this exception, Klein recanted his reservation as "a matter of sentiment" that was "halakhically immaterial and irrelevant." He fully endorsed gelatin that included pig skins, going so far as to remove the earlier qualification when he reprinted his gelatin teshuva in 1975.[45]

The Conservative acceptance of pork products in gelatin created a major disagreement with the Orthodox, which paralleled their increasing divergence in other areas of Jewish law and generated sharply different approaches toward application of kosher law to modern industry. For Conservatives, the implications of accepting gelatin quickly emerged in considering other products that, manufacturers argued, bore no resemblance to their source. In one case, Klein investigated the claim of Rich Products that its nondairy coffee whitener was in fact nondairy even though it contained sodium caseinate, a milk product. In defense of its claim, the company explained the process through which it extracted caseinate from milk and concluded, "the final product which is obtained is quite different from the original source."[46] Questions about lactic acid, glycerin, and mono- and diglycerides (derived from glycerin) came to Klein as well, as they too appeared to be transformed products.[47] It seemed to one especially perplexed rabbi that Klein had opened a veritable "Pandora's box" with his lenient application of *ponim chadashos*.[48]

INDUSTRIAL KOSHER BECOMES ORTHODOX

General Foods simply ignored the rabbinic debate. Relying on the *hecksher* of rabbis unaffiliated with any certification organization, it continued to claim Jell-O was kosher. In 1967 George Goldstein was still complaining that, among the "constant stream of telephone calls and letters" to his office, "most numerous are questions about JELL-O products."[49] The manufacturer, however, became more wary of kosher concerns and revised its standard information sheet to eliminate explicit reference to pork products, even though pork skins remained its principal source for gelatin.[50] To this day a *K* adorns Jell-O gelatin dessert packages. The capacity of a large firm to secure independent rabbinic endorsement and to use a *K* to suggest kosher status certainly was a great problem for systematic certification of kosher food.

A more subtle consequence of this struggle, however, offered better portents for the Orthodox. Jell-O's manufacturer continued to claim it was kosher, but food companies did not, more generally, see gelatin as a kosher ingredient. Since Conservative Judaism continued to view gelatin as kosher, and some Orthodox rabbis continued to certify gelatin products, this is a curious outcome. Why would the non-Jewish management of major food companies endorse, by their practice, the stricter standard of the Orthodox and thus make it harder to claim their products met kosher standards? Even more striking was the resistance of these same companies to the campaigns by Ralph Nader and other critics to tighter regulation of their activities. The higher expectations of kosher certifiers were consistent with the trend toward greater regulation of food in general, but their efforts occasioned far less resistance. How could this be so?

To some extent company actions reflected the way in which kosher consumers followed the lead of Orthodox certifiers. Dannon Yogurt offers an example. In 1985 the company reformulated its eight-ounce yogurts with fruit on the bottom to include gelatin, presumably to facilitate mixing. Unable to maintain certification from its previous kosher agency, the Triangle K, as it would not accept gelatin, the company turned to Rabbi Yehuda Gershuni, who along with Rabbi Telsner certified Jell-O. (Indeed, they were the only Orthodox rabbis to certify products that contained gelatin.) Notices in magazines followed by kosher consumers noted this change, and the experiment was a failure—kosher consumers simply stopped buying Dannon Yogurt, as there were many other kosher options. After a year the company removed gelatin from its products and returned to its original certification.[51]

The company evidently was chastened by the experience. While certainly capable of ignoring kosher rules, Dannon had learned that if it wanted to sell yogurt to observant consumers it needed certification from rabbis who did not accept gelatin. This insight resulted in a dramatic change of company policy. Three years later, Dannon shifted certification of its yogurts from Triangle K to the OU, doubtless incurring a considerable increase in certification costs but also seeking approval from the dominant Orthodox certification operation. And, accompanying this policy change, the company made no effort to claim that the yogurts in its product line containing gelatin (principally the low-fat varieties) met kosher requirements. The results, however, justified the firm's efforts to drastically reduce its use of gelatin and to comply with the mainstream Orthodox interpretation of kosher law. In 1991 the company told the trade magazine *Prepared Foods* that its sales to kosher consumers grew dramatically following its change in policies, including a 32 percent increase in number of Jewish households purchasing Dannon yogurt.[52]

Other firms followed a similar path. Their actions are only understandable if we add into this story the influence of Orthodox certification agencies, which grew rapidly after 1960. It is to their development that I turn next.

4

WHO SAYS IT'S KOSHER?

ON THE way to meeting Rabbi Menachem Genack, head of the Orthodox Union, the impending entry into the inner sanctum of Orthodox Judaism made me think of my very serious grandmother, Florence Horowitz. As a child, my limited contact with Orthodox Jews principally consisted of our regular Sunday afternoon visits to my father's parents' home on the Upper West Side. As I got a little older, I dreaded these occasions. While my father's father, Abe, was fun, with a sense of humor (he had a small stock of magic tricks and would delight in pulling a quarter from behind your ear), Florence was dour and strict. I remember sitting painfully on plastic slipcovers that protected their quasi-Victorian living room sofa and marveling at how she conserved whenever possible (reflecting her experiences in the Great Depression), even getting two or perhaps three cups of tea from every teabag. She radiated disapproval regarding most matters, often shaking her head at my family's much more liberal and, at least to her, profligate ways. I wondered if my reception by Rabbi Genack would be any better than it had been by Florence.

Once immediately outside the OU offices, however, another memory came to mind—my visit to the Washington, DC headquarters of the United Food and Commercial Workers in the mid-1980s while researching the meatpacking industry. Similar to the UFCW offices, the OU facilities breathed success and stability, signifying through a reputable address

FIGURE 4.1 Abraham and Florence Horowitz, 1950s. Personal collection of Roger Horowitz.

(lower Manhattan), tight security, and polite receptionists that the organization had authority, power, and stability.

However, once inside, the OU's austere culture was pure Florence. Rabbi Genack's functional corner office was small; a step up, perhaps, from the tightly packed cubicles where most seemed to work, but not on a par with the large, decorated offices of the UFCW top brass. He did not make me welcome. Genack barely looked at me during our perfunctory fifteen-minute conversation, constantly monitoring his e-mail and mobile phone as I explained my project and asked for the OU's cooperation. While indicating that the OU would respond favorably to my queries, he radiated disapproval (so reminiscent of Florence!) for my evidently non-Orthodox mode of dress and behavior.

Despite feeling put off by Rabbi Genack's chilly reception, my experience studying unions such as the UFCW made me appreciate the OU's success. It is quite an accomplishment for an organization to change the behavior of corporate America, as unions have known for some time. Yet here was an organization of Orthodox Jews, following a set of cultural practices far outside the mainstream of American life, that had persuaded huge corporations to permit rabbis to inspect, and in some areas dictate, corporate practices. And they did so without the supporting web of legislation and federal agencies (such as the National Labor Relations Board) that have proved indispensable to the success of unionism and without adopting the practices of the companies it monitored, quite unlike how unions too often assimilated corporate culture.

The growth of kosher certification organizations such as the OU was central to the expansion of kosher food. It was, of course, essential that Orthodox rabbis develop a clear understanding of what was acceptable and what was not in modern food, as in the cases of Coke and Jell-O. But their actions begged the question, how to enforce those decisions outside the Jewish community? And how could companies interested in reaching kosher consumers learn what was necessary to do?

Through a process of trial and error, the Orthodox Jews committed to advancing their creed learned how to create organizations that could enforce kosher standards in food manufacturing. But these organizations did even more—they established a formal structure in which kosher law could be adjudicated and enforced. The discordant debates in the 1930s, 1940s, and 1950s, fought out in public among feuding rabbinic factions, were brought inside new institutions—the certification organizations—and resolved behind closed doors between hierarchically organized rabbinic associations. With their symbols formally registered as trademarks under U.S. law, these agencies could grant—or deny—permission for firms to adorn food packages with the symbols certifying the product was kosher. The American legal structure encoded hierarchical decisions on kosher law with new meaning and power, since awarding the right to attach a kosher trademark to a package established a finality and decisiveness to debate that in Jewish tradition had been heretofore more open to minority opinion.

"ORGANIZED KASHRUS" BEGINS

As with so many of the features of modern kosher food, the reliance on rabbinic agencies to secure agreements with food manufacturers can be traced back to the initiatives of Abraham Goldstein. While the OU had a few agreements by 1930 (and ones negotiated by Goldstein), it was through his efforts that the contract-based certification strategy expanded under the umbrella of OK (Organized Kashrus) Laboratories in the 1930s and 1940s. Working through a network of rabbis, mostly based in the New York area but including some in New Jersey and Pennsylvania, OK rapidly expanded the range of products carried on its kosher food lists. In 1938 the *Kosher Food Guide* listed 238 kosher certified products made by 136 companies, ten times more than those included in the OU's magazine. While Goldstein, and later his son George, functioned as the full-time administrator, the *mashgihim* (kosher supervisors) for OK were active synagogue rabbis who conducted necessary inspections on a part-time basis.[1]

After Abraham Goldstein's death in 1944, OK's growth slowed significantly. By 1948, it had added only fifty more certified products and about thirty firms to its 1938 totals at a time when many new products were entering the large supermarkets sprouting in and around major American cities.[2] In part, such slow growth was understandable, as George did not have the connections and status of his father, who was personally known to many food manufacturers. But is also may have reflected OK's problematic structure: an organization that was not headed by rabbis and yet authorized placing its *K* in a circle trademark on kosher products. It tried to duck this problem by claiming the actual kosher certification came from the supervising rabbis and not from the OK's nonrabbinic administrators; nonetheless, this awkward arrangement, and the Goldsteins' difficult relationship with Orthodox rabbinic circles, may well have limited OK's effectiveness.

For its part, the Orthodox Union took over a decade to recover from the mid-1930s schism with Goldstein. Four years passed before the OU could find a replacement to chair its Kashruth Committee; not until 1940 did President William Weiss appoint attorney Benjamin Koenigsberg to fill this position. Not surprisingly, its certification program languished. The OU had only fifty-two companies under supervision in 1948, less than one-third of those supervised by OK.[3] A few years later, its certification

program was ridiculed by the *Jewish Observer*, published by the Orthodox (if irascible) Trude Weiss-Rosmarin. She skewered the OU's 1952
Kashruth Directory as consisting mostly of vegetable and mineral products, "which require no Kashruth certification," including seven brands of
salt. "The uselessness of the UOJC [Union of Orthodox Jewish Congregations, the OU's parent organization] Kashruth Directory," she continued, "is attested to the fact that *not even one Jewish owned food packer
of national scope and not one first class Jewish restaurant or hotel* has
cared to engage the Kashruth Supervision services of the UOJC."[4] In contrast to the OU narrative that it pioneered organized kosher certification,
it was not until the mid-1950s that the number of OU-certified products
finally surpassed those endorsed by OK Laboratories.

Complicating the OU's reorganization efforts were ongoing frictions
with the Rabbinical Council of America (RCA), the rabbinic association linked to the Union of Orthodox Jewish Congregations. The RCA
was a far younger organization than the OU, formed only in 1935 by
the American-born graduates of Yeshiva University, and more attuned to
American culture than its principal competitor among the Orthodox, the
Agudath Harabonim, which was dominated by European-trained rabbis.
Desirous of cementing its status within rabbinic circles, and wary of a
repeat of the Goldstein saga, the RCA pressed for exclusive control over
the OU's kosher certification program.

The issue in dispute was, in perhaps somewhat different form, the
same that had bedeviled Goldstein: the relationship between lay scientific
knowledge and rabbinic authority rooted in traditional Jewish law. In the
RCA-OU tensions it surfaced as struggles over lines of authority—who
controlled the relationships with firms under OU supervision? With the
OU insisting on the importance of lay leadership (usually drawn from
men who were leaders of their synagogues), tensions between the rabbis
and lay OU leaders are palpable in the Kashruth Division minutes. While
Benjamin Koenigsberg took a far more respectful tone than Goldstein,
he also sought to preserve avenues for experts familiar with modern food
production to influence kosher supervision.[5] The rabbis, for their part,
remained highly suspicious that the lay administrators would, like Goldstein, not accord the RCA exclusive jurisdiction. A dispute over certifying Spry, for example, erupted at a 1942 meeting when it turned out the

rabbinic supervisor approved by the Kashruth Division was not an RCA member. No doubt these mutual suspicions impeded outreach efforts by the OU.[6]

A series of agreements between the RCA and the OU in the late 1940s and early 1950s helped to smooth ruffled feathers on both sides. The RCA received what it wanted, complete control over decisions involving the *kashrus* of particular products; the lay administrators preserved the OU as the principal certifying body to which rabbis reported—and where all monies were handled so that surpluses would go to the Orthodox Union and not the RCA. These agreements created a Joint Kashruth Division (JKD), "joint" signifying the RCA's coequal participation with a rabbinic coordinator serving on an equal basis with the division's lay director. In time the RCA rabbis largely took over the administration of the JKD as the post of rabbinic coordinator assumed the functions once reserved for the division's director, and the OU simply let the latter position remain unfilled.[7]

In retrospect, creation of the JKD meant the rabbis had won, as the RCA's rabbis came to completely dominate major staff positions. In so doing, the RCA ensured its own relevance in the future expansion of kosher certification and, with that, its place as the preeminent Orthodox rabbinic association. Yet its victory also incorporated the innovations sought by Goldstein decades before and tied the rabbis irrevocably to Union of Orthodox Jewish Congregations. The JKD rabbis fully appreciated the importance of science in the tasks they had set for themselves; indeed, their standards for supervising factories and checking all ingredients were in full accord with Goldstein's concerns. A professor of chemistry at Yeshiva University was even on call to perform necessary scientific tests. The OU finally had a structure in place well-suited for the challenges of certifying modern food.[8]

KOSHER SHOPPING IN THE 1950S

With its internal politics finally settling down, the OU could turn fully to the daunting challenge of expanding its certification program. Its seemingly impressive numbers in the mid-1950s—471 products from 102 companies—actually barely touched the American food market. The OU trumpeted its success with many minor products, such as fish, macaroni, potato chips, and wine that either were relatively easy to produce in a kosher manner or were made by Jewish companies for whom observant Jews constituted a core market. Yet its listings contained huge gaps; for example, according to its 1955 *Kashruth Directory*, there was neither kosher cheese nor kosher milk available for purchase—even though observant consumers obviously obtained those items! The OU created this problem by limiting its listings to only those products certified by RCA rabbis through the OU. Its *Kashruth Directory* thus presented a highly inaccurate picture of kosher food's availability and was not especially useful to observant consumers. Indeed, into the early 1960s the OU symbol simply was irrelevant to shoppers looking for many kinds of processed foods.[9]

Something as evidently useful as baby food exemplifies the omissions in the OU listings. The JKD's 1950 report lamented that kosher baby food with meat was not available, despite the many inquiries it had received from observant mothers. A few years later, the Manischewitz Company met this demand with a complete line of kosher baby food, "including beef, lamb, veal, beef heart, and liver," that it assured consumers was of "strictest kashruth and highest quality that has made Manschewitz kosher foods so popular." Yet this Manischewitz baby food, as with all Manischewitz products, did not appear in the OU's *Kashuth Directory*.[10]

A broader choice of food with rabbinic endorsement appeared in the OK's *Kosher Food Guide*. While it listed many of the OU-endorsed products, OK Laboratories drew more generally from foods that, to its satisfaction, came from a trustworthy manufacturer or had endorsement from a competent rabbi. All Manischewitz products appeared (including the kosher baby food), as did many types of soft cheeses, frozen fish, and canned meats—all of which were absent from the OU directory. With over three hundred products in its pages, the *Kosher Food Guide* not only demonstrated the parochial nature of the OU's kosher directory, it also showed that observant housewives relied on a number of different methods to obtain food that they felt met kosher standards.[11]

One common technique was closely reading the ingredient labels that appeared on processed food. Following passage of the 1938 Federal Food, Drug, and Cosmetic Act, the Food and Drug Administration required packaged foods sold through interstate commerce to display clear information on their contents. While the legislation's main concern was curbing the use of dangerous additives rather than promoting consumer knowledge, listings included principal ingredients. Although imprecise in its disclosure requirements, the 1938 legislation did offer kosher consumers a means to judge for themselves whether processed foods met their religious requirements.[12]

The popularity of reading labels to ascertain a product's kosher status is attested to by the unrelenting stream of expert advice to *not* rely on ingredient listings for this purpose. "Of course our readers are careful label readers," George Goldstein granted in 1950, who "make certain that all the given ingredients are kosher ones." He warned repeatedly, however, that the ingredient listings were insufficient to understand if the product was kosher. Goldstein especially decried the "disturbing development" of Orthodox women buying baked goods "just because the label listed vegetable shortening as one of the ingredients." While these women clearly wanted to avoid buying products that contained lard, he warned the labels might not tell them about *treif* flavorings or other ingredients or whether the equipment had been used to make nonkosher products. The endless repetition of this advice is, inadvertently, good evidence that many women relied on their own judgment—not a rabbi's *hecksher*—to determine if the product could be used in a kosher home.[13]

Kosher shoppers also turned to reliable brands from Jewish-owned food companies that generally did not seek outside supervision of their products. Firms such as Manischewitz, Horowitz Margareten, Streit's, and Rokeach had long produced kosher food, and, when they expanded their product lines in the 1940s and 1950s, observant Jews generally felt the new offerings could be relied upon as kosher. Rokeach even asked for an evaluation of the merits of OU kosher certification in a massive 1961 study conducted by the renowned market researcher Ernest Dichter. Dichter found that while the OU symbol was widely recognized, kosher consumers nonetheless "used brands of Kosher foods that carry only the word Kosher and that employ neither the congregational nor rabbinical symbol." In his opinion, Rokeach's established Jewish lineage, its long history in the food business, and the preference for its products among older Jews "all carry a Kosher implication which employment of the word

"You mean, you didn't <u>know</u> we carry a complete selection of Passover foods?"

(Including Rokeach Fine Kosher Foods, of course!)

FIGURE 4.2 Rokeach advertisement with Molly Picon, 1950s. Notice the company asserts its products are kosher, but does not place a rabbinical *hecksher* on the advertisement. Molly Picon papers, American Jewish Historical Society, New York and Boston. Courtesy Manischewitz Foods.

'Kosher' is sufficient to reinforce and authenticate." Consequently, Dichter advised that outside certification was simply unnecessary to secure patronage from observant Jewish consumers.[14]

Cookbooks also indicate how observant kosher shoppers in the 1950s relied more heavily on their own judgment rather than visible rabbinic endorsement to obtain products they felt met Jewish dietary laws. When my mother had to set up her own kosher home after marrying in 1951, she turned to the immensely popular book *Jewish Cookery* by Leah W. Leonard. Widely reviewed (including in the *New York Times* and *Commentary*), Leonard's popularity among young Jewish housewives is attested to by the book's many editions; first published in 1949, it was already in its fourth printing two years later. By giving her book the subtitle *In Accordance with the Jewish Dietary Laws*, Leonard clearly reached out to observant women who wished to maintain a kosher household. Yet, in very modern language, Leonard also explained how the "kitchen engineer" could prepare recipes "handed down from countless generations" that would work with "modern techniques for food preparation."[15]

In her mixture of contemporary and traditional advice, Leonard sought to educate the homemaker about the task of preparing kosher food—but not in a manner that would have made Abraham Goldstein or the Orthodox Union especially pleased. A table of kosher meats and their uses adorned the inner frontispiece, followed by chapters on "Rules for Kashruth." Employing concrete language, Leonard instructed readers in the required separation of milk and meat, Passover's special rules, what animals (and parts of these animals) were kosher, and how meat had to be soaked and salted before it was acceptable for use. Still, housewives were left largely on their own as how to acquire these foods. Leonard assumed that meat came from a kosher butcher, but did not offer any directions on how to determine if a butcher was indeed kosher. Similarly, while she explained that there were packaged goods specially prepared for Passover "labeled *Kosher Shel Pesach* (for Passover use)," she did not advise that any rabbinic mark had to appear on the package. And her recipes, many of which used flavorings such as Worcestershire and soy sauce, did not include any admonition to seek out kosher-certified version of those items.[16]

The only nod to kosher certification came in the book's final chapter, seemingly tacked on at the end and with the curious title "Magic Meals Out of Cans." In it Leonard explained that the "kitchen engineer" should always maintain an "emergency shelf" of food for those occasions when there was no time to shop for dinner. She credited the canning industry for making "every type of essential food available" for quick preparation. And she also recommended to the "emergency cook" the new "ready-to-heat" frozen foods "plainly marked with the approved" OU label. Finally, on p. 461 in a 500-page volume, rabbinically endorsed food had made it into Leonard's cookbook.[17]

A closer look at even this very limited endorsement indicates how minimally the OU had made it onto the radar of Jewish cooking. Leonard restricted her recommendation to frozen food and did not admonish housewives to similarly look for the OU's *hecksher* on canned goods, such as soups and baked beans, where OU-certified Heinz products competed for shelf space with many other brands. And the OU items she recommended were so ethnically Jewish—gefilte fish, cheese blintzes, knishes, and potato pancakes—that they would serve only as substitutes for traditional food made from scratch. They were of little help for young Jewish housewives such as my mother who wanted to figure out if the very American processed foods of the 1950s could be brought into observant homes.

More traditional Jewish cookbooks of the 1950s also paid very little attention to kosher certified food, favoring instead the observant home-maker's ability to determine what items were kosher. Brooklyn's leading Jewish newspaper, the *Jewish Examiner,* maintained a regular cooking column edited by Leah Gross containing recipes that stressed the impor-tance of maintaining a kosher home. It collected prize-winning essays into a simple spiral-bound book in 1955 called *The Balabustas' Best*; by using the Yiddish phrase for homemaker as its title, the *Examiner* stressed the traditionalism of its advice. Ignoring other cookbooks, such as *Jewish Cookery,* that doubtless were widely available by then, the *Examiner* pro-moted *The Balabustas' Best* as "the first kosher cookbook of its kind" that was "not only a kosher cookbook but also a guide . . . to the meaning and origin of Kashruth." To make sure there was no mistaking its message, *Examiner* editor Rabbi Louis D. Gross stressed in the book's introduc-tion that in a "rapidly changing modern world" the "chief bulwark of the Jew" remains the "spiritual caliber" of the home—especially kosher observance. To him, it was not simply a matter of cooking or health; "kashruth" was a "traditional religious ritual" that served to bind "the Jew to his heritage throughout the centuries."[18]

Despite their claims, however, there was little difference in the advice offered for maintaining kosher standards. In *The Balabustas' Best*, house-wives read what meat was kosher and what was not and how to soak and salt meat to make it acceptable for use. Similarly, there were sections on how to observe the Jewish holidays and a virtually identical admo-nition on Passover to abstain from grains and cereals, and to only eat foods such as soda water and candy that had a "Kosher label." Neither cookbook explained what constituted an authoritative "kosher label," nor did housewives learn how to determine the validity of the "Kashruth approved" shortenings that they were supposed to use. Presumably such a determination was left to their judgment rather than an authoritative body of rabbis.[19] For all their efforts, the OU and its Rabbinical Council did not yet have the authority to which they aspired.

PROMOTING KOSHER

In their aspirations to provide guidance to the purchasing decisions of observant Jewish consumers, the OU and OK faced off against the considerable influence of the Joseph Jacobs Organization. Founded in 1919 by an aggressive advertising salesman for the Yiddish *Jewish Morning Journal*, Joseph Jacobs created an independent agency tightly connected to leading Jewish newspapers in New York and other East Coast cities. In 1926 the Hecker H-O Company praised Joseph Jacobs for planning an advertising campaign "proving that the Jewish field was a very good market for our product." His advertising agency grew dramatically over the next two decades by showing mainstream food manufacturers such as Maxwell House "how to do business in the Jewish market at a profit" through systematic advertising campaigns that bridged the ethnic-linguistic divide.[20]

The OK and OU gnashed their teeth at Joseph Jacob's success, however, as he neither accepted their authority nor their view of kosher standards. To Jacobs, all cereals, flour, dairy products, canned fruits and vegetables, indeed all packaged goods were kosher unless the label identified contents contradicting kosher law. Maxwell House coffee also was inherently kosher to Jacobs, but to allay concerns as to whether it was kosher for Passover, he relented and sought a rabbinic endorsement. The concerns stemmed from a Passover *minhag* (custom) widely accepted among Ashkenazi Jews that prohibited consuming beans and legumes called *kitniot* (such as corn, rice, or soybeans) during the holiday. At Jacob's request, Rabbi Bezalel Rosen ruled that the coffee bean was akin to a berry rather than a bean, thereby making it acceptable for Passover. But, outside of Passover's special requirements, Jacobs preached that rabbinic endorsement generally was not necessary to market a product to observant Jews.[21]

Jacob simply advised food companies that they could and should ignore certification organizations. He pointedly contradicted the *Kosher Food Guide*'s oft-repeated claim that endorsement by OK Laboratories would provide an "open sesame to the Jewish market" and advised firms to ignore Abraham and George Goldstein's queries, as they "have no obligation to answer questionnaires or letters regarding their products." Speaking to a meeting of food industry scientists in 1949, Jacobs went further and virtually dismissed rabbinic authority altogether, holding up instead the housewife as the true gatekeeper for *kashrus*. She "knows pretty well what is kosher and what is not," he explained, as many foods were "inherently kosher"; if there were doubts, the ingredient labels required by federal law "makes it an easy matter for the housewife to determine for herself." If still unsure, she could seek the advice of a rabbi. Even then, though, the rabbi "has no power to decree the Kashruth of the product," in Jacobs's view. "He merely expresses his opinion."[22]

Celebrating the housewife's authority was a useful strategy for Jacobs—she was, after all, the target of his advertising messages. Doubtless his audience of food industry scientists was comforted by his affirmation that they need not submit to the entreaties of rabbis to inspect their products and pay for a certification mark on the label. But his position was ultimately self-serving, as it was intended to build a wall against rabbinic influence and to protect claims that the three products Abraham Goldstein campaigned so hard against—rennet, gelatin, and glycerin—were in fact kosher.

Jacobs's reassurances to food manufacturers rested on the assertion that all three ingredients were kosher. Echoing the arguments of Rabbi Pardes (referred to as "a well-known Rabbi in Chicago"), Jacobs stressed the *ponim chadashos* defense that creating a "new chemical substance" such as gelatin meant it was not prohibited under kosher law. While granting that not all rabbis agreed, speaking in 1949 Jacobs was still accurate to say that many "do not contest his opinion." As the Orthodox consensus changed in the 1950s, however, Jacobs did not alter his views—or his advice to clients. Shortly after Rabbi Eliezer Silver orchestrated the widespread rejection of gelatin as kosher, Jacobs remained an advisor to Jell-O's manufacturer and an active promoter of it as a kosher product. A 1952 *New York Times* advertisement by the Jacobs organization boasted how Menasha Skulnik, "America's top-rated Jewish comic" used "Jewish-themed copy" to sell Jell-O to Jewish radio audiences. A couple of years later the chief executives of the firms making Jell-O and Junket

Rennet products joined other company leaders to thank Joseph Jacobs for his thirty-five years of "distinguished service" that had helped solve the "particular marketing problems of New York City."[23]

With its dismissal of rabbinic authority, and lenient views on kosher law, the Jacobs agency was in effect a competitor of the certification organizations. Its impressive client portfolio and suite of advertising services was an enormous stumbling block to the OU's mission, especially the views it held on what manufacturers might need to do to bring their products into compliance with kosher law. Why should a firm turn to the OU or OK when the Jacobs organization had a track record of success, and would promote its products without requiring those annoying changes in manufacturing methods that the rabbis might demand?

In a fateful decision, the OU decided to fight fire with fire by hiring an advertising man to refashion its appeal. In January 1956 the JKD turned over promotion, and in fact strategic direction, to Ben Gallob and his small public relations company, Galton Associates. With a journalism degree from the University of Minnesota and considerable experience working for United Press International in the Midwest, Gallob brought knowledge of modern marketing methods to the OU. While well-known in later years for his long involvement with the Jewish Telegraph Agency (the principle Jewish news service), his enormous influence on the OU's *kashrus* program is insufficiently appreciated.[24]

With his professional understanding of public relations, Gallob changed the OU's approach from passively waiting for firms to contact it to actively promoting kosher certification's benefits. Much as Abraham Goldstein had applied chemistry to modernize kosher certification, Gallob used contemporary marketing strategies to modernize the OU's profile, as well as the range of services it offered, and in so doing reduce the appeal of the Joseph Jacobs Organization. He understood, above all, that the OU had to show mainstream food companies that adding its label to their foods would increase sales.

His very first action, reflecting an advertiser's understanding of brands, was to submit an application on January 18, 1956, to formally trademark the OU's distinctive *U* in a circle symbol. When set in use in the 1920s, the OU's symbol could not be registered under U.S. trademark law, which held (in the words of the U.S. Patent Office) that an "'association' that neither produces goods nor trades in them cannot be the owner of any technical mark." In this respect, U.S. law was at odds with practices of other nations that generally permitted registration of "collective" marks such as union labels. After many years of debate, U.S. law finally caught up with the rest of the world with the 1946 Lanham Act and authorized certification marks to be issued by associations "not possessing an industrial or commercial establishment"; 15 U.S. Code 1127 defined such a mark in robust terms: "The term 'certification mark' means any word, name, symbol, or device, or any combination thereof used by a person other than its owner . . . to certify . . . material, mode of manufacture, quality, accuracy, or other characteristics of such person's goods or services." This broad definition would give the OU, the OK, and later other rabbinic organizations remarkable authority under secular law to promulgate religious standards.[25]

Gallob then moved systematically to create value in the OU label, a venerable advertising strategy. To best the Joseph Jacobs agency, he needed to be able to convince manufacturers that a visible sign of rabbinic certification was indeed the "open sesame" to the Jewish market. He began with the OU's greatest resource, its national network of synagogues, which, in addition to their religious function, also constituted a primary market for kosher-certified products. Here was a network that could be reached with targeted advertising that was far more efficient and much less expensive than the traditional approach followed by the Jacobs agency. Under his initiative, the OU began producing a glossy, one-page monthly called the *OU News Reporter* promoting newly certified products. Designed to reach observant Jews directly (if economically) by posting on synagogue bulletin boards, its distribution through Orthodox channels also showed firms the unique market they could reach through OU endorsement. For similar reasons, the OU altered its *Kosher Products Directory* from a supplement in the magazine *Jewish Life* to a stand-alone booklet that urged housewives to "HANG ME IN YOUR KITCHEN," using the convenient punch hole in the upper left-hand corner. A special effort went into disseminating the annual Passover directory; in 1963 the OU distributed 175,000 copies, principally through Orthodox synagogues and other institutions. These measures were intended to shore up the observant market that followed the OU symbol and thereby provide greater incentive for mainstream firms to explore certifying their products.[26]

Gallob then moved on to fact-finding discussions to ascertain what was necessary to increase media coverage of the OU's program. He discovered "strong" interest among women and food editors in general media outlets (e.g., *Good Housekeeping*) for information on what constituted kosher food and a quite different but promising audience in business journals (such as *Supermarket News*) on the technical features of the OU's certification program. However, he discovered surprising ambivalence toward the OU's kosher program among the Jewish media, both Yiddish and English. *Jewish Record* editor and publisher Arthur Wayne, for example, applauded how the OU symbol was "a vital service to Kashruth." Nonetheless, in careful language, he urged that certification expand to become a "total operation" that included "an advertising schedule—even if only of a token nature—to be linked with the Union's endorsement." Securing advertising revenue from food companies that had received OU endorsements would, he predicted, create "the most permissive kind of situation in the Jewish Weekly press" for favorable press coverage of the OU program.[27]

The JKD evidently gave Gallob a free hand developing programs based on his findings, as his media activities over the next few years showed close adherence to the needs he identified in 1956. Under his guidance, the JKD issued a steady stream of press releases on OU activities, such as newly certified products, "Food Fact Sheets" on Passover and other holidays, and information on food-related activities of the OU Women's Division. Dozens of newspapers picked up these often short announcements, from the *Los Angeles Examiner* and San Francisco *News-Call Bulletin* on the West Coast to the *Miami Herald* and *Knoxville Journal* in the South and the *Chicago Tribune* and *Detroit Free Press* in the Midwest. Naturally, East Coast papers carried many of these news items; indeed, the *New York Post* published more than thirty of the OU's announcements in the course of six years. Its steady stream of activities also generated press queries that lead to feature articles. Both the AP and UPI wire services carried stories picked up in local papers around the country. The *New York Times* and *Wall Street Journal* each carried several extended articles, as did *Good Housekeeping* and *Time* magazine.[28]

The OU also listened closely to Arthur Wayne's concerns and systematically sought to strengthen its ties with Jewish media. The OU started its own modest institutional advertising campaign promoting the OU symbol, especially around Passover, and strongly encouraged OU-certified companies to place advertisements in the Jewish press as well. Arthur Wayne must have been pleased with the result; by 1963 several OU-certified companies, including Thomas bread and Buitoni macaroni products, regularly advertised their products in Jewish newspapers. Proof that such advertising "helps to foster goodwill" was evidenced by the inclusion of an estimated one thousand OU-initiated items—from pictures to feature-length articles—in the Jewish media between 1956 and 1962.[29]

While this blizzard of articles in general interest and Jewish publications was impressive and unprecedented, inclusion of stories on kosher issues in business publications was simply phenomenal. Forty periodicals oriented to particular food business sectors carried JKD news, ranging from *Food Processing* (for manufacturers) to *Modern Grocer* (for retailers), and in some cases more than twenty times. *Food Business* and *Chemical Week* carried more extended articles; the latter doubtless intrigued its readers by pointing out that learning how to conform to kosher requirements "could open up markets now closed to specialty makers" of food ingredients.[30]

As *Chemical Week*'s advice indicates, the extensive media work had as its ultimate objective expansion of the OU's kosher-certified product line. In his initial 1956 research, Gallob learned that food company executives and their marketing and advertising advisers were "keenly interested" in learning about the kosher market: "how many Jews, in what areas, buy and use which Kosher products." Much of the coverage in the *OU News Reporter* served to answer these questions by including success stories of firms that had increased sales by certifying their products.[31] Quickly, however, Gallob and the JKC learned that simply educating firms about the kosher market was not enough to attract their business. To secure a competitive advantage against the well-established Joseph Jacobs Organization, Gallob persuaded the OU that it needed to dramatically expand its kosher certification services far beyond what an advertising firm could offer.

Using its expertise and authority as a nonprofit religious organization, OU systematically developed its ability to serve as a general consultant for firms considering kosher certification. Its 1967 publication, *The Key to the Kosher Market*, described in thirty-five detailed pages how a food company could get observant Jewish customers to buy its products. "EVERYONE BENEFITS," the pamphlet explained, "the Jewish consumer, the grocery industry, the food industry" from OU certification, as firms gained access to the growing kosher market and Jews could buy more products. And the pamphlet went on to delineate the assistance firms could receive from the OU in reaching this market.[32]

One dimension of these activities emulated, in large degree, the activities of a niche marketing firm. While the OU stopped short of preparing actual advertising copy, in all other respects it functioned as marketing consultants for how to enter the kosher field. Firms could receive extensive information on consumer preferences and demand for particular kinds of products, drawing on information from surveys conducted by the OU with a panel of observant homemakers. The OU also offered advice on store displays and advantageous advertising outlets (such as the Jewish media) and was willing to review advertising material, presumably to ensure there were no inadvertent mistakes that might offend observant Jews.[33]

Its largest departure from standard advertising agency services, though, was advising the engineers in firms that wished to explore the kosher market's possibilities, but were unsure how to fashion products that met necessary requirements. Such a company could draw on the expertise of OU rabbis who were not only knowledgeable "about Kashruth and technology" but also could "suggest new advances to the food industry." While respecting the proprietary concerns of manufacturers, OU rabbis were able to operate like production consultants, transferring knowledge from one firm to another, especially to suggest "dependably basic kosher ingredients for lack of which many familiar foods could not previously meet OU standards." The OU could tell firms how to make their products kosher, not only where and how they could sell to kosher consumers.[34]

The expansion of OU activities, first into public relations and then into production consulting, transformed the reach of its certification program. It took just two years for Gallob's efforts to double the number of OU-certified products to almost a thousand; within five years the OU had tripled the number of firms that used its certification program. While the statistics are not entirely consistent, it is clear that by 1970 the OU certified around twenty-five hundred products produced by approximately five hundred companies. Without doubt, the OU now was the leading kosher certifying agency in the country.

While the OU's efforts doubtless brought considerably more choices to observant consumers, the aggregate numbers conceal major limitations in the program's reach: 150 of its certified products were made by Rokeach and Horowitz Margareten, two Jewish firms that had long produced kosher food and only recently added OU certification. Similarly, a number of Israeli food companies were certified by the OU even though they had been kosher as well. An additional two hundred certified products were nonfood items such as aluminum foil, sandwich bags, and detergents, while another three hundred were various types of pickles and relishes. While these listings were certainly useful to kosher consumers, they did not add much to their ability to take advantage of "the great new field of convenience foods," as George Goldstein observed. The many labor-saving products entering the market in the 1960s, "so much desired by many working women," he observed regretfully, "are barred for our kosher tables."[35]

The presence of many private supermarket brands was a more promising development. As supermarkets were rapidly supplanting small neighborhood food stores (often owned by Jews) in the 1960s, their interest in OU certification portended great things. Many supermarkets participated, including once significant companies that have since disappeared, such as Bohack and Food Fair, and chains that have survived including Waldbaum's and ShopRite. A&P, the largest East Coast chain, had 275 of its products certified by the OU, certainly an accomplishment that New York kosher food shoppers appreciated.

While encouraging, the supermarkets obtained certification in only limited product areas. Fully one-half of the A&P's certified items were spices and candies, with various types of pasta and fruit jellies comprising an additional 20 percent. Shoppers wanting additional OU-certified A&P products were limited to coffee and tea, salad dressings, dessert puddings, and breakfast syrups, as well as company brands of mayonnaise, meat tenderizer, mustard, olives, pretzels, tartar sauce, and cooking oil. All this hardly made for a full shopping cart—and A&P's offerings were certainly the most extensive among supermarket brands. In time, though, the OU anticipated that it would be able to certify an ever wider range of products—and, indeed, that would prove to be the case.

The OU also made comparable, similarly modest gains with mainstream food manufacturers. Mothers could choose among an extensive array of vegetable and fruit baby foods from Beech-Nut as well as some meat items offered by the Erez food company. A wide range of Thomas's breads were acceptable, including the company's signature English Muffins and its white bread. Devonsheer and Dutch Maid had satisfied kosher requirements for their cracker product lines, as had Crosse and Blackwell and Polaner with their many jams and jellies. Some convenience foods also were available, though principally frozen potato products, soups, and spaghetti sauce varieties, along with frozen meals produced by Jewish companies Rokeach and Mother's. Skippy Peanut Butter and Wise Potato Chips were well-known national products headlining categories that also included small, local brands.

Large food companies were, however, absent from important categories. None of the major breakfast cereal companies or margarine manufacturers had OU certification; similarly, ice cream and soft drinks included only a few secondary firms. Kosher consumers who closely followed OU certification might have had lots of choices among pasta, pickles, and detergents, but could not buy Cheerios, Borden's Ice Cream, or Coca-Cola. Indeed, in many areas the OU's listings were inferior to what had been certified by OK Laboratories in the late 1930s, and had remained with OK for decades, such as Wheaties cereal and Breyer's Ice Cream![36] Missing too were firms widely associated with kosher food, such as Hebrew National and Manischewitz. Both companies relied on certification from individual rabbis, as did some national brands such as Coke. Much as OU aspired to make kosher food more widely available, observant Jews still faced sharply restricted choices around 1970 and, moreover, could not rely on the OU's kosher products guide to offer a full picture of available kosher foods. Much progress had been made, but kosher food still had a long way to go.[37]

KOSHER COMPETITION

Reporting on the advance of the kosher certification program to the Union of Orthodox Jewish Congregation's 1966 convention, JKD chairman Nathan K. Gross took a moment from his uplifting tone to disparagingly note the emergence of "imitators" who were seeking to emulate the OU's methods. Indeed, the very success of the OU's efforts to place its trademark on the products of processed food manufacturers attracted notice in the Orthodox world—and, with that, more competition. The Star-K agency began as the Vaad Hakashrus of Baltimore, literally a "kosher council" constituted by the Orthodox congregations in that city. Founded in 1947 to supervise locally produced items, Star-K expanded its activities under Rabbi Moshe Heinemann to include the suppliers of ingredients used in Baltimore's kosher food. In time its certifications would stretch throughout the United States and overseas. While the Star-K expanded outward, other agencies focused on particular sectors, such as the Kosher Supervision Service started by Rabbi Zecharia Senter in 1968. With particular strength in complex food technology, the agency, known as the K of K, soon became strongest for baked goods such as Levy's rye bread, which was marketed with the famous advertising slogan "you don't have to be Jewish to love Levy's." But, a few years after Gross's observation, the OU would find that its principal competitor could hardly be called an "imitator"—as it was a reenergized OK Laboratories.[38]

As the OU program blossomed in the late 1950s and early 1960s, OK Laboratories fell further and further behind. A local agency with an aging lay administrator was no match for an institution based on a national network of synagogues and with an affiliated rabbinic association to tap for *mashgihim* to supervise companies seeking certification. In what would turn out to be a propitious move, George Goldstein sold OK Laboratories to Rabbi Berel Levy in 1969.

At the time of the sale, Rabbi Levy had limited experience in kosher supervision. But he had spent a lifetime as a leading figure of the Chabad Lubavitch order. While born in New York City, Rabbi Levy's formative training took place at the Lubavitcher Yeshiva in Otwock, Poland, in the 1930s. Fortuitously, he returned to the United States just before the outbreak of World War II and received his rabbinic *semicha* (ordination) from the Lubavitch Yeshiva in Brooklyn. For much of the postwar years he was a leader of the Torah Umesora movement, creating schools in Connecticut and New Jersey and rising to director of development of the national organization.[39]

Rabbi Levy thus was an integral part of the rapidly growing American Lubavitch movement. Taking its name from the town of its birth in the late nineteenth century, Lyubavichi in Russia, the Lubavitch order was part of the Hasidic Jewish movement that stressed study and observance of the Torah as central to Jewish practice. After relocating its headquarters to Brooklyn during World War II, Lubavitch rebbe and leader Menachem Mendel Schneerson reshaped it into a missionary society devoted to returning nonobservant Jews to the faith. Emissaries known as *shluchim* moved throughout the United States, and indeed the world, to establish Chabad houses to disseminate traditional Jewish practices and serve as the core of an observant Jewish community. It was not surprising, then, that one of its trusted leaders began taking a close interest in kosher certification.

The immediate cause of the sale was the relationship that developed between Rabbi Levy and George's son Arthur Goldstein, who serendipitously took the same class on fund-raising at New York University in the late 1960s. Through their friendship, Rabbi Levy learned that George Goldstein, now in his late seventies, wanted to retire, and he offered to buy the business. Rabbi Levy's interest, however, was not merely opportunistic, as the Lubavitchers had been concerned about OU's standards of kosher certification for some time. Rumored to be acting on the urging of their rebbe, Rabbi Schneerson, to enter the kosher supervision field, Rabbi Levy found George Goldstein's interest in selling OK Laboratories the perfect opportunity to do so.[40]

Although OK Laboratories remained a private business rather than a not-for-profit religious organization like the OU, it was de facto a Lubavitch kosher certification firm. Its connections to the far-flung network of Lubavitch *shluchim*, who traveled regularly in their missionary activities, created a national and international network of potential *mashgihim*. In some respects, their mobility gave OK a competitive advantage over the OU, whose rabbis either led settled congregations or worked in

Orthodox Jewish institutions. As food chains—and the ingredients they used—stretched across national borders, the OK's close relationship with the Lubavitch movement gave it the means to track ingredients previously difficult to regulate.

OK's method for certifying kosher tropical oils reflected its special capabilities for international supervision; the results indicated that the Lubavitch rabbinic networks were an asset to operations. Oils produced in the South Pacific, principally palm oil, palm kernel oil, and coconut oil, were (and remain) very important for kosher foods as they pose no *kashrus* problems for either regular or Passover use. Rabbi Levy himself traveled to Malaysia in the early 1970s to certify palm kernel oil used by Wesson, solidifying the firm's previous use of OK's *hecksher*. A few years later, OK cemented its special international role by pioneering a method for certifying the tankers that carried the oil to American processing plants as well as the holding tanks located in Rotterdam into which oils often were placed waiting for transshipment.

Extending the principle of *b'lios* to international shipments, the OK developed a system of certificates to monitor the movement of oil-laden ships. It tracked bills of lading to determine what the tankers carried before taking oil into its containers and required stringent treatment of ships that had held previous shipments of nonkosher materials. To ensure that animal fat residues did not contaminate a tanker later filled with kosher tropical oils, it had to be thoroughly cleaned using OK-specified methods. A *mashgiah* would then place a seal on the empty container before it was sent to the South Pacific for its liquid cargo. The seal would have to remain in place until removed by a Lubavitch rabbi for the oil that was pumped into it to receive certification.

Having a far-flung network of Lubavitch *shluchim* to recruit for these duties was essential to the OK's operations. And with this network the OK was able to certify products from major health food companies Arrowhead Mills, Eden Foods, and Erewhon, as well sauces, ketchups, and mustards manufactured by Hunt and Kraft foods.[41]

While the OK could draw on the highly mobile Lubavitch to follow food production wherever it took place, the OU had to rely on synagogue rabbis to expand its supervisory network. This resource was a poor fit with increasingly decentralized industrial food production. The highway network's growth in the 1960s and development of national supermarket chains with central distribution warehouses encouraged manufacturing of many food products to shift into rural areas. At the same time, the Orthodox population remained concentrated in a few cities and towns, all too often at a considerable distance from the food processing plants that the OU hoped to be able to certify.

The mismatch was particularly acute when the OU looked for rabbis who could serve as kosher supervisors over certified plants. Employing congregational rabbis to visit, as a part-time sideline, factories nearby was one matter; but finding properly trained *mashgihim* to travel hundreds of miles to plants in the Christian Midwest farm belt was quite another. As the number of supervising rabbis on the OU's payroll doubled between 1958 and 1968 to 624, simply locating *mashgihim* for new facilities became a daunting problem. Moreover, it was not possible to accept new certifications without first conducing an on-site inspection so as applications for supervision steadily increased, it became harder and harder for the OU to respond in a timely manner. "I understand there are 57 Kashruth applications pending," recorded an unsigned 1978 memo in the files of OU executive vice president Rabbi Pinchas Stolper. In a frustrated, almost despairing tone, the memo concluded that "companies call daily in anger wanting to know when; if; what?" Without the personnel to properly supervise manufacturing plants, the OU was having grave difficulties keeping up with the interest in making kosher food.[42]

The OU also faced challenges from another direction—the higher expectations of observant Jews influenced by the Orthodox renaissance of the 1960s and 1970s. The formation of the state of Israel and its successive wars with Arab neighbors stimulated widespread identification with Zionism among American Jews and, among some Zionists, renewed exploration of Jewish religious practices. Extensive immigration of Jewish refugees following the end of World War II brought in large numbers of observant Jews deeply committed to saving the traditional cultures that the Nazis had tried so hard to exterminate. By the 1950s and certainly the 1960s, Jews seeking to educate their children in Jewish ways could turn to a network of private Jewish schools and yeshivas formed, "out of almost messianic zeal," by the Torah Umesorah movement. Among these Jews, as Jeffrey S. Gurock notes, Orthodoxy "was now pitching a narrower but stronger religious tent." And kosher observance was central to this revived Orthodoxy.[43]

The Orthodox renaissance created a dilemma for the OU. While welcoming the new members to its synagogues, and invigorated by what must have seemed a reversal of fortunes after the losses to Conservative Judaism in the 1950s, the OU now found itself criticized for insufficiently enforcing traditional kosher law. Writing in the pages of the Orthodox Congregation's journal, *Jewish Life*, in 1966, Michael Kaufman decried how the "orthodox 'right,' including the 'yeshivah world,' the Chassidim, and the organizations representing this vital—and militant—force, have tended to challenge the leadership of the Orthodox Union."[44] And it was in matters of kosher enforcement that the OU met with new competition as well as intense scrutiny of its real limitations.

In the winter of 1978 a stinging "Review of the 'O.U.,'" appeared in the journal *Madrich Lakashrus*, published by the Brooklyn Vaad Hakashrus. The cogently argued and carefully documented criticisms made for a thoughtful analysis of the OU's structural limitations that resulted in inconsistent supervision of kosher food production. The main problem it identified was that the OU had too few rabbinic supervisors on the ground to guide enforcement of its policies. It was simultaneously top- and bottom-heavy, with an overburdened staff in the OU's New York office and hundreds of field *mashgihim* supervising widely scattered plants, and with only a few regional officials to assist. Indeed it often was "very difficult to find *mashgihim* for factories which are located in small, remote towns," the report noted, leaving the OU little option but to hire supervisors who "may not always be relied upon in matters of kashrus." These shortcomings were compounded by the absence of controls over the far-flung *mashgihim*; left to their own judgment and with only limited contact with the OU's central office, "quite often a mashgiach will allow the use of a certain product, which he assumes is permissible but which actually might be incompatible with OU regulations."[45]

While it might have been tempting for the OU leaders to dismiss these criticisms as carping by newcomers to the kosher certification field, an internal revolt by its own *mashgihim* certainly placed problems of supervision front and center. Delegates to the OU's 1978 conference found an extraordinary anonymous flyer circulated at the event purporting to speak for the organization's *mashgihim*. In an echo of *Madrich Lakashrus*'s criticisms, the *mashgihim* decried poor communication within the OU, "not only when it pertains to their livelihood, but also when it pertains to important decisions which must be made." Such "breakdown in communication" had led to reprimands for *mashgihim* who made decisions counter to OU policy as well as to complaints from companies that their letters and phone calls had gone unanswered. The *mashgihim* also complained bitterly about their low pay and the absence of fringe benefits such as medical insurance. Sounding very much like aggrieved employees at one of the companies they were certifying, the *mashgihim* detailed efforts first to take their complaints to a religious court, then to form a labor union, and, finally, with those alternatives blocked by the Kashrus Division leadership, to reach out to directly to OU delegates, asking them to authorize creation of an internal grievance committee to permit the *mashgihim* to air their concerns. With such high levels of dissatisfaction, no wonder the OU was experiencing grave problems within its kosher certification operations.[46]

RESTRUCTURING, REVENUE, AND POWER

The confluence of a steady, indeed at times overwhelming, stream of requests for new certified products from food producers and the multiplication of criticisms brought profound, and effective, changes to the OU and other certification organizations. Following the appointment of Rabbi Genack as OU rabbinic administrator in the early 1980s, the Joint Kashrus Division underwent major restructuring. The office staff increased fivefold to thirty rabbis by 1989, and assigned not to monitor regions but instead to be specialists in particular manufacturing sectors, such as oils, flavors, baked goods, etc. These rabbinic coordinators, as they were termed, in turn supervised the rabbinic field representatives who inspected factories in a specific region. To address the challenges of properly monitoring certified plants, the OU increasingly hired full-time *mashgihim* and actively recruited from all Orthodox denominations, including the Lubavitch. At the apex of its supervisory structure, the OU retained two highly respected *poskim*, rabbis Yisroel Belsky and Herschel Schacter, to participate in weekly discussions on halachic issues that emerged from the field. With these shifts, the OU dramatically increased its on-staff expertise and, correspondingly, its ability to more closely guide the actual practices of *mashgihim*.[47]

With these changes, the post-1985 OU internalized both determination of *halacha* as well as implementation of rabbinic decisions. In so doing, it came closer to becoming a central church of Orthodox Judaism than at any other moment in American Jewish history. Debates that at one time took place between rabbis located in different regions and connected to different synagogues now were confined to the RCA rabbis in OU's leadership positions. Religious authority, once exercised through informal reputation and influence, became embedded in a hierarchical bureaucracy. Senior rabbis at the apex of the OU's structure exercised authority that was not debatable within the organization, while ladders for promotion and pay increases offered opportunities for younger rabbis to make a living, have career advancement opportunities, and expand their reputation within Orthodox circles.

The actual fees paid by firms to the OU constituted, in most cases, a negligible expense. A 1985 client list (the only one on record) offers some ideas of the costs for particular companies. Claussen, with pickles and canned tomatoes under supervision, paid $421.50 for the year. Haagen-Daz, with sixteen certified ice cream flavors, had annual payments of slightly under $1,000, as did Melitta coffee. Procter & Gamble, with many plants under supervision, paid the OU slightly over $5,000, still an insignificant amount for such a large company. Doubtless these low figures reflected the relatively simple supervision needs at these firms. Companies making products that required more active involvement, however, could pay substantial amounts. The largest client was Barton's candies, with a *monthly* fee of $2,500, reflecting perhaps costs associated with supervision of the company's retail outlets. Meat producers did pay proportionately more as *mashgihim* had to remain on-site while the plants were in operation; Empire Poultry, for example, paid the OU at least $10,000 annually to certify its operations. Keeping products kosher did cost considerably more in these instances.[48]

Accrued through its growing stable of certified products, the substantial funds that flowed through the OU's certification programs funded an expanded program to promote Orthodox Judaism. In its 1980–81 fiscal year, the last year for which financial records are publicly available, the Joint Kashrus Division had gross income of $2.5 million and a surplus of just under $400,000. Its revenues comprised 75 percent of the total income for the parent Union of Orthodox Jewish Congregations and its surplus subsidized a variety of programs designed to advance Orthodox Judaism, such as $306,000 spent on outreach to teens through the National Conference of Synagogue Youth. Since the JKD had contributed between 70 and 80 percent of the UOJC's revenue since at least 1958, it is easy to see how the expansion of kosher certification contributed substantially to the institutional development of this organization as the central institution of American Orthodox Judaism—and how it in turn could devote significant financial resources to strengthening the Orthodox denomination against its Conservative and Reform competitors.[49]

Orthodox Judaism benefited in other ways from certification-derived revenue flowing to the OU and other agencies. Regular employment as a *mashgiah* was an attractive career path for devout young Jews, especially those interested in ordination as a rabbi but wanting opportunities other than serving a particular congregation. Indeed, the hundreds of full-time *mashgihim* opened up new employment options for those who wanted to dedicate their lives to serving Orthodox Judaism. For synagogue rabbis who performed kosher supervision on a part-time basis, the supplement to their income was welcome and ultimately helped a congregation's finances. The geographic expansion of certifications to international outposts of food production, such as China, directly subsidized the travels of Lubavitch emissaries around the world, as they could become agents of the OU, OK, or other agencies (and sometimes more than one) and monitor some of their plants. As a peculiar form of Orthodox "government work," employment in a certification organization buttressed Orthodox religious institutions, created employment for Orthodox religious workers, and generated significant revenue for other Orthodox programs.

In a manner befitting their acceptance by major American firms, the "big four" kosher certification agencies—OU, OK, Kof-K, and Star-K— constituted a dominant oligopoly in the kosher supervision field. With their power to accept or reject inputs into the products they certified, they were able to enforce a set of standards for the many other small agencies that proliferated along with the expanding number of kosher certified products. In some cases certification agencies that did not meet the standards of the big four agencies found it hard to keep their customers, as it was inefficient for a firm to maintain supervision with an agency that was not accepted by the large ones. And, while Conservative rabbis had never attempted to create a national organization and generally limited supervision to local stores, the consolidation of an Orthodox kosher oligopoly precluded their entry into national supervision.

The increased authority commanded by certification organizations among kosher consumers is a measure of their success. While the cookbooks of the 1950s placed little emphasis on kosher symbols as a guide to obtaining kosher products and instead stressed the judgment of observant shoppers, similar guides produced after 1980 made it clear that, without a proper *hecksher*, the product could not be trusted as kosher. In *How to Keep Kosher*, published in 1980, author Bonne Rae London sternly advised kosher shoppers that they could not rely on reading of a package's label to determine if a product was kosher. While modern shoppers now had an "enormous variety" of items available to them, she warned that "the decision involved in determining if an item is kosher is very complex, requiring a detailed knowledge of biochemistry as well as *halacha* (Jewish law)." Consequently, she advised that "special rabbinical supervision" was necessary before a product "can be considered kosher" and offered examples of the OU and OK symbols as acceptable *heckshers. Kosher Cuisine*, published in 1984, contained similar advice but expanded the number of acceptable symbols to nine; *Our Food—the Kosher Kitchen Updated*, which appeared in 1992, endorsed fifteen symbols.[50] With these recommendations, authors endorsed not only these symbols but also the efforts of Orthodox rabbinic associations to establish themselves as the sole gatekeepers for kosher food.

The salutary influence of these organizations on kosher food's availability tended to obscure the dramatic changes they had wrought in Jewish practices. The kosher trademark became the measure of a product's conformity with Jewish law, not its contents; without the trademark, a product was not kosher even if its contents were. Certification trademarks thus aided a shift in the locus of judgment about a product's conformity with Jewish religious requirements from the purchaser and individual rabbi to bureaucratic religious organizations. In this way Jewish law paralleled the professionalization of knowledge so common in many areas of life in the modern era, with rabbis and their organizations obtaining new power through their capacity to determine, with the protection of secular law, what was kosher and what was not.

The standardization and legal protections accorded with this system aided the expansion of kosher food options, a true victory for the vision of Abraham Goldstein and Rabbi Tobias Geffen. But it also marginalized organizations and rabbis that did not agree with the dominant Orthodox interpretation of kosher law. Rabbis associated with Judaism's Conservative denomination lost the most with this centralization, as they were systematically denied access to those chambers and venues where the Orthodox-endorsed certifying organizations thronged. Buttressed with the authority to determine what was kosher, and the substantial revenues that came with that power, Orthodox certification helped to contribute to a greater renaissance of Orthodox Judaism in the latter part of the twentieth century. And it did so through increasingly close integration with industrial food producers.

5

INDUSTRIAL KASHRUS

ONE OF the celebrated advances of kosher certification in the 1990s, the prosaic Oreo cookie, was an item that never appeared on my families' tables when I was a child. Certainly Florence would not have served such a *treif* treat during our dreaded Sunday visits, instead relying on kosher-certified Barton's Barbonniere products obtained from its 96th Street and Broadway store, a short walk from my grandparents' apartment. While my mother was far from strict, the Oreo held no particular appeal as she wasn't exposed to it in her parent's house. So when I started to encounter Oreo snacks at school, camps, and the homes of friends, I didn't like the cookie at all. Kosher or not, I never became attuned to its taste during those childhood years when so many food preferences are established.

So decades later I wondered, "what is the big deal?" when the observant Jewish community began buzzing about the revolution finally coming home—the Oreo now was kosher. "The news came racing across the Internet with apocalyptic urgency," Rabbi Joshua J. Hammerman related in the *New York Times Magazine* in January 1998, a few weeks after the official announcement. As "the most infamous prohibition for observant Jewish children," Rabbi Hammerman claimed, acceptance of the Oreo was a "sign that Jews have finally made it." A decade after his essay, an entry by Natalie in the blog *stuffjewishyoungadultslike* emphasized that the Oreo was a watershed moment. "More than Kurt Cobain's death," she recalled, "more than the fall of the Berlin Wall, many YJAs [Young Jewish Americans] will select 1998, the year that Oreos became kosher, as a pivotal moment in their coming of age experience."[1] With the certification of the Oreo, kosher food, it seemed, had finally become as American as the proverbial apple pie.

Rabbi Hammerman's comment, that "Jews had finally made it," captured the deep symbolic meaning of the Oreo's acquiescence to Jewish religious requirements, along with a cascade of other American products. The world seemed to turn for kosher food in the late twentieth century; from Coors beer to the Oreo, many mainstream American processed foods found ways to add a kosher certification mark to its label. Yet the success seemed outsized for the market it was to serve; if many Jews like me were indifferent to the already spectacularly successful Oreo, why would Nabisco trouble itself with kosher certification? Surely the addition of observant Jewish customers comprising less than 1 percent of the U.S. population would have little impact on the firm's bottom line—especially considering the increased costs associated with rabbinic supervision.

Market research firms and kosher advocacy groups offered a straightforward "consumer demand" argument—significant numbers of non-Jews were seeking out kosher food. Inspired by the Hebrew National slogan, "We answer to a higher authority," consumers with doubts about the food system (and frequently naive about kosher certification) looked to kosher-certified products as somehow safer and cleaner than nonkosher varieties. Small numbers among these non-Jewish consumers were highly motivated—Muslims looking for assurances that foods contained no pork, lactose-intolerant consumers ensuring there was no milk residue in their food, etc. But, for most, kosher functioned as an assurance of quality, in some evanescent way, even if what they thought it meant bore no resemblance to what kosher certification actually entailed. The Oreo, after all, was just as full of sugar, fat, and calories after kosher certification as it was before.

The "consumer demand" explanation rested on simplistic notions of a food system consisting of producers on one side and individual consumers on the other. Instead, it is better imagined as a network of incredibly complicated chains, with myriad stops on the way between farmer and consumer and enormous varieties of institutional relationships bringing food to the table. The diversity among "producers" in such a system is matched only by the diversity of consumers. Indeed, food consumers may also be food producers, endlessly complicating the neat duality of "consumers want—and producers make" conjured up by believers in a responsive marketplace. Kosher food's successes—as well as failures—owe as much to the dynamics of the modern industrial food system as the preferences of *stuffjewishyoungadultslike*.

THE SUCCESS...

By the late twentieth century, kosher food was starting to resemble other sectors of American business. In addition to a widely respected trade journal (*Kashrus Magazine*), it had a quasi-trade association, the Association of Kashrus Organizations, that met periodically to discuss common problems, and an industry expo, the annual Kosherfest show, usually held in New Jersey. And, similar to the industrial sectors that it regulated, a more orderly competition emerged among the "Big Four" kosher certification organizations as they learned to live with each other as well as compete for clients. With these agencies certifying over ten thousand consumer products in the late 1980s, and additionally thousands of ingredients that went into those foods, certified kosher food had truly entered the mainstream of the American food industry.[2]

Befitting its advance, kosher food finally received attention from secular market research firms who saw that there was money to be made by selling reports detailing if, and how, companies could enter this field. *The Kosher Foods Market*, published by Packaged Facts at the end of 1988, was the first systematic study of American kosher food by a company without a stake in the industry or the Jewish religion. Its findings were dramatic. The study estimated that the market for kosher certified goods exceeded $1 billion, would double to $2 billion in five years with steady growth of 8 percent annually, and there would be an even more dramatic increase in the number of kosher-certified ingredients.[3] Its most noteworthy discovery was the substantial non-Jewish market for kosher food, which, in sheer numbers, was far greater than observant Jews. It was the first study to demonstrate, systematically, that kosher food had secured a substantial following having nothing to do with Judaism. Remarkably, there were at least three non-Jewish kosher food consumers for every observant Jew!

While kosher food producers had insisted for some time that nonobservant Jews sought out their products, these anecdotal claims had not been supported by impartial and well-grounded research. Packaged Fact's 1988 report did just that, and in so doing generated extensive coverage in the food industry trade press.

To explain this finding, the report pointed out that the 1980s was a decade of rising consumer anxiety about food. Producers sought to engage with and capitalize on consumer's concerns by placing a variety of claims on packages: "healthy," "natural," or "heart friendly." Yet consumers were understandably skeptical about claims made by companies that had an interest in selling their products, as well as harboring considerable doubt about the veracity of government-mandated information on packages. A 1989 study that asked consumers who they could rely on to ensure food safety found that only 14 percent felt they could trust food manufacturers and 20 percent believed that government regulations could make food safe.[4]

Kosher food certification seemingly answered this need—without intending to at all. The struggles over stringent requirements for ingredients ensuring that no suspect animal fats entered kosher-certified foods positioned kosher food effectively, if inadvertently, to attract nervous secular consumers. The non-Jewish market included not only those guided by religion, such as Seventh-day Adventists and Muslims, but more significantly vegetarians and other "diet-conscious consumers" who, Packaged Facts explained, have come "to equate the term 'kosher' with superior quality." Orthodox rabbis guided not by the profit motive but instead by belief in their deity seemed a far more reliable inspection force than fallible government employees, and their *hecksher* immensely more trustworthy than a firm's own self-interested product labels.[5]

Packaged Facts, eager to sell its studies to food companies with prominent brands, drew a straight line between individual food preferences and the surge in kosher-certified products. Doing so, however, glossed over the processes through which kosher certification received a boost from changes in food provisioning that had nothing to do with kosher food per se. Hidden from the market research on individual consumer preference was the enormous influence of institutional food consumers, the impact of thousands of anonymous private label manufacturing firms that made kosher food, the food chain effect that stimulated producers of basic food ingredients to make their products kosher, and fundamental changes in food manufacturing technology that made creating kosher food a great deal easier than in Abraham Goldstein's era.

THE PROBLEM...

Controlling the ingredients brought into the food system by hidden manufacturers was a daunting task for kosher certifiers. The issues central to certifying kosher Coca-Cola by Rabbi Tobias Geffen rested in control over inputs, specifically glycerin, and how it was produced and processed. The heated debates over Jell-O and comparable "kosher" deserts similarly turned over knowledge of the source, and method of manufacturing, for gelatin. But contemporary processed foods were far more complex than Coke or Jell-O, usually including a wide range of coloring agents, flavors, stabilizers, and preservatives. The careful steps taken by Rabbi Tobias Geffen to trace glycerin's source had to be repeated for all of the ingredients for a food to be kosher—a complex task in an era of industrial food production.

A scandal involving allegedly kosher vinegar brought home the far greater scale of the ingredient problem. The vinegar in question came from Sofecia, a French company that had for many years used ethyl alcohol derived from synthetic sources to make kosher-certified vinegar. Sofecia's vinegar was widely used in kosher products, as, with its synthetic base, it avoided the requirement that grape juice–based vinegar had to be made by observant Jews to be kosher. While kosher consumers didn't have Sofecia's vinegar on their tables, they did unknowingly consume it in products such as mayonnaise, ketchup, and salad dressing. Its role as an essential ingredient in many products made it a critical link in the kosher food chain.[6]

Early in 1986, kosher certification agencies learned to their horror that, without prior notification, Sofecia had been shipping vinegar derived from grapes to the United States for the past six months. Since observant Jews were not involved in the manufacture of the grape-based vinegar, it was not kosher. Hundreds of products were compromised, affecting all major certification organizations. Large informational meetings held in major Jewish communities immediately after Passover shocked observant Jews when they learned how many products had been affected. The scale to which kosher food had been compromised was unprecedented.[7]

In the aftermath of the Sofecia scandal, the *Jewish Observer* published a sensational exposé that dramatically showed the great difficulties of certifying kosher ingredients. Modestly titled "The Nine Days—My Introduction to Industrial Kashrus," the story gave a shocking picture of lax supervision at a chemical factory that produced ingredients for hundreds of kosher-certified products. Written under the pseudonym Gershon Monk, and with places and names changed, the article nonetheless had an authentic air; in a preface the magazine explained it had showed it to several "experts" who agreed that while "the situation described in the article is not typical, it is also not that exceptional."[8]

In in, author Gershon Monk explained that he was a rabbinic student who had studied kosher law but had no experience in kosher supervision and had been recruited in desperation by the certification organization "United Kashrus" as the *mashgiah* for "Northbridge Chemicals" (a three-and-a-half-hour drive from Monk's home) to replace one Rabbi Alter, who was retiring. But what seemed like a convenient way to fill his depleted bank account, albeit with a few long days, turned out to be a nightmare. Monk had no sooner arrived at the plant after a grueling nighttime drive, his "mental alacrity" admittedly diminished "by exhaustion and hunger," when he was presented with a dilemma. Not all the tanks used for nonkosher materials had been emptied, cleaned, and allowed to sit idle for twenty-four hours as United Kashrus required before production of kosher materials could begin—but the company wanted to start kosher manufacturing operations immediately. The plant manager argued that cleaning the tanks with detergent without waiting the full day would be good enough—and Rabbi Alter handed the decision to Monk (an admitted "rookie mashgiach") as to whether this new procedure was acceptable. Monk reflected that, as he considered the issue, "American kashrus stood breathless. If I were to decide in the negative, hundreds of products would be invalidated." Feeling he had little choice but to acquiesce, Monk decided he could consider the plant post factum (*b'dieved*) kosher since the same procedure was followed before. Later he was to learn that detergent was not in fact acceptable for kosherization—and that this issue, however troublesome, would be one of the lesser challenges he faced.

With this immediate crisis resolved, Monk learned that his main assignment was to somehow devise a "fool-proof" automatic system that would permit Northbridge to make kosher and nonkosher ingredients in the same plant, but without a *mashgiah* stationed on-site twenty-four hours a day. Doing so entailed learning how the plant operated, the complex system of pipes that conveyed fluids from one tank to another, and receiving procedures such that only appropriate products entered the system. Yet Monk had no training in production engineering, chemical manufacturing, or the procedures followed by the plant to make its products kosher. Neither could he draw on diagrams of the plant operations, as many jury-rigged connections between pipes did not appear on official blueprints; nor could he receive cooperation from the company to sequence acceptance of products so that, at least for that stage, a *mashgiah* could be present to ensure proper controls over the materials that entered production. He also could not receive guaranteed control of labels attached to finished products, leaving the "possibility" that "the company could affix kosher labels to some non-kosher products."

After several days of fruitlessly trying to devise a "fool-proof" system, Monk concluded that he had been given an impossible task. In an attempt to humorously communicate his dilemma to the UK kosher supervision agency, he recalled complaining "that I was only being paid for hasgacha [supervision]; nevius (prophecy) would require a much larger salary." When he recommended that UK maintain three *mashgihim* at the plant so that Northbridge would have around-the-clock supervision, the certification agency turned him down for reasons he suspected had to do with concerns that the increased cost would provoke Northbridge to drop kosher certification entirely. At this point Monk gave up; he told Rabbi Alter that the "situation was much more difficult than I had originally anticipated" and he asked UK to find a replacement. Chastened by the experience, Monk closed his essay by imploring consumers to be willing to pay the true costs of kosher certification, and for certification organizations to accept an "impassioned commitment" to upgrading their supervision.

SOLUTIONS...

Exposés such as Gershon Monk's tale and consternation over the Sofecia scandal forced the OU and other certification organization to improve their control over the ingredients going into kosher food—while simultaneously attempting to keep costs as low as possible. Much as Gershon Monk may have wanted three full-time *mashgihim* at Northbridge Chemical, the added expense might well have prompted the company to drop certification altogether. More critically, if the ingredients for consumer kosher products could not be procured affordably, the growth of kosher products available for consumers might stall.

The Sofecia incident was a lesson that the first step was for certification organizations to put their own house in order. A widely distributed editorial in *Young Israel Viewpoint* used the scandal to upbraid them for "publicly disavowing any knowledge of the nature or reliability of products under competing supervision" when, in fact, "every major kashruth organization must be dependent on the reliability of its competitors who supervise the raw materials whose use they approve in products under their supervision." Greater communication was the solution offered so that agencies "inextricably linked" through shared suppliers of raw ingredients could remain true to their, ultimately, religious obligation to make kosher food available for Jews who wished to follow observant practices.[9]

These pressures gave an impetus to the efforts of the Chicago Rabbinical Council to create a trade association for certification organizations. A series of meetings in 1986 and 1987 drew in the main national agencies as well as many local *vadim* (councils) that supervised restaurants and small businesses in their communities. After struggles over its authority and whether to include the OK (the OU at one point threatened to walk out if OK leader Rabbi Berel Levy attended a meeting), the Association of Kashrus Organizations finally settled down in the early 1990s to become a typical trade association that exchanged information and offered a private forum for discussion and resolution of disagreements among agencies and problems confronting all kosher food certifiers. The result was a more orderly form of competition and greater cooperation.[10]

The kosher certifiers also adopted an independent magazine, the *Kashrus Newsletter* (later *Kashrus Magazine*) as their de facto trade journal. Launched in 1980 by Rabbi Joseph Wikler as "the source of authentic kashrus information," the magazine had a muckraking quality revealing the many problems that until then had been kept quiet. The *Kashrus Newsletter* published information on newly certified products, the touchy subject of products that had shifted from one agency to another, and the all-important topic of products that had lost certification and were no longer kosher. Befitting its self-appointed role, *Kashrus Magazine* not only reported on the Sofecia scandal and published information on affected products but also pushed certifying organizations to improve their practices so there would be no repetition of this grave incident. Its dissemination of information, while occasionally angering the secretive rabbis, became generally accepted as a critical way in which kosher producers, consumers, and certifiers could cooperate.

While OK was the agency that had missed the nonkosher Sofecia vinegar, the OU came under fire for stubbornly denying that its effectiveness depended, in part, on what other agencies did. It finally addressed this concern by systematically classifying tens of thousands of ingredients that were used, similar to the problematic vinegar, in a plethora of consumer products. Aided by a vast computerization project that took several years (and $500,000) to complete, the OU sorted ingredients into three categories. Class 1 required no certification at all, class 2 were acceptable with most certifications, and the more sensitive class 3 could be accepted upon review of the certifying agency's guidelines. (Subsequently, the number of categories would proliferate so as to make finer distinctions among ingredients, but the principle of accepting certification from other agencies was the same.) Such recognition was a breakthrough, doubtless relieving many firms that finally could see some order developing out of the chaos of obtaining acceptable kosher ingredients.[11]

Generating better cooperation and moderating competition were positive steps, but not enough in themselves to solve the problem of ingredients and control over their use, especially in manufacturing plants that made both kosher and nonkosher products. It was all too easy for firms to violate kosher rules—willfully or in ignorance—as they moved between kosher and nonkosher production operations. Without the development of automated "fool-proof" systems such as that imagined for Gershon Monk's Northbridge Chemical, there was little alternative to a more sustained presence by kosher inspectors, and with the additional costs so entailed.

Help came from an unexpected, underappreciated, and inadvertent ally—federal food regulation. Curiously, the seemingly ever expanding inspection regime demanded by government regulators proved a great asset to kosher food's development, even as kosher requirements as such remained outside those rules. To satisfy regulatory requirements, firms developed sophisticated inventory and production control systems to closely track the materials used in a production facility. Doing so gave them the capacity to add kosher requirements to already strict compliance practices. Uniting these seemingly separate developments was widespread concern over the safety of modern processed food.

Kosher food's advance thus received a major boost from government requirements that firms closely monitor ingredients and their food manufacturing processes. In 1986 the Food and Drug Administration implemented extensive "Good Manufacturing Practices" regulations that required firms to document their sanitary procedures in manufacturing, warehousing, and distribution. Then in 1990 Congress adopted the Nutrition Labeling and Education Act requiring inclusion of ingredients and nutritional content on product labels. Following closely, over the next fifteen years regulatory agencies steadily expanded mandates for many firms to develop a Hazard Analysis and Critical Control Point systems (HACCP) for controlling pathogens in food production. Intended to shift responsibilities from government inspectors to the company, the practice required firms to develop a HACCP protocol to monitor food safety and maintain records of their findings. Finally, the Food Allergen Labeling and Consumer Protection Act, which took effect January 1, 2006, adding requirements that food labels declare major allergens and that products labeled allergen-free needed documentation for such claims.

These new rules, often criticized by consumer advocates for relying on food producers rather than government inspectors for implementation, nonetheless had a major impact on company practices. The HACCP and allergen control requirements generated widespread changes in control over food operations, as companies had to systematically document all food inputs as well as how these were handled in their factories. Records may have been maintained within firms rather than deposited with government agencies; but the technology and infrastructure needed to generate those records was a bonanza for kosher certifying agencies seeking to automate, to the extent possible, maintenance of kosher standards. Such record keeping was exactly what they demanded for kosher certification; now firms were investing in the necessary hardware and software without having to be asked by the OU and other agencies.

These regulatory pressures—and the record keeping so entailed—facilitated securing kosher certification of institutional food providers and the private label manufacturers that supplied them. Their interest in following kosher practices provided, in turn, a stimulus for ingredient suppliers to obtain kosher certification. This food chain effect magnified interest in kosher food immensely, as interdependent networks of food suppliers, manufacturers, and retailers found that securing kosher certification opened doors for their products.

The sheer purchasing power of institutional buyers (known in the trade as the HRI—hotel, restaurant, and institutional—market) gives them enormous influence in the food industry. Institutions such as the military, prisons, school systems, restaurants, and intermediate food distributors received 40 percent of the shipments from American food manufacturers in the mid-1990s. Put differently, almost half of all food consumed took place in settings where institutions, not individuals, selected the ingredients that were turned into meals.[12]

Institutional consumers, in turn, rely on what are called private label food manufacturers for much of their supplies, as the customers they serve are not selecting among branded products for personal consumption. Private label companies make products to order for other firms based on recipes they develop or that are supplied to them; while ubiquitous, they are virtually invisible to consumers unless implicated in a food contamination scandal. Private label production for restaurants and cafeterias goes back well into the nineteenth century; someone, after all, had to make the fancy pickles and condiments displayed on the tables of fine restaurants and classy hotels. The school lunch program's remarkable expansion after World War II, along with the growth of restaurant chains in the 1950s, boosted demand exponentially for these anonymous producers. Making products sold under supermarket names offered another growth opportunity. Not surprisingly, established food manufacturers interested in boosting their brands were reluctant to make the A&P and ShopRite store varieties that would be sold alongside their products at lower prices. By 2000 private label products (generally sold as supermarket brands) absorbed 12–15 percent of consumer spending for food in supermarkets; in the case of Kroger, private label food items contributed 25 percent of total food sales.[13] And, of course, since they were making food for someone else, detailed records of their operations were essential.

Private label manufacturers also could fudge the line between themselves and the traditional food companies. Firms with well-known brands could contract with private label manufacturers to make their products, either to test demand or handle sudden shortages. Conversely, branded goods could become ingredients in private label products sold through institutions. Regardless of whom they supplied, the advanced technology employed by private label companies allowed them to serve many different masters—and also made it possible to ensure that those products which could be kosher were indeed kosher to the satisfaction of the principal certification agencies. Kosher agencies in turn developed a specific set of requirements for private label goods, requiring a tripartite agreement between the actual manufacturer, the firm contracting for the specific items, and the certification agency.

VENTURA FOODS, CHAMBERSBURG, PENNSYLVANIA

Seeking a way to understand the very complicated food chain effect on kosher food, I spent a day at the Chambersburg, Pennsylvania plant of Ventura Foods in 2010. This private label operation produces a wide range of kosher ketchups, mayonnaise, sauces, and salad dressings; none carry Ventura's name. Yet in all likelihood millions of Americans have at some time eaten foods made at its unimposing Chambersburg facility. Those dining in a cafeteria, school, hospital, military commissary, or even prisons have eaten Ventura products, as it is a major supplier to some of the largest food service operations in the country (Ventura asked that its customers not be named). So too have the huge number of consumers who grab the small condiment packages (made in Chambersburg) in some of America's major burger, sandwich, and pizza chains. Others have eaten mayonnaise from the Chambersburg plant in major brands of potato salad or its French and Italian salad dressings bearing the names of supermarkets' house brands. And the vast majority of these products are made in conformity with kosher requirements.

Built in 1990, and conveniently located near both rail lines and a major highway, the Chambersburg plant was designed with strict controls over inventory, manufacturing, and product labeling so that it could compete in the highly regulated food business and sell to its principal customers, large institutional buyers. The facility is large and sprawling, with manufacturing and packaging operations limited to one level except for production stations reached by open metal walkways from the main floor. Pipes snake throughout the plant, conveying ingredients to industrial processing equipment and then the resulting mixtures to bottling areas where final products are readied. Tight control through a central computer system and close supervision over raw inputs, mixtures, and outputs—essential for making private label products to exacting requirements—also permits tracking allergens and enforcing kosher requirements. Quite unlike older plants, such as the chemical factory that "Gershon Monk" valiantly sought to certify, the very structure of the Chambersburg facility aids segregation of materials in a manner that makes it easier to satisfy kosher requirements, and for a *mashgiah* to efficiently supervise.

Production controls start in the receiving area, where quality assurance staff inspects all deliveries—including kosher certification documentation. Each day the plant receives approximately one million pounds of oils, corn syrup, and high fructose corn syrup in rail cars, as well as additional amounts conveyed by trucks. Tanker rail cars are easy to control as they are dedicated only for specific products—oil, syrup, etc. They arrive with a kosher seal that records the place and time when filled, along with documentation that the oil was kosher. Some truck tankers are similarly dedicated for specific products, such as vinegar; but many are not and can be used for many types of liquids. For the latter vehicles, the driver must produce a kosher wash certificate attesting that the tanker was cleaned at a certified facility before loading its content bound for Chambersburg. The liquids are emptied into tanks that supply, via pipes, areas of the plant where they are needed. Flow meters on those tanks record how much was pumped in and out and can be matched against the amount remaining. A discrepancy alerts the supervising rabbi to check to see where the additional product came from.

Similar close controls govern handling of dry products delivered on pallets by trucks. Quality assurance staff checks for kosher certification and halts the shipment for further verification if there are any doubts. If acceptable, they code pallets with colored labels indicating whether they are "sensitive" (for allergies), kosher dairy, or other categories requiring special attention. The inspectors attach a "pallet tag" with a bar-coded label that the driver scans to determine where to store the product. Software governs storage locations: potential allergens are kept on lower levels or separate aisles, and kosher dairy products in a separate area as well.

Ventura seeks out kosher-certified ingredients so long as their price is not significantly greater than nonkosher versions. It only buys kosher oils and syrups so it does not have to create additional production controls to segregate nonkosher versions. For similar reasons, the tomato paste used by the plant has to be kosher. Correspondingly, all eggs are certified kosher; they are sourced from a plant that commercially breaks eggs and creates mixtures for commercial use, using electric eye technology to monitor for blood spots that would render eggs nonkosher. Flavoring, food colors—all are kosher certified if they can be. The main exception is cheese, as commercial kosher cheese is far more expensive than nonkosher versions and cheese is an important ingredient in some popular salad dressings.

Enforcing kosher certification requirements continues through the manufacturing process. The central computer system ensures that only kosher ingredients are used to make kosher salad dressings, mayonnaise, and ketchup. A computer-issued "pull tag" is necessary before any materials can enter production; it gives the precise location of ingredients in storage so that only the proper ones are obtained. A work ticket, also computer generated, then regulates each processing stage. Included in the precise information they contain is the designation "kosher parve," "kosher dairy," or "non-kosher" heading each ticket. Once the particular operation is completed, a worker has to enter corresponding information into the computer; otherwise the next production stages are blocked.

Computer controls are particularly important to regulate production such that Chambersburg can make kosher, kosher dairy, and nonkosher products in accordance with kosher requirements. The principal challenge is *b'lios* (taste), which lingers in pipes and on equipment after each product run and can then contaminate subsequent operations. Nonkosher products leave *b'lios* that renders any product made thereafter nonkosher; and kosher dairy residue makes it impossible to run kosher pareve products subsequently. Efficient scheduling while accommodating these kosher requirements is one of the plant's greatest challenges—and a task that is embedded into production control software. "The computer system actually schedules everything based on input information indicating which products are kosher and which ones are not," explained Gerry Kean, director of quality assurance for Ventura Foods at the time of the tour.[14] Typically pareve products are made first, followed then by kosher dairy; doing so in reverse order would delay production by making it necessary to eliminate milk residue on the equipment between product runs. Nonkosher products such as blue cheese dressing (using nonkosher cheese) are produced after kosher ones for the same reason. To prevent errors, the computer is programmed to simply not permit nonkosher products to be made prior to kosher ones, or kosher dairy before pareve, without prior kosherizing operations.

Similar to how existing production control systems facilitate manufacturing that respects kosher law, Chambersburg's industry-standard CIP (clean-in-place) technology can kosherize equipment in accordance with OU requirements. Such systems are designed for nightly cleaning and sanitation of manufacturing equipment to prevent bacterial contamination; as with all processes, the computer system regulates, and records, the temperature of the water to ensure it is hot enough (at least 170 F) to satisfy government regulations. These cleaning practices are sufficient to eliminate the *b'lios* from equipment used to manufacture products through a cold process never exceeding 110 F, as they do not cross the important *halachic* threshold of *yad soledes bo*, or "cooked." In these cases (which apply to most of Chambersburg's products), the nightly cleaning is sufficient to kosherize equipment used to make kosher dairy and nonkosher products so that the next morning anything can be made on them.[15]

Products made through "hot" methods that exceed the *yad soledes bo* threshold pose greater challenges; but the same CIP technology is still sufficient to kosherize the equipment. These OU-mandated procedures are derived from two kosher rules originally developed for personal kitchens. The first, the principle of *hag'olah*, provides that the same operations creating *b'lios* can eliminate it; thus *b'lios* generated by cooking nonkosher or kosher dairy food in a pot with boiling water can be eliminated by boiling clean water in the same pot. The second principle, *ayno ben yomo* ("not of the same day"), addresses the conundrum that some of this *b'lios* would remain in the very water boiled to kosherize the pot. Kosher law assumes that *b'lios* in a pot left unused for twenty-four hours becomes foul tasting and is thus "insignificant at any level," according to Rabbi Yusef Blech's authoritative tome, *Kosher Food Production*. To put this into the dense jargon of industrial *kashrus*, once the pot (or equivalent manufacturing machinery) became *ayno ben yomo*, it could be kosherized using the principle of *hag'olah* with its *b'lios* completely expunged.[16]

To ensure Ventura complies with these requirements (which may well have mystified its gentile production managers), the computer schedules manufacturing of "hot" process nonkosher products for the Friday afternoon shift, permitting kosherizing of equipment over the weekend. Beginning on the midnight shift, the CIP system cleans equipment in a conventional manner, finishing by Saturday morning. The equipment then sits idle for twenty-four hours so it can become *ayno ben yomo*. On Sunday the CIP technology kosherizes the necessary hardware with water hot enough to satisfy the requirements of *hag'olah*; the temperatures are recorded by the plant's computer system to document compliance. By Monday morning the equipment is fully kosherized, ready to make anything the company needs.

The label department, located immediately adjacent to the bottling room, is the final staging area for controls over products and their kosher status. Relying on the schedule lodged in Ventura's computer system, the operator issues the appropriate labels the day before product is run and only makes them available when production actually begins. Such close coordination is necessary to avoid many possible complications. The same Ventura product can appear in up to five separate brands and in different sizes all requiring their own label. Connecting the right label with the right package obviously matters enormously; to do so is especially sensitive for kosher certified products. Companies with OU private label agreements can include the OU symbol on packaging material, while firms selling the same Ventura-made product but without such an agreement cannot display a kosher endorsement—even if the product is in fact kosher. It is a fitting irony: even as the total number of kosher-identified products has increased dramatically, manufacturing systems create even more that meet kosher requirements, but do not carry a rabbinic *hecksher*.

Chambersburg's efficient production control system was a great asset to the OU's rabbinic field representative responsible for the plant at the time of my visit. Simply put, the record keeping intrinsic to the system made kosher supervision easier and less expensive. On his regular—and unannounced—inspections, the OU's rabbi "will check our production schedules when he comes in to make sure that, in fact, everything is sequenced properly," explained Kean. He also can download the plant's schedule A that lists all the ingredients it uses in manufacturing and verify what he sees in the storage areas against it. Walking through the plant, the rabbi spot-checks work tickets at production stations to make sure they match what the plant's computers say is being made. If he needs to investigate a product manufactured before his arrival, the rabbi can access the computer system to determine what was done when, where, and at what temperature. "This company," Chambersburg's rabbi reflected, "has a computer system that is a dream, because I can review a pipe and say, what did you run through this pipe at 3:46 A.M. three days ago, and they pull up the history and show me." When he inspects the label room, the rabbi can compare the labels scheduled to go onto products with the company's schedule B (downloaded to his computer), which contains a complete list of the private label products that can carry the kosher certification mark.

Ventura's place in the modern food chain helps to explain why so many private label companies choose to make kosher products. "Most of the products are kosher because then we can sell them anywhere," explained Kean. Making as many products kosher as it can permits recruitment of customers who "feel that that's important" and does not foreclose any options. In this sense, Ventura's attitude is similar to all "large food service distributors" who want "their products certified kosher if they can be because it opens up the marketplace." As some institutions want kosher food—Jewish nursing homes, for example—it is easier for distributors selling to nursing homes to simply make those products kosher that can be kosher. Stocking as much kosher food as possible reduces the complications of tracking two types of the same food item (kosher and nonkosher)—an obvious benefit to large operations.

Even when those served by an institution have no direct means to influence its food selection, there are still compelling reasons to favor kosher food. Prisons, for example, are "the largest purchaser of kosher products" in Kean's experience, even though obtaining kosher food is not for the purpose of feeding observant Jews. Although many of the ingredients on hand are kosher, most prisons do not actually serve kosher meals, as doing so would entail observing additional requirements for food handling and cooking. (Typically, inmates wanting a certified kosher diet receive specially prepared meals from outside vendors.) Instead, prisons prefer kosher goods because they are certified to be free of any trace of pork, making the food acceptable to observant Muslim prisoners.

Given the size of the institutional market, it is simply good business for Ventura to make kosher-certified products for the institutional suppliers—to the extent possible. (Kean did have to disappoint one client who had trouble understanding why Ventura was unable to supply kosher-certified lobster soup base.) With their preference for kosher products, Ventura and similar private label firms in turn influence decisions by the primary producers of oil, syrups, flavors, food colors, spices, and other ingredients that similarly, as Kean puts it, "never want to cut out any segment of the marketplace." This food chain effect expands, correspondingly, the options for firms looking for ingredients that will allow them to make their food kosher.

Kosher certification agencies, for their part, have sought to encourage the food chain effect by developing greater integration with manufacturers' supply chains. The Universal Kosher Database, created by the OU and other agencies, establishes a universal kosher number for each product; in 2008 it contained over 340,000 approved ingredients.[17] (The OK has a similar Digital Kosher system.) OU companies can access the database through the online OU Direct system, thereby reducing delays associated with satisfying certifying agencies' documentation requirements. If Ventura finds that one of its approved ingredients is unavailable, production supervisors can access OU Direct to obtain alternative supplies that are already acceptable to kosher supervision agencies. In the event a new customer needs a product in a hurry, the UKD can be used to create a recipe acceptable to the OU, allowing a new private label agreement to be executed in less than an hour.

The relative ease with which kosher requirements can be integrated into contemporary plant operations and control systems encourages firms to create more kosher food, as the price difference and supervision annoyances have steadily declined. Even Chambersburg's impressive twenty-year-old control systems look relatively antiquated compared to current technology. The hardwired computer system, despite its remarkable capacity, is now archaic; at the time of my visit the company was in the process of updating to a Windows-based system. More recently constructed plants install wireless computer systems that allow their rabbinic field representative to download production and ingredient information in advance of a visit. Contemporary production management software from companies such as Advanced Software Designs permit close control over information on all food inputs and can "automatically" determine regulatory information for "kosher, allergen, and GMO status."[18]

THE INDUSTRIAL OREO

As it turns out, it was the food chain effect that stimulated the celebrated kosher milestone of the late 1990s, the decision of Nabisco to make its Oreo cookie kosher—along with most of its cookie line. The proximate cause stemmed from problems created by the integrated nature of food manufacturing, in which Oreo cookies were an input into another product—in this case, cookies-and-cream ice cream. Created in the late 1970s, cookies-and-cream ice cream made with Oreos was one of America's most popular flavors—but, annoyingly, it could not become kosher. Ice cream manufacturers could obtain bulk supplies of Oreo cookies made in a private label factory under contract with Nabisco that met kosher requirements and combine those with ice cream that was equally acceptable under Jewish law. However, since the Oreo cookies available for consumer purchase were not kosher, the major certification agencies would not permit use of *Oreo* in the name of kosher-certified cookies-and-cream ice cream under their supervision—even if that combination technically complied with kosher law. Ice cream companies could, however, create kosher versions of this ice cream flavor by the simple expedient of including a kosher Oreo analogue and selling it as generic cookies-and-cream ice cream. The disadvantage of so doing is obvious—they could not add the name of a cookie that had made the flavor so popular and link their product to a potent national brand.[19]

The pressure for Nabisco to address their competitive weakness in this area came through its food service division. Its manager learned that large institutional purchasers were annoyed that the lack of kosher certification for the Oreo complicated offering cookies–and-cream ice cream in places such as schools and hospitals. Having to offer two versions of this popular product, one kosher and one not, complicated manufacturing, inventory, and delivery and increased the chance of making an error with kosher customers—as indeed occurred in one case in the early 1990s.[20] As a result, Nabisco found itself unable to sell Oreos as an ingredient in cookies-and-cream ice cream to some large food distributors who only wanted to handle a kosher version.

As it was her responsibility to advance Nabisco's market share in this crucial sector, the food service division manager decided to see if it was feasible to create a kosher Oreo. With input from Cornell food science professor Joe Regenstein, a respected authority on kosher food manufacturing, she convinced Nabisco that the ingredient changes necessary to secure kosher certification involved only a minimal expense. The company already had made a transition from lard to vegetable oils a few years earlier, removing the most problematic obstacle. "The re-formulating was not the hard part," Regenstein later recalled, as by the 1990s it was possible to switch to kosher ingredients without much trouble. The expansion of kosher certification—the very factor impelling Nabisco to seek the OU's assistance—also made it economically feasible to bake a kosher Oreo.

Nonetheless, Nabisco still faced a considerable expense, as it had to kosherize over one hundred ovens used to make Oreos and other Nabisco products. As these ovens baked cookies using direct heat, rather than through the medium of water or steam, kosherizing them required using the principle of *libun chamur* ("to heat severely"), heating every surface to 900 F. The belts used to move products continuously through the ovens constituted the most daunting obstacle, for, as Regenstein recalled, they "could not be koshered and each belt was worth over $150,000." The belts simply had to be replaced; to save money, Nabisco allowed them to wear out before kosherizing each oven. In a process lasting several years, once a particular oven's belt was ready for replacement, special OU "blow-torch crews" would kosherize the metal ovens by heating them to a white-hot temperature sufficient to satisfy the *libun chamur* requirement. Late in 1997, the OU was finally able to announce that the Oreo cookie was indeed kosher.[21]

It may have been on overstatement that, with the Oreo's certification, "Jews had finally made it" in America. Certainly there were other markers of Jewish success! Nonetheless, Rabbi Hammerman pointed to an important truth: making it possible for Jewish children to have Oreo cookies—and many other previously nonkosher products—was a victory for assimilation on Jewish terms. With steady growth of consumer kosher food products exceeding 10 percent annually, by 2000 it was possible to be observant and to participate, as well, in the great bounty of American food.[22] This was a great accomplishment, without doubt.

Nonetheless, explaining the increase in kosher products as a direct outgrowth of non-Jewish consumer demand generates an overly optimistic picture of kosher food's acceptance. Such expansion also reflected the vast reduction in costs for doing so and the capacity for kosher certification practices to be appended to other manufacturing management systems, again at minimal cost. What would happen, then, if the costs were not minimal and embedding kosher practices in factory architecture and control systems proved far more difficult or controversial? The journeys of kosher wine and beef charted in the next chapters offer a cautionary coda to the success story of kosher food.

6

MAN-O-MANISCHEWITZ

OUR ANNUAL Passover Seder was, as for most Jewish families, an opportunity to eat traditional food, retell the story of Jewish liberation from oppression, and, for grown-ups, to drink the required four glasses of wine as well as other celebratory beverages. But as the children reveled in the special opportunity to guzzle Coca-Cola, my father could not restrain his disdain at the sweet kosher wine, usually Manischewitz, that seemed mandatory for the occasion. As he grew more successful in business in the 1960s and 1970s, he developed a taste for fine French wine. While he was not troubled about drinking nonkosher varieties while eating out, Passover was about Jewish tradition—and the meal often included other family members who would have been offended at using a nonkosher wine to toast Moses's passage from the land of Egypt.

Then, one year my father made a great discovery: kosher French wine! As a child I do not recall the vineyard, but I can remember the gusto with which he announced his discovery at the Seder. Indeed, we all cheered, as the sweet Manischewitz or Mogen David had become a standing joke among the children accustomed to my father's complaints. The Seders continued even after my parent's divorce, as my mother and father remained on amicable terms, and I noticed that the range of kosher wines available for Passover kept expanding.

Our switch from sweet to dry kosher wines paralleled the experience of many Jewish households. Millions of nonobservant American Jews viewed Passover as the one meal each year where items had to be kosher, and it thus provided a ready (if seasonal) market for dry wines produced in accordance with Judaism's religious requirements. Increasingly affluent observant Jews, while a far smaller group, offered a more stable market, consistent with their interest in taking advantage of the increasing range of kosher products and kosher restaurants to more readily participate in American food culture.

The progression of kosher wine from sweet to dry seems a straightforward success story, similar to the expansion of other kosher food options. What was lost, however, is less appreciated. By the late 1940s Manischewitz was the first crossover kosher product, attracting not only substantial consumption from non-Jews but also considerable cultural visibility through widespread print, radio, and television advertising. The dry kosher wines that took their place on Jewish tables have not, by and large, made their way into Christian households, and their branding as kosher is indeed a detriment in the wine marketplace, quite unlike the benefits such association served for Manischewitz. Dry kosher wine may have been "better" by the standards of discerning consumers such as my father, but it was far more marginal to American culture than sweet kosher wine in its heyday—and sold far less. Kosher wine's progression thus is also a story of contraction to a Jewish core market, a movement strikingly at odds with the contemporaneous advance of kosher processed food.

BOREI P'RI HAGAFEN—THE FRUIT OF THE VINE

The sweet taste of traditional kosher wine had nothing to do with European Jewish traditions. Instead its character stemmed from the materials at hand for kosher winemakers—the inexpensive Concord grapes grown in New York State close to East Coast Jewish communities. Derived from the hardy domestic *Vitis labrusca* genus, the Concord dominated the grape market in northeastern United States. It was a reliable product, resistant to the phylloxera plague that devastated European varietals in the late nineteenth century and tough enough to endure all sorts of growing conditions, such as the chilly weather of upstate New York. Originally shipped to cities in small lots intended for direct purchase by consumers and retail stores, growers shifted to bulk railcar lots around the turn of the century as the "inexpensive wine" market burgeoned. The producers of such "inexpensive wine" were immigrants flooding into Eastern cities (especially Jews and Italians), both small entrepreneurs making commercial brands and families crafting wine at home.

The Concord's popularity did not mean it was a good wine grape. Highly acidic, making even "sour wine" from Concord grapes required adding large amounts of sugar so that it would ferment adequately; then more would be added to the mixture to create a palatable product that masked its "foxy" taste.[1]

The large Jewish demand for Concord wine was not, however, primarily to drink it with meals. Instead, wine fulfilled important ceremonial religious functions in the home. Wine was part of the weekly recognition of the Sabbath and integral to the Purim and Passover ceremonies. Wine helped to mark major life passages, from the *bris* (circumcision) of a male infant to the blessings recited in marriage ceremony, and was served to mourners at the first meal following burial. To immigrants coming from Eastern Europe, where grapes could not grow and most wine had to be made from raisins, the plentiful supply of purple Concord grapes (and the cheap sugar that could make it into wine) was yet another example of the plentitude of their new home.

Accorded its own particular blessing, *blessed are thou, oh Lord our God, King of the universe, who created the fruit of the vine*, wine preparation had its own complex set of rules designed to ensure it was for Jews—alone. It was not enough that all the ingredients used to make wine, such as clarifying agents, were kosher. Jewish ceremonial uses could be traced to ancient times, the same era when their Greek and later Roman rulers also used wine in ceremonies to their pagan gods—and imbibed quite a bit themselves. To firmly separate the Jews from their polytheistic neighbors, rabbis imposed stringent requirements to ensure that the wine drunk by the Jews was not *yayin nesech* (wine employed in pagan rites) or *stam yeinom* (wine made by non-Jews). Aside from ensuring that pagan ritual wine never touched Jewish lips, this prohibition also was inspired by *chatanut*, concern that social interaction over wine with non-Jews could lead Jews away from the Torah and perhaps even result in intermarriage.

To build a fence against such transgressions, rabbis mandated that only Sabbath-observant Jews could participate in making kosher wine from the time the juice began to flow from the grape to when the container holding the fermented liquid was sealed. After the barrel or bottle was opened, the smallest touch and movement of the container by a non-Jew would render the wine nonkosher. As promulgated in the ancient Middle East, Jews could neither consume nor benefit from *yayin nesech* or *stam yeinom*. With the decline of pagan religions, rabbis under Christian and Muslim rule moderated these rules to permit Jews to benefit from *stam yeinom*, that is, to become growers and dealers of nonkosher wine. [2]

Averting the pitfalls of non-Jews handling open kosher wine required making *yayin mevushal*—cooked wine. Maimonides explained that "if the wine of a Jew is first boiled and then touched by a heathen, it may be consumed, even from the same cup used by the heathen, because boiled wine is not suitable for a libation for an idol." Presumably since boiled wine was meant for cooking, not sociability, young Jewish men and women also would not drink *yayin mevushal* with those from other religions. For the early twentieth-century immigrants who either made their own wine or bought wine from Jewish wine dealers, the question of what constituted "cooked" wine was not a pressing issue. In most cases kosher wine of this era was not *mevushal*, made as it was by Jews and for Jewish consumption at home or in religious ceremonies. But, in time, how to define *yayin mevushal* would become a major *halachic* concern.[3]

Prohibition was a watershed for kosher wine. Article 7 of the National Prohibition Act permitted home and commercial manufacture of wine for sacramental purposes, but under strict limits. Households could make no more than ten gallons annually, and complicated procedures governed distribution by rabbis to their congregants. Consider what Atlanta's Rabbi Tobias Geffen had to do to obtain wine for Passover. With an estimate in hand of what the Jewish community needed, he would contact a company licensed to make sacramental wine to see if it could supply that amount. Once he received confirmation through return mail, the next step was to bring the receipt to the local federal alcoholic beverage bureau for endorsement and permission to ship. After receiving legal approval, Geffen would write again to the manufacturer to confirm the order. Upon receipt of the wine, he then sold it to congregants from his home so he had the money to remit payment. If Rabbi Geffen ordered too much, he would have to dig into his pocket to pay the bill; if too little came in, the whole process had to be repeated so that sufficient wine would be available for ritual use. Not surprisingly, this cumbersome system encouraged widespread home manufacturing of kosher wine.[4]

Prohibition also made kosher wine a convenient way to avoid alcohol restrictions, especially by organized crime. Jenna Weissman Joselit has documented that demand for "kosher" wine skyrocketed in the early years of Prohibition, with shipments to New York City tripling between 1922 and 1925 to almost 1.8 million gallons. The evident fraud behind such demand resulted in a tightening of federal control over rabbis' abilities to obtain wine for sacramental purposes, with shipments plummeting to just under four hundred thousand gallons in 1932, prohibition's final year. This successful effort to suppress illicit "sacramental" wine use also meant, in all likelihood, that commercial kosher wine supplies were inadequate for New York City's Jews. Shipments in 1932 were just enough for each Jew in New York to have the required four glasses of wine during Passover, and nothing more, hardly sufficient given wine's other ritual purposes. Home production must have filled the gap—and, when Prohibition finally ended, entrepreneurs seized the opportunity to satisfy pent-up demand with new brands for Jewish use.[5]

"WINE LIKE MOTHER USED TO MAKE"

The Monarch Wine Company was the strongest entrant among the new kosher wine firms. Its founders were two friends who were in the paint business in the 1920s, Leo Star and George Robinson; they recruited George's younger brother, Meyer, to be the new company's attorney. When George died in 1935, Meyer took his place as the firm's co-owner. Star kept a home in Fredonia, New York, in the heart of the upstate grape region, giving him the connections to make sacramental wine in the later years of Prohibition. Eager to expand sales when liquor once again became legal in 1933, the astute owners realized, as Robinson's daughter Gale recalled, that "they needed a name that was well known in the Jewish world." In an astute marketing decision, they sought out the Manischewitz food company, whose products were widely used among Jews, and negotiated an agreement to license the name for their wine.

Monarch also relied on Manischewitz's rabbis for kosher certification, ensuring that it benefited from the high regard among Jews for Manischewitz products, even though its namesake had nothing to do with actually making the wine.[6]

Befitting its association with Manischewitz, the wine bottle's label was steeped in religious traditionalism. A light blue Jewish star dominated the brown label; inside the star a rabbi with a white beard, holding a prayer book in one hand and a glass of wine in the other, verified the wine's branding as "New York State SACRAMENTAL Concord Grape Wine." In the Hebrew text, Rabbis Itzchak Halevy Segal and Menachem Mendel Hochstein affirmed that this "wine from the fruit of the vine" was made

FIGURE 6.1 Manischewitz wine bottle label, 1940s. From the Archives of the YIVO Institute for Jewish Research, New York.

under their supervision and "is kosher for Pesach for all of Israel." Immediately below, if there was still any doubt about the wine's kosher bona fides, the slogan emblazoned along the bottom declared, "WINE LIKE MOTHER USED TO MAKE," connecting Monarch's Manischewitz to the women during Prohibition who had made sure there was kosher wine available for their family's use.[7]

It was not until the end of World War II that Monarch's Manischewitz emerged as the leading U.S. kosher wine. Before then the company's products were not among those advertised by liquor stores and shopping emporiums for Passover use. Macy's pushed its house Red Star brand of Concord grape wines, while liquor stores favored kosher wines by Marmok, Wirklich, Blue Diamond, and the Carmel brand produced by Jewish colonies in British Palestine. Hearns, which called itself "America's Largest Liquor Store," finally added Manischewitz "fine Passover wine" to its advertised specials in 1944, trumpeting its "special reserve quality" while warning it was only available in limited quantities. Gimbel's and Macy's added Manischewitz soon thereafter; in 1946 Manischewitz was the only brand promoted by Macy's aside from its much cheaper Red Star varieties.[8]

Monarch's wine made rapid progress in the late 1940s. The effectiveness of the Manischewitz brand name as an advertising device led two other kosher food producers, Rokeach and Streit, to offer their own varieties of kosher wine. Small brands also found space on the shelves of Jewish liquor stores, such as Shapiro's California Wine Company, Hersh's Hungarian Grape Products, and the Monterey Wine Company, but none had Manischewitz's promotional resources or visibility. Regular *New York Times* advertisements during Passover stressed that Manischewitz was "the traditional wine for Passover." Reaffirming the messages conveyed on its bottle label, advertisements asked readers to remember "Seder night at mother's house, the way it used to be . . . and on the table, wine like mother used to make . . . Manischewitz Kosher wine." Radio and even television advertising conveyed to a wide audience Monarch's claim that Manischewitz was "America's Largest Selling Kosher Wine."[9]

Certainly, my family participated in the postwar demand for Manischewitz on Passover night. But its use did not extend far outside the Seder itself. For us, serious drinking on Passover meant imbibing slivovitz, a powerful 100-proof plum brandy that was made throughout Eastern and Central Europe, including Romania where my mother's ancestors hailed from. As far back as I can remember, we would drink several shot glasses of slivovitz before sitting down for the Seder service and dinner. Evidently many other midcentury New Yorkers had a similar informal Passover ritual, as there were far more varieties of slivovitz advertised for Passover use in the 1930s and 1940s than brands of kosher wine. For all of Monarch's success becoming the "traditional kosher wine," its sales to Jews remained connected to specific rituals and holidays.

Reflecting the pattern of Jewish demand, Manischewitz sales spiked in September with the High Holy Days of Rosh Hashanah and Yom Kippur and then again in the early spring with Passover and Purim. It had to accept returns from stores after April, as there was little demand until the end of summer. But during the 1940s the company noticed a curious phenomenon—returns actually were decreasing among retailers who held on to the wine after Jewish holidays. Clearly other customers wanted it. Then, stories began to circulate about New York's African Americans requesting bottles of a kosher wine they called "Mani" that had a man with a beard on the label. By the early 1950s the pattern had become clear—there was substantial demand in the black community for Manischewitz wine such that Thanksgiving, Christmas, and Easter sales far exceeded Passover. Manischewitz had become the first crossover branded kosher product, several decades before Levy's rye bread or Hebrew National hot dogs.[10]

African American affinity for kosher wine was national in scope. With a population five times the size of the Jewish community, their purchases stimulated a remarkable increase in kosher wine production. Manischewitz sold especially well in Washington, DC, Detroit, Los Angeles, and the South, while Mogen David, a similar wine made by the Wine Corporation of America, dominated Chicago and other Midwestern cities with large African American populations. Sales even grew internationally, as Monarch found customers throughout the Caribbean and northern Latin America, as well as a few locations in Asia. Kosher Concord grape wine, a product whose "annual output was once so negligible that it wasn't isolated very carefully from the over-all statistics," comprised 10 percent of all wine produced in America in 1953 with a total production of ten million gallons.[11]

The African American market for Manischewitz puzzled Morris Freed-man, author of a long 1954 article in *Commentary* about the Monarch Wine Company. His curiosity was further piqued by the presence of reporters from African American newspapers at the inaugural tour of Monarch's upgraded Brooklyn facilities, where the company unveiled suf-ficient capacity to make five million gallons annually. His own theory was that African Americans had learned of the wine through domestic ser-vants receiving bottles of Manischewitz for the holidays from their Jewish employers. He didn't follow up on the hint offered by one unidentified black reporter. Manischewitz is "like the wine their mothers and grand-mothers used to make down South," the unnamed reporter explained in an aside to Freedman. "Scuppernong grapes are much like Concord. You've got to add sugar." It was an astute insight.[12]

The scuppernong grapes referred to by the reporter were the Concords of the South—or, if primacy as a wine grape is considered, Concord grapes were the scuppernongs of the North. Just as Concords grew well in chilly upstate New York, scuppernongs were unperturbed by sweltering southern weather and resistant to the fungus that devastated European grapes. Derived from native *Vitis rotifundia*, or muscadine grapes (much as Concord grapes were descendants of the domestic *Vitis labrusca* vari-ety), scuppernongs provided wine for Southerners generations before New Englanders learned how to turn Concords into a beverage. While scupper-nongs were carefully cultivated to drape over arbors, muscadine grapes were its wild cousin, growing prolific over trees, along hedgerows and fences, wherever there was enough water and sun. Scuppernong arbors were so commonplace that they provide a location for children's play in Harper Lee's classic *To Kill a Mockingbird* (1960). While used for other products, such as jams and fruit cakes, their availability meant that mus-cadine and scuppernong wines were widespread throughout the South.

Scuppernong grapes shared with Concords a high acidity and a musky flavor; hence the reporter's observation that, to make wine from either grape, "you've got to add sugar." Adding abundant sugar permitted com-pletion of fermentation and made the product palatable. And the home recipes used to make wines from *Vitis rotifundia* grapes were remarkably similar to those for *Vitis labrusca*, even though widely separated in time and place. A mid-nineteenth-century North Carolina recipe directed that for "every gallon of juice take three pounds of white sugar" to make muscadine wine. Several generations later, the 1913 *Dishes and Beverages of the Old South* similarly recommended using three pounds of crystallized sugar for each gallon of liquid from crushed "dead-ripe" muscadine grapes to make a wine that was "a peculiar but indescribably delicious flavor."[13]

Mid-twentieth-century kosher wine recipes were remarkably similar, even as they relied on Concord grapes. Located in the Passover section of cookbooks, these wines clearly were a complement to the special foods for that holiday and replicated well-worn home recipes. Leah Leonard recommended almost the same proportion of sugar—a little over two and a half cups per gallon—and advised that it would take three months for the wine to mature, enough time to make it in the late fall and have it ready for Passover. Little wonder these domestic wines, albeit made from different grapes, tasted similar.[14]

African Americans used wild and home-grown grapes to make wine even after national Prohibition ended, as many areas of the South retained a ban on alcohol sales. Robert Taylor, who grew up on a farm in Utica, Mississippi, in the 1950s and would enter the wine business himself, recalled that as a youth he helped to "climb the trees" to collect muscadine grapes, which his grandmother would turn into wine. The well-off white Southerners who enjoyed scuppernong wine at home also relied on the knowledge of their African American kitchen staff. "Two black women named Josie and Lena" presided over the kitchen of Mary Elizabeth Sproull Lanier's grandmother and doubtless were the ones who prepared her scuppernong wine, made with the conventional three pounds of sugar for every gallon of juice. Either way, knowledge and experience of home winemaking was widespread among rural African Americans, including the hundreds of thousands who traveled to New York and other cities to seek better employment opportunities.[15]

As the African American migrants to northern cities moved into neighborhoods that had Jewish residents—and Jewish-owned liquor stores—it was easy for them to discover the sweet wine known as Mani. Whether introduced to it through holiday gifts (as Morris Freedman surmised) or through other means, sweet Manischewitz wine tasted familiar—and was easy to obtain. Its prominent religious overtones, and label copy describing it as a sacramental wine, eased acceptance by the often devout African Americans. Similarly, the appeal to Jewish traditions through the marketing slogan "Wine like mother used to make" unintentionally carried a welcome message for African Americans with southern roots, familiar with home-made scuppernong wine, and now wanting to enjoy a northern lifestyle that included access to brand-name consumer products.

"MAN-O-MANISCHEWITZ"

Manischewitz avidly pursued black consumers in the 1950s with a multimillion dollar advertising campaign created by the Emil Mogul agency. Print advertising emphasized Manischewitz's popularity among leading culture figures and the qualities imbued by its kosher status. The Ink Spots, a prominent African American vocal group of that era, endorsed Manischewitz in a 1950 *Pittsburgh-Courier* advertisement. "Manischewitz kosher wine . . . harmonizes with us—sweetly!" they declared. "It's our favorite wine, too." A 1954 advertisement in *Ebony* used endorsement by bebop artist Bill Eckstein to declare that those drinking Manischewitz "drink with the stars of the entertainment world to whom nothing but the finest is good enough." The "quality and taste" enjoyed by these performers reflected how Manischewitz was "the *traditional* kosher wine" that could trace its history "back to Biblical days." And to make sure there was no doubt of the connection with the wine's kosher character, a prominent picture of the Manischewitz bottle graced both advertisements, with the serious rabbi on its label dominating the foreground.[16]

The company also poured money into radio spots intended to embed proper pronunciation of the Manischewitz name in the minds of black consumers—and, in so doing, add to brand recognition. Using the syncopated tag line, "Man-O-Manischewitz, What a Wine," the Emil Mogul agency "gave very careful pronouncing instructions to the announcer," including a phonetic spelling of the wine's brand name, "Man-i-shev-itz" so that consumers knew how to ask for it. These promotions were placed in programs that played "race" music and were conducted by "popular local personalities" in the black community, such as Jack Surrell, the legendary DJ for Detroit's WXYZ radio station. And these promotions always linked the wine's quality with its kosher status; listeners were reminded that "Manischewitz is kosher wine. . . . That means it's so pure, it's also used for sacramental purposes."[17]

Manischewitz advertising oriented toward Jewish consumers maintained the "Man-O-Manischewitz" tag line, but in other respects followed completely different themes. Maintenance of tradition, and of the established ways of celebrating Jewish culture, dominated its messages. "If it weren't Manischewitz, Grandma wouldn't serve it for Passover," declared a 1956 advertisement in the *New York Times*. By including promotion for Manischewitz matzoh, gefilte fish, and macaroons and declaring "Passover-Time is Manischewitz-Time," the advertisement also linked Monarch's Manischewitz wine with venerable kosher products made by an entirely different company—a distinction invisible to readers.[18]

In the late 1950s a new advertising agency, the Lawrence Gumbiner firm, briefly tried to reposition Manischewitz as "everybody's wine . . . because it tastes so good." These efforts sought to expand sales among white consumers by deemphasizing its Jewish association and kosher status. Gumbiner shifted expenditures away from radio shows that reached African Americans and toward mainstream television. Similarly, it suspended the *Ebony* advertising campaign in favor of using almost its entire magazine budget for full-page glossy *Life* magazine advertisements featuring men and women who did not look particularly Jewish. It even halted the Passover-series *New York Times* advertisements that had been a centerpiece of Monarch's promotional strategies towards Jews. These deliberate efforts to increase sales by "shatter[ing] the image of Manischewitz as a Jewish ceremonial wine" failed to make sustained headway among non-Jewish white consumers. Monarch fired the Gumbiner firm in 1960.[19]

With a solid and yet limited niche market among Jews, and little evidence of interest from other white groups, the company reverted to the strategy of expanding African American demand for its products. Monarch recruited its former account executive at the Emil Mogul Advertising Agency, Nort Wyner, to become the company's director of sales and advertising. Meyer Robinson "adored this guy," his daughter recalled, as the creative Wyner was schooled in the new world of postwar advertising methods. Under his direction, magazine advertising shifted back to focusing on the African American market, with *Ebony* absorbing 85 percent of the entire magazine budget by 1973. And, in a brilliant stroke, Wyner recruited Sammy Davis Jr. (made famous as a member of the rat pack through his movies with Frank Sinatra and Dean Martin) as Manischewitz's television front man. Nattily dressed and filmed while knocking out a seemingly impromptu tune on the piano, Davis encouraged African American men to be a bon vivant like himself by drinking Manischewitz on the rocks. A convert to Judaism who was hardly a "Richard Pryor," as one former company executive reflected, Sammy Davis was not likely to scare off consumers who drank Manischewitz for traditional purposes.[20]

To increase sales, Monarch even expanded its product line directed toward African Americans. Sustained efforts went into the launch of Cream White Concord in 1968, a year whose events might have discouraged

FIGURE 6.2 From left to right: unidentified, Sammy Davis, Jr., Meyer Robinson, and Jack Carter. Collection of Gale Robinson.

other white firms from seeking to grow sales among black consumers. While featuring the Manischewitz name, the bottle's shape emulated a VSOP brandy, rather than the traditional design, and bore a simple and elegant label with gold lettering—and a much less visible rabbi. This appeal to upscale style reflected a common judgment among advertisers that African Americans preferred to buy the best kind of alcohol, rather than cheap brands. Seeking to build on its positive brand image, its *Ebony* advertisements introduced Cream White Concord by asking, "How do you tell wine lovers about a *different* Manischewitz wine"? While its kosher status was less evident (though still confirmed on the front label), the wine's connection to Manischewitz and its traditional Jewish wines was a centerpiece of the company's marketing efforts.[21]

The contrast with efforts to sell white consumers on the new wine could not have been greater. Rather than building on Manischewitz's reputation to promote Cream White Concord, the company sought to minimize its association with the new product. *New York Times* advertisements featured a hand hiding the bottle's label, reinforced by text that advised, "Don't let them see the label until after they taste the wine." Consumers seeking to introduce it to their friends were counseled to dispense sips before revealing the brand so that its connection with Manischewitz would not detract from appreciation for its taste. "This is terrific," the advertisement quoted an anonymous consumer saying. "Y'know, if I'd seen the name, I might never have believed it," he then admits. Such pessimism conceded the circumscribed appeal of Manischewitz wine to Jews—and to all white Americans.[22]

Cream White Concord quickly became the company's sales leader, largely due to African American demand—and an advertising budget that reached $4 million by the late 1970s. "The African American community was dedicated to the Manischewitz name," reflected former company executive Marshall Goldberg, "and when they saw a new product that was packaged so beautifully, it gave them a whole new product to drink." In 1981 *Forbes* magazine could declare that the typical Manischewitz drinker was an urban blue-collar African American man rather than an ethnic Jew.[23]

As a brand built through savvy marketing, Manischewitz wine had an outsized presence in American popular culture. In addition to displaying billboards, placing magazine, radio, and television advertisements, and developing extensive in-store displays, company president Meyer Robinson was an inveterate promoter. "When he would go someplace and introduce himself," his daughter Gale Robinson recalled, he always would put out his hand and say, "Meyer Robinson, Manischewitz wine." (She kidded her father that someday his approach would generate the comeback, "how do you do, Mr. Wine.") With his wife Roslyn, Robinson frequently drove into Manhattan from their Long Island home to "go to the Copacabana and the Latin Club and that kind of thing because of the people involved"—especially disk jockeys. Robinson personally got to know prominent radio personalities such as William B. Williams, who favored playing singers such as Lena Horne and Frank Sinatra on his WNEW shows, and Barry Gray, an early pioneer of talk radio on WOR. Knowing their influence, Robinson cultivated these relationships, with the objective that they would "in some way mention Manischewitz" on the air. While the wine's clientele may have been predominantly African American and Hispanic, its prominence was that of a kosher wine, a

FIGURE 6.3 Buddy Hackett, Jackie Robinson, and Meyer Robinson. Collection of Gale Robinson.

Jewish wine, lending a visibility to kosher products that permeated the wider American culture. When astronaut Buzz Aldrin invoked the by then iconic phrase "Man-O-Manischewitz" to capture the awe he felt stepping on the moon in 1973, he also inadvertently certified the remarkable success of a quarter-century of company marketing efforts.[24]

Among Jews, though, Manischewitz was not doing so well. While my father may have turned up his cultured nose at sweet kosher wine, my mother increasingly viewed it as fit for "winos" rather than upwardly mobile Jews. She would tell us that alcoholics drank sweet kosher wine because it was a way of getting drunk quickly and imbibing enough calories to avoid having to spend money on food. Her prejudice was fanned by the movement of poor Puerto Ricans and African Americans into our Upper West Side neighborhood and the visible cultural changes this entailed. Business names on store fronts switched from English to Spanish, and streets that had been sedate and quiet when she walked them as a child now were lined, in the summer, with people sitting on stoops, some drinking from bottles in paper bags. Her fear was such that we were forbidden to walk between Broadway and Central Park West, except along the wide east-west crossings at 86th, 79th, and 72nd streets. In her anger at these changes, my mother did not distinguish between Manischewitz and those kosher brands that aggressively catered to the "wino" market, such as Mogen David, which produced MD "Mad Dog" 20/20— twenty-ounce bottles containing wine that was 20 percent alcohol—to compete with Thunderbird, Ripple, and other fortified high-alcohol wines. Sweet kosher wine, regardless of brand, had become a beverage tolerated only for tradition's sake on Passover and was not to be seen in the house at other times.

Among the Orthodox, Manischewitz suffered a more fundamental challenge—doubts that it was kosher at all. For decades, the Monarch Wine Company had relied for certification on the same rabbis employed by the Manischewitz food company. The OK certification agency included Manischewitz in its *Kosher Food Guide,* but the Orthodox Union steadfastly refused to endorse it. "The rabbis always were the issue," recalled Marshall Goldberg. "The Orthodox would not recognize our rabbi and the K with a circle around it on the label." As OU's certification program expanded, and the observant community became more demanding,

Monarch's Manischewitz suffered under a whispering campaign that it did not meet kosher norms.

Monarch faced relentless criticism from the Orthodox, as Gale Robinson recalled, for "having non-Jews working in the winery." As job opportunities for Jews improved following World War II and new migrants moved to Brooklyn, the composition of the plant's workforce changed accordingly. By the 1960s there were in fact "many, many non-Jews working at the plant," Marshall Goldberg admitted, with most of the remaining Jews working "upstairs" in the chemical and scientific research areas and as salespersons, and not in the production jobs that actually made the wine. Among the Orthodox, these changes violated one of the first rules for making wine kosher—that only Sabbath-observant Jews could play a role in production from the time the grapes were crushed to when the bottle was sealed.[25]

Conservative Judaism, the variant that my family adhered to, was firmly behind Manischewitz. At the behest of its governing Rabbinical Assembly, Rabbi Israel Silverman delved into Jewish law to determine if the ancient requirements governing kosher wine were still applicable in the modern era. His 1964 responsum, "Are All Wines Kosher?" argued that modern production methods rendered the ancient rabbinic prohibitions obsolete. Rabbi Silverman held that mechanized operations in large factories meant that gentile production workers could not touch the wine "from the moment the grapes are placed in the crusher machine until the entire production process is complete and the wine resulting from it placed in sealed containers" even if they managed those operations. While such wine might still be *stam yeinom*, wine made by non-Jews, the absence of any physical contact with gentiles meant it could be permitted for Jewish consumption. Drawing on a long lineage of lenient opinions, especially those of Moses Isserles, Silverman nonetheless emphasized how dropping the rabbinic restriction on *stam yeinom* did not extend to permitting its use on Passover—as unacceptable leavening agents might be in the wine—and for other religious functions so as to "enhance the ritual of the mitzvah." Manischewitz thus was not only acceptable, but, along with other Jewish-made wines, preferred for traditional uses. Conservative Jews drew on Silverman's responsum to argue, as Rabbi Meyer Hager did a few years later, that Manischewitz was "kosher in every respect."[26]

The breach between Conservative and Orthodox over non-Jewish workers in wineries was compounded by profound differences over *mevushal* requirements. All Manischewitz wines were *mevushal* to the satisfaction of its supervising rabbis—a status they translated as "boiled" rather than cooked. The machinery at the company's disposal, however, did not heat wine to anything close to 212 degrees. Monarch relied on commercial technology initially developed to pasteurize milk to "boil" its wine; to comply with U.S. Public Health service rules, this equipment heated liquids in large vats to 145 F for thirty minutes. Since Monarch already relied on vats connected by hoses and pipes to mix wine with sugar, adjust color, and filter impurities, it was relatively straightforward to incorporate the milk pasteurization technology into its manufacturing operations. "The wine is bottled at 140 degrees," company scientist Monroe Coven told visitors, immediately following pasteurization. Once *mevushal*, opened Manischewitz wine could be passed by a person of any religious persuasion at an event without compromising its kosher status. Rabbi Silverman, along with other Conservative rabbis, was satisfied that Manischewitz's *mevushal* methods were in accordance with Jewish religious requirements.[27]

The Orthodox did not agree. Barely a year after Silverman's essay, Rabbi Moshe Feinstein issued what was in essence a sharp riposte, though without mentioning him by name. His responsum's timing and content, though, indicates that it was a rejoinder to Silverman's leniency. In it Feinstein concentrated on the issue whether conventional pasteurization was sufficient to render a wine *mevushal*. His challenge was to translate the traditional sensory criteria of "cooked" into a modern numerical standard. After evaluating several areas of rabbinic debate, Feinstein concluded that a reduction in wine's volume was the proof needed to determine if it had been heated enough to be "cooked" in compliance with rabbinic requirements. Citing a chemist for support, Feinstein determined that 165 degrees F was the minimum temperature required—that is, twenty degrees warmer than the pasteurization achieved by Manischewitz using vat technology. While Rabbi Feinstein did not comment on Manischewitz explicitly, the implications of his ruling were clear; given his views, the Orthodox Union would not extend certification to Manischewitz.[28]

Compounding his differences with Silverman over *mevushal* require-ments, Feinstein also did not agree that the automatic processes used by Monarch changed the traditional requirement for observant Jews to be involved in winemaking at all stages of the process. While Monarch con-tinued to find individual Orthodox rabbis to certify its wine, without the OU seal of approval doubts remained about its *kashrus*.[29]

Monarch wine made no efforts to satisfy its Orthodox critics, even as its sales stagnated in the late 1970s. Since "the die had been cast as far as whether Manischewitz was acceptable," reflected Goldberg, "it wasn't really worth it" to go through the expense of obtaining OU certification. With Jews comprising at most 15 percent of Manischewitz's customers, an advertising campaign saying, "look, we have changed," designed to attract Orthodox consumers, didn't make sense. "We're certainly not going to let the tail wag the dog" was the unfortunate description of the wine's Jewish consumers offered by Manischewitz's advertising agency in 1981—a telling if undiplomatic admission about its consumer base.

Instead, the company looked outside the Jewish market. It acquired highly profitable distribution rights to the Chinese Tsingtao beer and invested heavily in flavored domestic wines oriented to its African Amer-ican and Latino customers. In 1981 three-quarters of the company's $4 million advertising budget went to promote Piña Coconnetta, a piña colada–flavored wine beverage, which *Forbes* wryly noted was "not exactly what you would call a sacramental drink."[30]

With its focus remaining on sweet wines, Monarch's owners denied in vain that there was a shift underway among assimilated Jews such as my father, along with other Americans, toward dry varieties. It may be "chic to be dry," company sales director Cliff Adelman lectured *Forbes* in 1981, but in his opinion the "upward mobility-group" that preferred dry wines "represent *zilch* population-wise." He would be proven wrong. The interest in French wines and California varieties made from European grapes accelerated in the 1980s, such that by 1985 80 percent of the wine consumed in America was table wine. Black consumers began to switch to dry wines as well, sending sales of Cream White Concord into a tailspin and frustrating the company's investments in Piña Coconnetta and simi-lar products. The reversal was so sharp that, just three years after he rid-iculed *Forbes* for suggesting "that people drink dry," Marshall Goldberg admitted to the *New York Post* that the company's association with sweet wine "blocks some consumers from buying." Shortly thereafter, the partners gave up and sold the Manischewitz brand to the Canandaigua Wine Company at a considerable profit, where it became just one of its stable of Concord wine brands, thereby ending this remarkable saga in American Jewish wine culture.[31]

"KOSHER DOESN'T HAVE TO MEAN SWEET"

The French kosher wine we started serving for Passover came, in all likelihood, from the Royal Wine Company, better known as Kedem. Initially established as the Herzog Wine and Spirits Company in Czechoslovakia in the early 1800s, the firm was one of many European wine companies created by Jews to serve both their own communities and to reach a gentile market. Austro-Hungarian Emperor Franz Joseph even took note of the company, making it a supplier of wine to the crown and anointing company president Philip Herzog a baron. In the 1930s, however, the rise of Nazism forced the Herzog family into hiding, with several dying in the Holocaust. Philip's grandson Eugene survived the war years, only to find his company in the crosshairs of the pro-Communist Czech government and its program to nationalize private firms. In 1948 Eugene fled Europe, his family's fortune gone, and sought to create a new life in America.

Eugene joined other Jewish refugees on New York City's Lower East Side where he looked for opportunities to use his particular expertise. While Manischewitz dominated the market, enough customers were interested in variety to support a half-dozen small companies making sweet Concord grape wines. With his knowledge of the wine business, Eugene joined the Royal Wine Company as one of eight partners in 1948; it received certification from the *Kosher Food Guide* in 1954.[32]

The founders of Kedem and Manischewitz could not have been more different. Meyer Robinson was a quintessential product of mid-century Jewish culture, descended from immigrant parents and proudly Jewish as well as deeply embedded in American culture. He was an avid Brooklyn Dodgers fan, often bringing the team to the winery for meals, and a friend to Jackie Robinson when he broke baseball's color line. While kosher at

FIGURE 6.4 Brooklyn Dodgers at Monarch Wine. Collection of Gale Robinson.

home, and a firm believer that the Friday Sabbath dinner was sacrosanct, he was comfortable in nonkosher settings and enjoyed lobster and other dishes that were, without doubt, *treif.*

The Herzog family was instead part of a post–World War II Jewish refugee generation that carried with them lived experiences and vivid memories of the efforts of the Nazis and Soviet Communists to eradicate Judaism. Deeply embedded in Jewish Orthodoxy, the five Herzog children attended yeshiva; one became a rabbi. While Monarch Wine's owners looked to associations with American life to brand their wine—selecting the well-known Manischewitz name to aid marketing efforts—Eugene Herzog's choice was embedded in Jewish tradition and his family's European odyssey. He drew from the emotional Hashiveinu prayer familiar to synagogue-attending Jews, sung by the congregation when the traditional scrolls of the holy Torah were returned to the ceremonial ark where it was kept between services. Its closing stanza, *Chadesh yameinu ke-kedem,* translates as "renew our days as before," with *ke-kedem* meaning, "as before." "It was a wish," reflected Eugene's son David. "That's what my father wanted," for the family's fortunes to return, "as before." The name was both a brand and an expression of hope among a particular generation of Jews, the post–World War II refugees, that their life in America would permit a restoration of the pious Orthodox communities wiped out by the Holocaust.[33]

While the wine's name may not have had meaning for consumers unfamiliar with Jewish synagogue rituals, it did telegraph to postwar Jewish immigrants that Kedem was a wine for them, one produced by observant Jews from their own community. Nonetheless, the Royal Wine Company struggled for several decades. Each partner produced and named their own wine; adding so many choices to an already crowded marketplace meant none did very well. The company survived largely due to its contract to distribute the Israeli Carmel wines, which naturally had distinctive appeal. Gradually Herzog bought out his associates, finally becoming sole owner in 1958 when the final partner left, amicably, taking with him the Carmel distribution business.

Herzog turned the Royal Wine Company into a family business, depending heavily on his sons' labor. "He had his kids working their butt off," recalled David. As a yeshiva student in his early teens, David Herzog would return home to help harvest grapes in the fall, then again to help the company through the busy Purim and Passover season. "Seven days after my wedding," he reflected with a smile, "I was loading trucks."[34]

Seeking new market niches for his grape products, Eugene Herzog developed Kedem grape juice in the late 1950s. It was a boon for the company, with sales boosted by Passover consumption and crossover demand in Puerto Rico and in other Latino markets. For its core kosher consumers, Herzog produced a new naturally sweetened Concord wine, using grape juice concentrate rather than sugar to improve its taste. Together, these products gave the Royal Wine Company something distinctive in the marketplace, generating both income and visibility for its Kedem brand.

Herzog also sought to make inroads among the Orthodox—already skittish about the *kashrus* of Manischewitz—by securing OU certification for Kedem wine and grape juice in 1970; by the mid-1970s, Kedem was the only wine producer with the OU's imprimatur. At the same time that Manischewitz was aggressively seeking non-Jewish consumers, Kedem was busy consolidating its position as the Orthodox Union's preferred kosher wine.[35]

Kedem also began to explore alternatives to sweet kosher wine entirely, especially as David Herzog assumed a larger role in the company's operations. The youngest of Eugene's sons, David had left the family business to work as a Wall Street analyst for almost six years. Upon returning to Kedem in the early 1970s, David brought a new attention to marketing to a company that had been principally focused on production. "Because of my Wall Street background," he recalled, "I saw the world in different angles." What he especially learned was that in order to reach new customers "you have to give them something unique." Since Kedem was too small to "beat up" on bigger companies by competing directly, it had to look for market niches that were not yet occupied.

Dry kosher wine would become just that "something unique" for Kedem. In the late 1970s, David fortuitously encountered a Jewish winemaker from France who was touring Kedem's upstate New York winery; he asked if Kedem would be interested in distributing his kosher Bordeaux wine in the United States. David's brother Yankel demurred, as he felt the French wine would cut into their own sales; but David argued for experimenting with a dry wine the company had not actually made. "The world is changing," he recalled telling his brother. "People start to drink more dry wines." So he gambled by buying one shipping container amounting to 750 cases; at the time "a lot of money to us."

For a leading Jewish company to sell dry French wine for use on Passover was news—at least among those who followed wine. The *New York Times*'s well-known wine critic, Frank Prial, took note of Kedem's audacious move. The "Royal Kedem line of kosher wines," he announced in his April 5, 1978 "Wine Talk" column, "now includes three imported Bordeaux" all of which, he quickly reassured startled readers, were "strictly kosher" and "bordeaux superieure in rating." To those "elderly traditionalists" who wrote in to him promising to "wreak various types of mayhem" if forced to drink anything but traditional kosher wine, he admonished, "we are talking about dry wine. Dry is not the opposite of wet in the wine world; it is the opposite of sweet."[36]

Prial's widely read column was a sensation in the New York metropolitan area. By the end of the day Kedem had sold out its entire stock, much to the frustration of some liquor stores, which had been initially wary of this peculiar new thing, dry kosher wine. "That was the beginning of our imported wines," Herzog recalled.

With this success, David Herzog sought to expand the company's imported wines to include Italian vintages. Going through his father's old files, he discovered one labeled "Italy" that contained an unsigned agreement to make a kosher Asti Spumante wine through the Bartenura winery. While the Italian company was interested, Eugene explained that Kedem had been unable to locate the Sabbath-observant Jews it needed to make the wine as required by kosher law; the deal had fallen through. With his father's encouragement, David tried again. He located the winery, and then secured help from the Orthodox rabbis for Milan's Jewish community to recruit workers to handle operations for a special production run of kosher wine. Kedem paid for this help, thereby funding significant improvements in the facilities available to Milan's Jews.

With a growing stable of dry kosher wines, Kedem decided to go on the offensive. In 1982, just as Manischewitz's troubles were growing, Kedem launched a remarkably successful marketing campaign around the slogan "Kosher needn't be sweet—just special," and declared, in case readers didn't get the point, that "special means Kedem." Large advertisements reinforced the company's message by including pictures of its "special" wines: a French Bordeaux, Italian Bartenura Soave, Spanish Ararbanel Rioja, and Kedem's own California Chenin Blanc. The advertisements, appearing in small Jewish periodicals such as the *Jewish Chronicle of Pittsburgh* and the *Kashrus Newsletter* as well as the *New York Times,* appealed to refinement rather than tradition, promising that Kedem's wines were "specially selected for the finesse and character that lingers happily on your palate." The slogan was so compelling that New York's Garnet liquor store used a slightly modified version, "Passover wines (needn't be sweet just special)" and listed its kosher inventory by nation of origin—just as it did nonkosher wines.[37]

The Royal Wine Company steadily expanded its stable of dry wines with a strategy of adding more imported varieties. Drawing on its successful Bartenura experience, Kedem sought out relationships with Orthodox synagogues abroad whose rabbis and members could be drawn on to produce kosher runs of local wines. "In most places we have local communities who have been trained to do the work," Herzog explained to Montreal *Gazette* wine critic Bill Zacharkiw, doing so "under the supervision of the estates' winemaker." Some of these relationships developed into virtual international outposts of the Kedem Company that could be flexibly enlisted to make wine. Its crew of Argentine Jews also did service in Chile to create kosher wine there, and a pool of thirty-five reliable Sabbath-observant Jews based in Western Europe produced kosher wine on fifteen to twenty estates in France, Spain, and Portugal. It was a brilliant way of economically expanding Kedem's inventory; using already active vineyards to make kosher wine allowed the company to benefit from the credibility of established brands. The appeal of Kedem's wines among observant Jews is apparent; Passover sales that had once comprised 80 percent of the company's business had fallen to 35 percent by 1990. The company was now selling a great deal of its wine throughout the year to Jews wishing to have it with dinner and on special occasions.[38]

While expanding its line of dry wines, Kedem also sought to increase sales of its traditional Concord grape vintages by eroding Manischewitz's standing among observant Jews. Its advertisements prominently displayed the OU symbol, the endorsement denied to Monarch's wines, a quiet but unmistakable affirmation of Kedem's superior adherence to kosher standards. In public statements, Kedem spokespersons consistently reinforced Jewish doubts about Manischewitz by emphasizing its nonwhite customer base. "We target the Jewish market," David Herzog told the *New York Times* in 1984. "Manischewitz targets the entire sweet wine market, which includes many blacks and Hispanics." A couple of years later he made the same point to a Long Island paper widely read by observant Jews, asserting (with slight exaggeration) that "90 percent of their [Manischewitz's] sales are not going to the kosher market." As Kedem also sought sales among non-Jews, Herzog's comments were disingenuous. But they did serve the objective of branding Manischewitz as a wine that was not really meant for observant Jews, despite its kosher lineage.[39]

Kedem continued to air similar themes even after Manischewitz's new owner, the Canandaigua Wine Company, secured OU certification. A radio and point-of-sale campaign in 1991 purported that Jewish consumers had selected Kedem over Manischewitz in a head-to-head competition—sponsored, of course, by the Royal Wine Company. The radio advertisements featured two men with Yiddish accents expressing their preference for Kedem, while point-of-sale ads showed, as the *Los Angeles Times* reported, "a bottle of Kedem standing upright over a knocked down bottle of Manischewitz, and was headed, 'The chosen one.'" The attack, not only on Manischewitz's taste but on its legitimacy as a kosher wine, was reaffirmed by a Kedem spokesperson who, according to the newspaper, "sought to question Manischewitz's Jewish credentials by noting that much of its success derives from the popularity of Manischewitz among non-Jews, especially blacks." Outraged by the campaign, conducted during the 1991 Passover season and based on a dubious competition, Canandaigua secured a court order forcing Kedem to remove the advertisements from radio stations and liquor stores. By that time, however, the damage already was done.[40]

Despite its success among Jewish consumers, wine critics nonetheless viewed Kedem's early dry wines as "mediocre," in the blunt statement of Baltimore wine columnist Michael Dresser. Frank Prial, generally one of Kedem's boosters, nonetheless advised wine consumers in 1991 to just "try the lower-priced" of the company's Herzog Cabernets, as "it may fulfill all your needs."[41] Recognizing the need for greater winemaking expertise, the Herzogs hired Peter Sterns to head up the company's wine operations. After a career with the large California companies of Robert Mondavi and J. Lohr, Sterns had made a name in kosher wine through his work with the acclaimed Israeli Golan Heights Winery in the 1980s. Familiar with both California grapes and kosher practices, he was able to steer Kedem toward far better vintages, and, in 2005, to open its own California winery in Oxnard, just north of Los Angeles.[42]

Kedem's owners realized as well that improving *mevushal* technology was integral to creating better wines. The best wine grapes and vintages could be undone by the demands of heating wine to make it *mevushal*. In so doing, however, the large Royal Wine Company actually lagged behind newer innovative companies. The true breakthroughs in making high-quality kosher dry wine took place among small winemakers who figured out how to adapt technology developed for pasteurization of fruit juice to make kosher wine *mevushal*. And these winemakers came not from the Jewish traditions of the East Coast, but instead from California's efflorescent new wine industry.

THE "MEVUSHALATAR"

Ernest Weir's Hagafen winery (still in operation) was the pacesetter among the new California-based kosher wine operations. Weir had twenty-four years of experience in California wineries such as Domain Chandon before he set out, in 1980, to create his own kosher vineyard. He later attributed his inspiration to memories of attending Passover Seders in his late teens, "our best holiday of the year," and yet having to drink "this wine that we hate." Schooled in the boutique wine making methods that had proliferated in California since the late 1960s, Weir was able to create high-quality kosher wine at Hagafen. After a decade of operations, the *Wine Spectator* accorded his kosher Cabernet Sauvignon a strong 91 rating (out of 100)—far better than Kedem's California and European wines, which it termed merely "reliable."[43]

Not far from Hagafen, another influential vineyard drew on European traditions to make some of its wine kosher. The St. Supery Winery was founded by Robert Skalli, heir to a wealthy French-Algerian family with deep roots in the wine trade. Seeking a foothold in California as part of the family's global wine business, Skalli established St. Supery in California's Pope Valley in 1981 and appointed Michaela Rodeno (who had worked with Ernie Weir at Domain Chandon) as its CEO. Drawing from European practices familiar to the Jewish Skalli family, St. Supery brought in rabbinic supervision so it could prepare a short run of a kosher for Passover wine called Mount Madrona.[44]

Hagafen and St. Supery quickly had to address the difficult challenge of making their wine *mevushal*. Weir originally resisted, concerned that doing so "might be harmful to the quality of the wine." But the initial "acceptance—or lack of acceptance" of his new kosher wine made him realize that making it *mevushal* would allow it to be "served in a hotel or in a restaurant" and thus increase sales, as "it really wouldn't matter who touched the wine." Still concerned about the effect heating wine would have on its quality, Weir departed from past *mevushal* practices by adapting the flash pasteurization methods used in fruit juice manufacturing. Employing fundamentally different technology than Manischewitz's large, heated vats made it possible for Hagafen to produce high-quality *mevushal* wine.

Vat pasteurization, by all accounts, was hard on wine, much as it might have worked adequately for milk. The contents of the large tanks (holding up to fifty thousand gallons) took time to heat to 145 F and then had to be held at that temperature for thirty minutes, a slow process with deleterious effects. In a typical complaint about vat-pasteurized wines, *Chicago Sun-Times* wine critic Dee Coutelle complained that most "had a boiled character, lacking weight and body." These were damning phrases for consumers wanting good wine.[45]

Flash pasteurization, known as "high temperature short time" (HTST) pasteurization by the trade, had more potential to produce good *mevushal* wine. The technology first emerged in the U.S. fruit juice industry when scientists determined that sterilization at high temperatures required far less time than at lower temperatures; pasteurization that took thirty minutes at 145 F could be achieved in a few seconds at 185 F. The HTST systems relied on heat exchangers that used closed pipes containing the juice to pass adjacent to plates or coils heated by scalding hot water; the two liquids never touched. Heating destroyed enzymes and bacteria that could spoil the juice, and units also typically contained cooling sections that could reduce the temperature rapidly to avoid discoloration or loss of nutrients. With skyrocketing demand for apple and orange juice in the 1950s and 1960s, equipment firms developed sophisticated systems that allowed precise control over the temperature to which the liquid was heated and the length of time it remained in that state; the appeal for winemakers seeking a gentler *mevushal* process is evident.[46]

With California's large agriculture industry, Weir had ample opportunity to experiment with flash pasteurization units. In 1985 he rented the HTST equipment of an apple juice manufacturer located an hour away to successfully produce his first *mevushal* wine. He recalled that the unit "could set the temperature to exactly where I wanted [180]," so it met Rabbi Moshe Feinstein's standard, and then "chill it immediately" to 60 F. In an extraordinary contrast to the slow (and damaging) vat procedure, the HTST unit could bring a quart of wine to the *mevushal* temperature in under two seconds and then cool it down just as fast. Soon Weir discovered a more convenient unit—one at St. Supery, just twenty minutes by car. St. Supery had in turn bought it from the Weinstock winery, a short-lived kosher operation, which in all likelihood had obtained it from a juice producer. In the mid-1990s St. Supery's "mevushalatar"—as workers referred to it—was used by Kedem as well as by Hagafen and St. Supery to create *mevushal* wines.[47]

Modifying HTST systems designed to make apple juice for the exacting production of wine was not as easy as it may sound. For HTST systems to heat (and cool) liquids so quickly, consistently, and thoroughly, filtering systems needed to first remove solids and impurities that could impair the machine's effects. Additionally, pipes had to be designed in such a manner that complex fluid dynamics rotated the liquid to ensure equal exposure to the heating elements. Wine producers had to choose between parallel pipes or plates to heat and cool the liquid and decide the placement within the manufacturing process: just after pressing the grapes and before fermentation or as the last stage before bottling. Modifying HTST systems for *mevushal* purposes and to create high-quality wine quickly became a place for widespread tinkering with existing technology to better adapt it to wine production—and to create competitive advantage.

Kedem's initial efforts to adapt HTST technology began in the late 1980s and continued steadily thereafter. "We did a study with UC-Davis," David Herzog recalled, and "spent a lot of money with them on the *mevushal* process." (Some sources indicate that these expenditures were in excess of $1 million.)[48] While the Davis researchers helped the company, there were "certain things they didn't pick up"; subsequent improvements were developed internally by "knowledgeable people" on its staff. Kedem experimented with "different systems of chilling, different systems of heating, different systems of filtrations," Herzog explained, "so that everything just works right." Knowledge and techniques accrued through these efforts were proprietary and not shared publicly. "There's only three people, four people who know it," Herzog explained about Kedem's closely held *mevushal* technology, "and all the last name is Herzog."

Ernie Weir similarly experimented with several HTST systems for his *mevushal* process. After using the old Weinstock equipment for a number of years, he bought an "off the shelf" unit the manufacturer had adapted for his specific requirements and "integrated into a new system of heating and cooling." While successful, Weir remained watchful of opportunities to improve his technology. Similar to Herzog, Weir explained that he "was not at liberty to describe" the machinery, as doing so might give other firms a "competitive advantage."

Driving the expensive process of creating *mevushal* wines was the desire to expand sales to hotels, restaurants, and caterers for large events. The likely presence of non-Jewish staff whose touch would render non -*mevushal* wine nonkosher compelled this choice. "We can't sell a caterer or restaurant wine which is not *mevushal*," Herzog explained. Simply opening up the bar mitzvah and wedding market was a boon, as maintaining the *kashrus* of these events when there was a non-Jewish wait staff required serving *mevushal* wine.

Systematically making kosher wine *mevushal* helped reach additional markets—but it also placed new burdens on its acceptance outside observant Jewish circles. Heating wine, albeit briefly, to 180 F profoundly affected its chemistry; if performed before fermentation (the usual practice for white wines), new enzymes had to be introduced to replace those destroyed in HTST systems. Heating wine after fermentation (the general practice for reds) killed the enzymes that aged it, significantly affecting maturation in the bottle. In the case of Manischewitz, the *mevushal* process was an asset, as it meant the wine kept longer without spoiling, even if not refrigerated. But halting wine's aging process was abhorrent to discerning consumers and vastly reduced *mevushal* wine's appeal outside Jewish circles.

Wine commentators universally panned *mevushal* processes as damaging to wine, no matter how carefully it was done. Few were as blunt as Jay McInerey, who advised wine buyers "to look at the label, and if the label is mevushal, pass it over. Walk on by. Or, better yet, run." Even Israeli wine critic Daniel Rogov, with evident sympathy for kosher wines, nonetheless wrote that, with "very few exceptions," *mevushal* wines "are incapable of developing in the bottle" and unfortunately often impart "a 'cooked' sensation to the nose and palate." Non-*mevushal* kosher wine did not encounter the same disdain. The same commentators who heaped abuse on *mevushal* wines exempted non-*mevushal* wines from their complaints. McInerey (presumably having run away from wines with a *mevushal* designation) had only the highest praise for Israel's Yarden, whose wines of "real distinction and character" were good enough "to tempt the heathen palate."[49]

The very success of the relatively small number of non-*mevushal* wines, however, only entrenched *mevushal* wine's status as kosher's poor cousin. Winemakers unintentionally reinforced this distinction by generally placing lower quality—and hence less expensive—vintages in their *mevushal* line. "Bad wine pasteurized is still bad wine" Weir complained; making it so created "a self-fulfilling prophecy" that *mevushal* wine was "the worst wine in the winery." The economics of the kosher wine business drove this practice. Since *mevushal* wines were intended for use in social settings, especially large events where the sponsors chose the wine rather than those who actually drank it, less expensive wines were the clear choice for this purpose. And since *mevushal* wines could not achieve the same prices as non-*mevushal* varieties, it did not make sense to use better vintages for these occasions. Instead, more expensive, non-*mevushal* wines were more likely to be drunk by observant Jews in private settings where the presence of a non-Jewish wait staff was not an issue—and where the higher price point was a less important concern.

Kosher wine advocates sought ammunition against critics by supporting research challenging the "anti-*mevushal*" consensus. With funding provided by several kosher wine companies, University of California-Davis graduate student Shlomo (also Shiki) Rauchberger conducted taste tests to see if a panel of judges could discern the difference between *mevushal* and non-*mevushal* Cabernet Sauvignon. Sampling included a recently bottled Cabernet and one aged for one hundred days; in both cases the panel could not taste the difference. As his 1992 study remains unpublished either in print or on the Internet, its methodology could not be reviewed, leading many oenologists to question its veracity. As some pointed out, aging wine just over three months was hardly enough time to test the *mevushal* process's effect on a wine's maturation after bottling. Nonetheless, Rauchberger's study has lived on as an asset for pro-*mevushal* positions, morphing from an unpublished paper prepared by a graduate student with industry funding into a study graced by the salubrious lineage of coming from "one of the top wine-making schools in the United States."[50]

The spin on the Rauchberger paper did not convince critics; but diligent efforts by kosher winemakers did soften a few hearts—and even palates. Daniel Rogov endorsed Hagafen's *mevushal* wines as "among the very best kosher wines anywhere" and thus as proof that "in some cases" the *mevushal* process was not harmful. Even Jay McInerery granted that among the wines on Kedem's Baron Herzog label there were a few *mevushal* varieties (such as its "outstanding" Special Reserve Chardonnay) where there was "little, if any, deleterious effect on the finished wine." In these cases the great care with which winemakers deployed flash pasteurization technology allowed their *mevushal* wines to pass muster.[51]

Kedem was able to ride the Jewish component of the remarkable increase in dry wine consumption after 1980; David Herzog, in that respect, was as insightful as Meyer Robinson in seeing and pursuing new opportunities and, in so doing, built a thriving and dynamic company.

Such success, however, did not alter the broad consensus among wine authorities—and wine consumers—that kosher wine was, in general, inferior to nonkosher varieties. Disdain among tastemakers for the sweet Concord wine of Manischewitz cast a long shadow, and the muttering about cooked *mevushal* wine hindered any dramatic reversal of attitudes. Not surprisingly, then, the new dry kosher wines did not generate much interest outside the Jewish market. A large New York purveyor of kosher wines admitted in 2008 that "his clients instinctively go to the non-kosher section when they want to buy first-rate wines." His few "converts" to dry kosher wine tended to be Reform Jews who wanted to support the "kosher movement."[52] The kosher designation may have helped kosher wine producers gain sales among non-Jews for a generation following World War II, but by the late twentieth century kosher was instead an obstacle to breaking into the gentile marketplace.

PASSOVER, AGAIN

Attending my mother's 2010 Passover Seder, the last one before her death, we were able to enjoy a wide range of kosher wines to complement our meal. After getting ready for the service with glasses of slivovitz, we experimented with several French Burgundies and a California Cabernet as we celebrated, in the way we had for forty years, the Jewish exodus from Egypt. Elijah certainly would have had a fine wine to sip if he entered when we opened the door for him, certainly better than the days when Manischewitz or Mogen David filled his cup. And with the discussion naturally turning to my kosher food book, which seemed to be taking so long to complete, my mother reflected on the extensive selection of kosher wine in her neighborhood liquor store.

The family Seder moved to my southeastern Pennsylvania home after her death in 2011; obtaining kosher wine for those events was a far different experience than in Manhattan. Pennsylvania's state liquor stores in my area scarcely seemed to notice the existence of dry kosher wine, and the private wine stores in nearby northern Delaware relegated kosher wine to an obscure section in the back where it battled organic and local wines for shelf space. Kedem's Baron Herzog reds were for sale and offered a welcome alternative to Manischewitz, but it is doubtful that the stores' non-Jewish patrons even noticed that kosher wine was available unless they stumbled across it looking for other unusual varieties defined by how they were made rather than where they were from.

My personal experience indicates how kosher wine's great contemporary success providing quality wine for the Jewish market took place alongside its marginalization in non-Jewish circles. Sales figures, to the extent available, show that dry kosher wine was far less able than Manischewitz and Mogen David to attract non-Jewish consumers. While Kedem does not make its annual sales public, journalistic accounts give a rough picture in 2010: around 1 million gallons of grape juice, 1.5 to 3 million gallons of traditional Concord grape wine, .5 million gallons of dry kosher wine from its Oxnard plant, and an unknown quantity imported from its many international affiliates. Taking the highest estimates and assuming that imports were equal to Kedem's entire domestic production of dry kosher wine gives annual sales of 5 million gallons—half of total kosher wine production in the early 1950s and far less than Manischewitz's peak output of 13 million gallons in the late 1970s. Indeed, industry estimates in 2010 of a $28 million national market for kosher wines are still less than half the value of Manischewitz's wine sales in 1979—even if the effect of inflation is ignored.[53]

Kosher wine's visibility faded even more dramatically than its consumption by non-Jews. A 1957 survey of five hundred people in New York City, Los Angeles, and Detroit, composed equally of Jews, white gentiles, and African Americans, showed an astonishing awareness of Manischewitz: 72 percent recalled seeing a Manischewitz advertisement on television, almost half had heard a radio spot, and one-third remembered a newspaper advertisement.[54] Such prominence allowed Manischewitz to be invoked in comedy routines, songs, and even by an astronaut standing on the moon. Indeed, its cultural presence remains strong enough for Lauryn Hill to feel confident listeners would understand the lyrics "Now I be breakin' bread sippin Manischewitz wine" in her 1998 apocalyptic ballad "Final Hour."

Kosher wine's evolution from sweet to dry is thus not a simple story of "success." Every Passover, newspaper recommendations for Passover wines contain a similar refrain—once we suffered with Manischewitz, but now we need not suffer anymore with the many good kosher wines available. The story of my family's switch from Manischewitz is regularly echoed in other writers' recollections and indeed constitutes a tried

FIGURE 6.5 Rabbi and Meyer Robinson at Monarch Wine. Collection of Gale Robinson.

and true narrative for how kosher wine is better than it used to be. Such an argument usually is discursively connected to the wider success of kosher food in the past twenty years as a type of product appealing not only to observant Jews but also to middle-class consumers who believe that kosher certification makes the food better—healthier, safer—than nonkosher varieties.

Such a narrative hides in plain sight the remarkable achievement of Manischewitz wine as the first crossover branded kosher product. It was so successful in American culture that 80 percent of its customers in the mid-1950s were not Jewish—even though it was an aggressively kosher product. With such dramatic accomplishments, why isn't Manischewitz considered a kosher success story? Why is it a negative reference point, its very rejection by Jews and other Americans a sign of progress?

Manischewitz's success, very simply, disrupts the narrative offered by contemporary promoters of kosher food who stress its attraction to consumers with disposable income willing to pay more for food that seems healthier—especially the white middle-class consumers who also buy organic foods for the same reason. These were not the people who made kosher wine so popular. Instead, Manischewitz's remarkable appeal was principally to African Americans, not middle-class whites. Seeing blacks as a market for kosher products is not part of this narrative—for that matter, neither is a wine favored by Sammy Davis Jr. as well as blue-collar African American men kicking back after a day of work.

That said, there is an additional complication to the "success" story of dry kosher wine—the enduring antipathy among non-Jewish white Americans. White gentile consumers were never particularly interested in kosher wine, even when they drank sweet Concord grape products that differed little from Manischewitz, instead preferring brands not associated with Jews. With the widespread growth of kosher varieties since 1985 that are easily as good as conventional dry wines, the kosher designation nonetheless continues to carry a stigma. Such deep-seated attitudes suggest that the integration of kosher food with American culture remains fraught, with a troubling incompatibility remaining between some Jewish ritual food practices and mainstream American culture. Kosher wine's challenges, however, would find an even deeper resonance in the difficult saga of kosher beef, detailed in the next two chapters.

7

HARRY KASSEL'S MEAT

SHORTLY AFTER my mother's marriage in 1951, she received proper indoc-
trination into the preferred method for kosher meat shopping from her
new mother-in-law. Florence took Louise to her butcher on the corner of
85th street and Columbus Avenue and then into the rear cooler that held
kosher meat. There Florence made sure kosher marks were attached to the
carcasses and selected one for cutting into a rib roast, meanwhile warning
my mother (as she recalled) never to buy the cuts placed by the butcher
in the display case.

When shopping on her own, my mother did not insist on first seeing
the carcass, but she did continue to buy meat at her mother-in-law's preferred butcher shop until we moved to 82nd Street and West End Avenue
shortly after I was born. As a young boy I remember walking with her to
another kosher butcher on Broadway closer to our apartment and not far
from a little Jewish delicatessen called Zabar's, which was at that time a
narrow, crowded shop and not the fancy food emporium it would become.
Chicken came from a butcher on 85th and Broadway who specialized in
poultry; in the 1950s birds were sold with feet attached, which my mother
would have to remove before cooking. Kosher meat was easy to find and
very, very local.

My family's experiences were fairly typical for Jews in early and mid-
century New York City. While kosher-certified processed foods remained
quite limited, kosher meat was generally available. But, curiously, at the
same time as processed kosher food became more prevalent, kosher meat

became harder to find. The neighborhood shops patronized by my mother gradually closed, and the new supermarkets did not carry kosher-certified meat. As our family was not observant after my parent's 1972 divorce, my mother simply switched to conventional meat. By the 1980s, kosher meat was much, much harder to find in America's most Jewish large city.

Kosher meat's dwindling presence offers a dramatic contrast to the expansion of processed kosher food options, as "in the eyes of many," kosher authority Rabbi Zushe Yoseph Blech perceptively notes, it is "the paradigm of Kosher food."[1] Early in the century, all major meat companies produced kosher meat, along with many small firms; remarkably, in the 1920s approximately 25 percent of the steers slaughtered in American were killed in accordance with kosher rules. A half-century later, no more than 6 percent of American beef underwent *shechita*, the intricate ritual process necessary to create kosher beef. Moreover, the handful of plants creating kosher beef were minor operations on the fringes of America's meat industry. Hebrew National's motto, "We answer to a higher authority," may have helped processed kosher food (and its hot dogs) attract non-Jewish consumers, but did little to arrest fresh kosher meat's precipitous decline.[2]

In search of an answer to this conundrum, I discovered a 1973 *New York Times* reference to a man named Harry Kassel, identified—in passing—as the president of a wholesale meat firm whose "sale of more than 400,000 pound of beef a day is largely for the kosher trade."[3] Intrigued at identifying the man who was once the largest kosher meat wholesaler in the city, I managed to locate him, still in excellent health at the age of eighty-nine. His experiences, along with those of my family, help to unlock the puzzle of what happened to kosher meat.

HARRY KASSEL AND NEW YORK CITY'S KOSHER MEAT

Born and raised in Wisconsin by a moderately observant Jewish family, Kassel's path to the New York meat industry began with a blind date. Recently discharged from the Army Air Corps after service during World War II, he finally succumbed to his aunt's repeated entreaties to meet her best friend's niece, Zeena Levine. On April 6, 1946, he brought the

FIGURE 7.1 Harry Kassel, 1970s. Courtesy of Harry Kassel.

beautiful University of Wisconsin freshman to a tavern on Wells and 12th street in Milwaukee. "We hit if off right away," she recalled almost sixty-five years later, even though she kidded him about being a "cheapskate" who took her to a "rundown bar" rather than out to dinner. She left college after finishing her sophomore year; they married soon thereafter. Harry joked that he had taken her out of school "so she would go to work; she wouldn't, so I had to go to work." In his self-deprecating manner, he explained he took "the easy way out" by getting work with her father, who operated several kosher and nonkosher butcher shops.[4]

Zeena's father Joe Levine, in association with his partner Sam Cohen, had entered the butcher business in the late 1920s. They operated two large kosher shops in Brooklyn that employed dozens of butchers and bore the name Cohen & Levine, plus several nonkosher stores under the appellation Sunlight Markets. Their large establishments were unusual; most of New York City's seventy-five hundred butcher shops were small operations with an owner and one or two employees.[5] And all New Yorkers, kosher or not, could walk short distances to obtain meat from stores scattered throughout the city's neighborhoods.

Cohen & Levine entered a bustling kosher meat industry. In the 1930s, ten kosher slaughterhouses operated in Manhattan, with most clustered between 38th and 42nd Street along the Hudson River on the West Side, with the rest situated across the city on the East River between 42nd and 48th Streets. Seven more killed kosher cattle directly across the Hudson River in New Jersey, and one operated in Brooklyn. These plants sold to 25 factories making processed meats such as frankfurters, 1,550 delicatessens serving a kosher clientele, and an estimated 6,500 kosher butcher shops located throughout the city's five boroughs. While larger operations such as Cohen & Levine bought supplies directly from the slaughterhouses (Joe Levine was a "terrific buyer," Kassel recalled), most butcher shops relied on 75 meat jobbers to obtain their supplies, while 110 provision wholesalers supplied delis and sausage factories.[6]

Beef and veal were, of course, the principal meats consumed by Jews. With pork forbidden by kosher law and poultry relatively expensive, Jews ate far more beef per capita than any other American ethnic or racial group. In 1909 a national study showed that Jews, regardless of income, ate close to one hundred pounds of beef and veal annually. With almost two million New York City Jews in 1930 (even if many were not observant), there was an ample market for kosher meat.[7]

The firms supplying this demand did so through the filter of Jewish law. Kosher rules governing beef slaughter were extensive and exacting, having roots in the Torah and Talmud and refined through intricate rulings by generations of Judaism's leading authorities. The *Shulchan Aruch*, the compendium of Jewish law compiled by Joseph Caro, consolidated these rules into a series of prohibitions against use of beef cattle that were damaged in any manner before slaughter, either by other animals, through illness, or due to accidents. Rabbis interpreted the biblical admonition that only a healthy animal could be slaughtered to mean it had to be conscious at the time of death; this ruled out preslaughter stunning, a standard practice in the modern meatpacking industry.[8]

Consequently, meat companies had to alter their procedures to accommodate kosher requirements. Stunning in a tight "knocking" pen was the first stage in conventional slaughtering operations; immediately afterward, cattle were shackled, hoisted into the air by a hind leg, and killed by a "sticker" who severed the neck veins and arteries. Since kosher-killed cattle could not be stunned, they were shackled fully conscious while confined in a pen, dropped to the ground, and then partially hoisted by a rear leg into the air with their forequarters remaining on the floor. Helpers then placed a muzzle over the snout, and drew back the head to expose the neck for the *shochet*, who used a long knife, known as a *chalef*, to cut through the major blood vessels, gullet, and windpipe in a smooth, continuous motion.

Precise requirements governed the *shochet's* killing stroke and blade; if not fulfilled, the slaughtered animal was not kosher. The knife had to be at least twice the width of the animal's neck, honed as sharp as a razor, and without nicks so that there was neither *ikkur* (tearing) of the flesh nor *derasah* (pressure) when the blade touched the skin. It was the *shochet's* duty to keep the *chalef* sharp and to test it for imperfections by drawing a finger nail across the edge before each use. His stroke had to be uninterrupted; halting even momentarily committed *shehiah* (pausing), another violation. And the cut had to be made in a narrow area of the throat, the upper boundary marked by "two berry-like structures" that constituted the protrusion of the thyroid cartilage and the lower limit set by the meeting place of the upper lobe of the lung and the trachea. Deviating outside of this area was *hagramah*, another proscribed error. Handled properly, the *chalef* severed the trachea, esophagus, jugular veins, and carotid arteries (but not the backbone), bringing on "a sudden and voluminous evacuation of the blood vessels, an acute anemia of the brain, unconsciousness, and then death." Not surprisingly, these regulations made kosher killing slower than conventional slaughter.[9]

Fifteen centuries of rabbinic rulings governed the crucial postmortem examination of the carcass by the kosher inspector, called a *bodek*. The *Shulchan Aruch* actually contained detailed rules proscribing animals with many kinds of defects; but modern inspection focused on the lungs, especially the presence of scars, punctures, or lesions. The *bodek* was especially interested in lung adhesions called *sirchas* that might conceal damage left by disease. Relying on his sense of touch, he felt the lungs while they remained in an animal's chest cavity; if he found *sirchas* significant enough to place its kosher status in question, he would pull the carcass off the production line for a visual examination. With the lungs removed from the body, the *bodek* would peel off the *sirchas*, place the lungs in a bucket of water, and inflate them with air. If air bubbles escaped, then the animal was unacceptable; but if the lungs still held air, then the animal was kosher. In either case, the *bodek* needed to be satisfied before the next production stages could commence, adding yet another set of delays peculiar to kosher meat production.

Given their importance, kosher law also defined the requirements for the positions of *shochet* and *bodek*. They had to be Sabbath-observant men who had trained for their positions under rabbinic supervision and passed a test that demonstrated, in practice, an understanding of their craft. They were religious functionaries as well as craftsmen practicing their trade; often they were ordained rabbis as well. Hence these men were not part of the regular packinghouse workforce and were treated in some cases as independent contractors and not employees.

The complex rules governing kosher meat production also kept the industry on the fringe of midtown Manhattan, even though the "slaughter-house odors" of plant operations "sometimes annoyed" residents of the toney neighborhoods along the East River and theatergoers on the West Side.[10] One of the most important requirements for kosher meat was elimination of *dam hanefesh*, the "lifeblood" from the flesh. The requirement could be traced to the Torah, in Leviticus 17:11 and 22:2 and Deuteronomy 15:23; its repetition led rabbis to view this as one of the most fundamental interdictions in kosher law. In furtherance of this biblical edict, Chullin 113a of the Talmud required meat to be "salted very well and rinsed very well" to fully drain all blood. Rabbis subsequently interpreted the Talmud's requirement in precise terms, requiring that these procedures (generally termed *kashering*) take place within seventy-two hours of slaughter. As a *minhag* originating in medieval Germany, the seventy-two-hour rule gained wide rabbinic acceptance, with the judgment that after that time the meat would be too hard and dry for the salting process to be effective. Kosher law did permit rabbis to extend the seventy-two-hour limit if they *begissed* (washed) the carcass, but this cumbersome procedure had little appeal for the early twentieth-century meatpacking firms as meat so treated brought less in the kosher marketplace.[11] Since beef carcasses sent from the Midwest took more than three days to reach New York and other East Coast cities, firms wishing to supply the lucrative kosher trade maintained operations close to Jewish consumers.

The kosher market was so strong that New York's beef slaughter-houses simply encoded Jewish religious requirements into routine plant operations. Plenty of nonkosher Western-killed cattle also entered the city as well; but "city-dressed" kosher meat commanded a premium of $2 per cattle forequarters, an incentive for meat companies to keep their kosher operations running. While the bulk of the nation's meat came from Mid-western plants, satisfying the kosher trade made the New York area the USA's fifth largest beef producer in 1920.[12]

Not all of the kosher-killed carcasses, however, could enter the kosher trade. Kosher law's preoccupation with blood meant Jews from eastern Europe removed the major blood vessels, along with the *helev*, "forbidden fats" that were delineated in the Torah for use in temple sacrifices and the *gid hannasheh* (sciatic nerve) that Joseph injured in his struggle with God (Genesis 32:33). Collectively termed *nikur* (to pull or cut out), these tasks were left to the retail butchers, but still affected the packer's use of the car-casses. While trimming the blood vessels in the forequarters was relatively straightforward, the veins and sciatic nerve in the hindquarters were much harder to remove without "such mutilation of these parts as practically to destroy their identity."[13] Hence the men who performed *nikur* on kosher-killed cattle in New York City (and throughout the U.S.) restricted their work to the forequarters, leaving the hindquarters to the nonkosher trade.

New York's observant Jews thus had plenty of ribs, chucks, and bris-kets to eat, but could not consume tenderloins, T-bones, or porterhouse steaks—generally considered the best beef cuts. The influence on Amer-ican Jewish foodways was enormous. Limiting acceptable beef to the forequarters meant, as home economist Florence Kreisler Greenbaum explained in 1918, that "the cuts of meat which are kosher are those which require long, slow cooking." Doing so properly, she reassured Jew-ish housewives, could still make them "as acceptable as the more expen-sive cuts of meat." Thirty years later, Leah Leonard similarly advised homemakers on how to give "special consideration" to cooking the "less tender parts" available to observant Jews. To guide meat purchases, Leo-nard offered a quick summary of the proper use of cuts typically sold by kosher butchers: necks and plates could be turned into soup, flank cuts and chuck were best for stews, shoulders and rib cuts for roasts, and briskets for pot roasts. For housewives wishing to quickly broil beef for dinner, *The Complete American Jewish Cookbook* included methods for "tenderizing meats and for preparing delicious steaks from kosher cuts." While sauces, spices, and ingredients could create enormous variety, the limitations on kosher meat defined the parameters of twentieth-century kosher cuisine.[14]

Greenbaum was right—kosher meat dishes could be as good as (if not even better than) those prepared from the "more expensive cuts." My mother remembered that, as a young housewife, she and my father planned their Sundays around the evening dinner of a standing rib roast at her mother's house. Just the thought, she recalled, made their mouths' water. In my own childhood memories, my mother's pot roasts stand out, as the delicious meat would seem to fall apart with just a touch from a fork. To reduce cooking times of two to three hours to just one, she used a pressure cooker, perhaps using recipes similar to those in Leonard's book showing how this device could cut cooking times in half.[15]

To generate good beef from relatively inferior cuts, it was necessary, as a leading meat industry authority noted in 1929, "to use high grade steers for kosher meat."[16] Conveniently, this meant that, while the kosher forequarters entered the Jewish market, the hindquarters and delectable loin cuts went to the white tablecloth restaurant trade to satisfy the voracious appetites of the city's upper and middle class. Similarly, the forequarters of cattle that did not meet kosher requirements could be sold to nonkosher butchers and turned into corned beef, stews, and roasts for New York's blue-collar Catholics, who also liked their beef. Doubtless these diners did not know that their meals came from cattle slaughtered in accordance with Jewish religious requirements.

Handling both kosher and nonkosher meat made perfect sense for the meatpacking companies, but created a paradox for kosher consumers: how could they be sure that the two types of meat remained segregated from one another? Kosher meat could never be isolated from nonkosher meat in the manner, for example, that an entire production run of a processed food could be made kosher. In a way, the very notion of a kosher meat business was a misnomer; kosher meat is better understood as just one of the meat industry's many products, since portions of the same animal had to be sent into different, if parallel, commercial streams. And tracking those streams of meat became harder and harder the further meat traveled along the distribution chain away from the slaughterhouse—and any connection with the animal from whence it came.

Since a relatively small number of well-regarded rabbis supervised the city's packinghouses, observant Jews could feel reasonably confident that *shechita* was performed properly. When the meat left the plants, however, controls were far less reliable. Rabbinic regulation relied on affixing marks on kosher meat that would tell butcher shops and provisions manufacturers whether the meat they purchased was indeed kosher. But there was little direct supervision of the retail butchers; that was left to local rabbis. And with only several hundred rabbis in a city with thousands of kosher butcher shops, the mathematics precluded comprehensive supervision of meat retailing.

Fraud was the predictable outcome of the inherent incentive to seek the higher prices garnered for kosher meat products. In one symptomatic case, the Union of Orthodox Rabbis protested to city authorities in 1928 when they learned that the Jerusalem Sausage Factory had obtained nonkosher meat from the Wilson & Company packing plant and mixed it with kosher meat to create so-called kosher sausage. For many years such cases were not unusual, as Harold Gastwirt detailed in his monumental book, *Fraud, Corruption, and Holiness*. These repetitive instances of fraudulent kosher meat sales stirred Jewish concerns about the true nature of the food that was such an important marker of their identity.[17]

Some fraud could be ascertained by tracing the meat orders supplied by the large companies. In the case of the Jerusalem Sausage Factory, Wilson readily cooperated with the rabbis' investigation, doubtless concerned that its reputation might suffer among kosher consumers. But small fly-by-night meat operations too often were willing to try more underhanded methods to garner higher profits for kosher products without having to pay more for the meat itself. A 1933 prosecution of the Jacob Branfman & Son meat operation indicates how difficult it was for rabbinic authorities, without additional aid, to prevent intermixing of kosher and nonkosher meat once it left the packinghouses.

The case came to light because Board of Health inspectors—who were not responsible for ensuring kosher standards—suspected the company was putting unwholesome meat in its allegedly kosher products.

On March 22, department inspectors, rabbis, and U.S. Department of Agriculture operatives staked out a marginal cutting and trimming factory located in a basement on East 21st Street (described to the court as having floors and walls "encrusted with fat and dirt") and watched as a Branfman truck loaded thirteen barrels of meat. To aid in the deception, the truck's driver concealed the firm's name (and its unintentionally ironic slogan, "The Name Deserves the Fame") with an oilcloth flap bearing the text "S&E Motor Hire Corporation." The "raiding party" of rabbis and inspectors followed the truck to the Branfman's Delancey Street factory and charged into the loading dock, confronting company officials who were unloading the illicit cargo. Upon opening the barrels, they discovered briskets without kosher marks and government stamps identifying the meat's source; the latter had been trimmed off.[18]

Rabbinic leaders struggled without success to create communal structures that could put an end to such fraud. In the 1930s, efforts to create a Kashruth Association overseeing meat certification collapsed due to internal divisions between the rabbis and court rulings that denied a rabbinic body the power to regulate commercial—and civil—affairs.[19] To a wider Jewish public, the rabbis also seemed to be doing more than just protecting kosher meat supplies. The Kashruth Association sought to ban sales of meat produced outside the greater New York region— even if certified kosher by other rabbis—leading to suspicions they were protecting personal income garnered by certifying New York slaughterhouses. Abraham Goldstein denounced their effort as "a criminal offense" as it was a restraint of trade and also "against the Jewish law."[20] He need not have worried; the rabbis did not, on their own, have the power to control the flow of kosher meat. But this left the kosher meat supply chain woefully exposed to purveyors willing to introduce illicit substitutes.

This history helps make sense of my grandmother's insistence in the early 1950s on seeing the kosher symbols on the meat she purchased. By then Florence had maintained a strictly kosher household for thirty years and had lived through all the battles and uncertainties concerning the *kashrus* of the meat she provided for her family. No wonder she wanted proof that the meat had been killed in conformance with kosher law. My mother, though, did not have those same concerns; for she had come of age in an environment where kosher regulation had dramatically improved, imparting a new confidence to observant consumers that the meat they ate was indeed kosher.

A NEW DEAL FOR KOSHER MEAT

When my mother's father, Charlie Schwartz, began to prosper from his law practice, he displayed his success by moving to a large apartment on the Upper West Side, and soon thereafter buying a waterfront property in Lake Placid, New York. His wife and three children spent summers there, away from the city's heat, at times joined by friends and business associates.

The Lake Placid house, though long gone, holds a special place in our family's history, as that is where my parents met. My father David met my mother's older brother Stuart at Columbia University, and the two became close friends. Stu invited him to visit Lake Placid when my mother was fifteen; she was smitten, and he must have been too. They married four years later. My grandparents owned the house until Charlie's death in 1969. I visited several times as a young boy and remember, through a child's perception, what seemed a huge rambling house with a wraparound porch and, best of all, a boathouse with two wood motorboats. The particular odor of maritime engines and damp wood can still take me back to those memories.

Getting kosher meat to Lake Placid, though, was a problem. There were no kosher butcher shops and, even if there had been, the house was only accessible by boat. So my mother recalled that when she was a teenager her mother Bertie would begin every summer by ordering large quantities of meat from an Albany slaughterhouse. Once delivered to the house, she and her kitchen staff cut it into large pieces that could undergo the kashering process required under kosher law. Placing the meat in large galvanized tubs, they soaked it for at least thirty minutes, drained the water, and then thoroughly saturated it with coarse granulated salt before moving the meat to large wooden boards placed on an incline to allow blood to drain. Afterward it was rinsed, cut into meal-sized pieces, and frozen for use over the summer.

FIGURE 7.2 Charles and Bertie Schwartz, late 1940s, in front of their house in Lake Placid New York. Personal collection of Roger Horowitz.

The availability of meat from an Albany slaughterhouse, and my grandmother's confidence that it was indeed kosher, reflected dramatically improved regulation in postwar New York State. While older observant Jews like Florence remained wary, a new stability took hold in kosher meat distribution. Reflecting in its own way a New Deal system of industrial organization that typified many industries following World War II, an interlocking set of institutions brought order into what had been chaos.

State regulation was the centerpiece of kosher meat's New Deal. New York State first inserted rules into its penal code governing kosher meat's distribution and sale in 1915. The regulations truly became effective in 1924 after surviving a strong legal challenge.[21] The state did not, however, actually employ regulators to enforce the law for another decade.

Until then, it took private complaints to trigger legal action, such as those pressed by Abraham Goldstein against butcher Hyman Schnapp.[22] Moreover, as kosher law violations were a criminal offense, the legal process required appointment of a grand jury to hear the charges, usually occasioning a delay of several months. Then, all too often, the end result was dismissal for, as one New York State official noted, "a Grand Jury is frequently reluctant to indict local persons."[23]

Creating an effective enforcement mechanism had to wait for the New Deal. Sparked no doubt in part by the agitation about kosher food's reliability, in 1934 New York State established the Kosher Law Enforcement Division of the Department of Agriculture and Markets, headed by Orthodox rabbi Shepherd Z. Baum. By 1940 Rabbi Baum supervised what was, in effect, a kosher "police agency" of twelve inspectors (ten stationed in New York City) that had the power to investigate and inspect food establishments claiming to serve, sell, or manufacture kosher food. A Kosher Advisory Board under the chairmanship of Orthodox rabbi Leo Jung provided a means for the rabbinate to influence the interpretation and application of kosher law by state inspectors. Two years later the legal regulations were expanded and incorporated as civil statutes into the Agriculture and Markets Law, allowing local magistrates to issue fines and jail sentences without having to empanel a grand jury. While eighteen states and the District of Columbia adopted statutes regulating kosher food before 1960, only New York had an enforcement agency.[24]

The state agency—and stronger state legislation—put backbone behind the previously less effective regulation by New York City's Department of Public Markets. With a staff of six in the mid-1920s, the city's enforcement unit conducted between four and five thousand inspections annually, an average of slightly less than one visit a year to kosher food purveyors. Convictions dwindled from slightly over one hundred in 1926 to just thirteen in 1934, and fines were usually in the range of $25 to $50. Kosher consumers, transfixed by the controversies over the authenticity of kosher food, might have been surprised at the department's sanguine conclusion in 1927 "that violations are becoming fewer." But, with the establishment of the state agency, New York City's inspectors now had support from the top in their efforts to regulate kosher food.[25]

Kosher consumers benefited enormously from these new institutional arrangements. To track the flow of kosher meat from packinghouse to retail stores, the state stipulated placement of *plumbas*—distinctive metal tags—on the carcass immediately after the *bodek* ruled it was kosher. To hinder fraud similar to the Branfman case, state law required that the *plumbas* remain attached to the meat until cut into consumer-sized pieces—creating a veritable forest of tags on kosher-killed forequarters. Kosher livers, tongues, and even offal such as hearts, brains, and intestines had to be marked as well so their kosher provenance was easily discernible. State inspectors tracked the movement of these kosher-identified products through the meat distribution chain; indeed, as the division summarized in its 1953 annual report, "everywhere that kosher meat or food is processed, distributed, sold or served."[26]

Occasional court cases offer glimpses of the regulatory system's operation. On December 27, 1949 (a year in which the state enforcement personnel conducted 16,650 inspections, and city agents an additional 14,000),[27] a city inspector on his normal rounds discovered two strips of nonkosher meat weighing 214 pounds in a kosher restaurant's cold storage locker. He informed the owner that this violated state law, prompting a series of frantic phone calls (in the inspector's presence) first to the wholesale distributors who had brought in the meat as part of a one-ton shipment and then to the slaughterhouse that had provided it. Doubtless deeply concerned for his reputation, the distributor's owner came to the restaurant to explain to the inspector that the entire shipment should have been kosher, as his company only dealt in kosher meat. As the slaughterhouse, of course, sold both kosher and nonkosher meat, the fault originated there; indeed the meatpacking company later confirmed that it had inadvertently included the nonkosher pieces in the shipment. Upon hearing this evidence, the Manhattan magistrate's court ruled that the violation was an honest mistake, and the restaurant did not have to pay a fine.[28]

Such careful monitoring of kosher meat's movement from slaughterhouse to consumer was typical. "We had irregular visits on a regular basis" recalled Kassel, who opened his own meat distribution company in the 1950s; "you never knew when the State Inspector would be there." In 1961 a meat wholesaler received a $500 fine for selling "meats which did not contain the necessary Kosher marks of identification" to a provision house that sold only kosher products. In another instance, state inspectors staked out a sausage manufacturing plant suspected of putting nonkosher products in "kosher" sausage. Armed with revolvers, the inspector stationed on the roof signaled his companion near the rear door when the nonkosher meat was moved into the plant so he could make the arrest. In these varied venues, inspectors put teeth into the state regulations and halted fraudulent activity. But their simple presence, and surety of a surprise inspection, doubtless discouraged many more purveyors from contemplating similar dishonest behavior.[29]

Corruption and fraud were not eliminated, of course. The temptation to sell meat that was not kosher at kosher prices remained an enduring temptation. In 1960 a Rabbi Felshin was convicted of trying to bribe a state inspector who had found nonkosher meat in an establishment he was supposed to be supervising. And the power of inspectors to hinder a firm's operation certainly tempted them to take advantage of their position. "I suspect that at the very least plenty of the inspectors took home meat on Fridays," Kassel reflected, "but I can't prove it; but for sure they never got it from us." Since the documented incidence of such cases is small, especially compared to the large number of inspections, indications are that the system worked quite well overall. Kassel credited Kosher Law Enforcement Division chief supervisor Shepherd Z. Baum for much of this success. "I had the greatest respect for him, because there was no fooling around with him," Kassel remembered. "He was truly legitimate, really, and it was a political job, or it could have become very political."[30]

This powerful state agency was not the only institution regulating kosher food. Rather, the Kosher Law Enforcement Division was the keystone of a trustworthy structure of kosher meat distribution that curtailed the anarchy and eased the worries that had plagued New York's observant Jews since the late nineteenth century.

Harry Kassel's father-in-law was one of the butchers who helped to create a more stable order for kosher meat. Beginning in the mid-1930s, Joe Levine served for several decades as vice president of the New Deal Kosher Butchers Association, one of nine employer groups in New York's kosher meat trade. His organization represented butcher shop owners throughout the New York City area who operated more than one shop. Other associations were constituted geographically, representing owners of individual stores in the Bronx, Brooklyn, Manhattan, and Long Island, while the Fresh Meat Retail Dealers Association took in kosher butcher shops elsewhere in New York State. Together these associations comprised the Federation of Kosher Butchers.[31]

While competitors in the market place, these butchers shared a desire for consistent application of kosher standards to inhibit fraud by unscrupulous merchants. Consequently, they generally favored measures that would eliminate opportunities to sell as kosher meat which actually was not. In the early 1930s, for example, the Federation of Kosher Butchers agreed to cooperate with a central rabbinic board that would provide kosher supervision and *heckshers* for stores, rather than rely on individual rabbis, as it could create a uniform and enforceable set of kosher requirements.[32] When that failed, the kosher butchers used the 1933 National Industrial Recovery Act's authority to draft a code of conduct that they hoped would standardize practices. It was similarly ineffective, as, in the absence of enforcement mechanisms, relatively few stores observed its provisions. It disappeared along with the rest of the NIRA in 1935 when the U.S. Supreme Court declared the legislation unconstitutional.[33]

With the code's disappearance, Joe Levine and the kosher store owners found that the best opportunity to stabilize the kosher meat industry ironically lay in an organization they had initially opposed—the Amalgamated Meat Cutters and Butcher Workmen, a union affiliated with the American Federation of Labor. This was quite a change for Levine. He began his store, Kassel relates, in an effort to evade unionists who were seeking to recruit him. Then, as a store owner, one of his first encounters with a "union" came from the efforts of mobster Tootsie Herbert to assert control over the poultry trade.

Herbert, nominally business agent of the *shochetim's* union affiliated with the Amalgamated Meat Cutters, actually was a mobster seeking to limit the wholesalers supplying kosher butchers to those associated with his gang. Relating a story no doubt told many times, Kassel explained that one day Herbert came into the store and confronted Sam Cohen, insisting that he only buy his poultry from a particular supplier. "Sam Cohen is six-two, husky" recalled Kassel, "and he was not about to listen to Tootsie Herbert tell him where to buy his chickens." But when he rejected Herbert's directive, "Tootsie Herbert . . . pulled out a pistol and put it on the butcher block and he says, 'Look, I can't tell you what to do, but that's what you do starting Monday.'" Knowing full well that Herbert would follow through on his threat, Cohen and Levine convened a meeting of all twenty butcher shops on 13th street in Brooklyn that decided to resist his demands. To do so, "Sam Cohen with an armed guard went to Lakewood, New Jersey with a truck, bought chickens down at Lakewood because it was out of the reach of Tootsie Herbert and the mafia."[34]

In this story told to Kassel by his father-in-law, it took just a few months for Herbert to abandon his effort to control poultry distribution in the Brooklyn area where the Cohen & Levine stores operated. If indeed rebuffed so quickly from this neighborhood, it took a more sustained effort to break Herbert's control of the *shochetim* union. Under constant pressure from New York courts and government agencies (especially District Attorney Thomas E. Dewey's office), the Amalgamated Meat Cutters finally forced Herbert out of his position in 1937.[35]

While Herbert's eclipse may have placated Sam Cohen and Joe Levine, this encounter doubtless reinforced their strong antiunion inclinations. So when they finally accepted collective bargaining, it was not voluntary. Instead, it reflected a grudging coming to terms with unionism that was too strong to resist. In a mid-1930s organizing drive filled with violence from both employers and unions, Amalgamated leaders Max and Louis Block secured agreements with employer associations throughout the New York area. Their efforts included a shadowy rapprochement with elements of the mafia, one that kept the mobsters neutralized as an antiunion force, but also provided ways for gangsters to infiltrate some of the Amalgamated locals over the next three decades. Max, a former boxer, relied on strikes by unionized meat truck drivers to force employers to bargain with butcher locals, as without meat supplies a store could not operate. Their support made it possible for the Amalgamated's Hebrew Butcher Workers Local No. 234, headed by Joseph Belsky, to secure collective bargaining agreements with the main employer associations, including Levine's, even though it could only claim a minority of the kosher butchers as members.[36]

By the end of World War II, the stability facilitated by union and employer agreements persuaded the once antiunion Levine, perhaps grudgingly, to accept the kosher butcher union. Levine even invited Belsky and other Amalgamated union leaders to his daughter's wedding to Harry Kassel. Representing Local 234, Joseph Belsky sought to cooperate with employers and use collective bargaining agreements to ensure that new butcher shops had to pay their employees the same wages as established operations, protecting establishments such as those operated by Cohen and Levine from low-wage competitors. Moreover, there were no hard lines between store owner and union butchers. Max Block actually owned a butcher shop throughout much of his tenure as a union official. Conversely, the president of Levine's New Deal Kosher Butchers Association, Emil Horn, had once been president of Local 234. Such crossing of the putative line between employer and employee was typical; in 1952 hundreds of butcher shop owners remained card-carrying members of Local 234. Little surprise, then, that the kosher butcher shop owners and the union that represented their employees were able to come to an understanding.[37]

Even the once mob-controlled *shochetim* union achieved a new legitimacy after the war. George Lederman, described by the *New York Times* in 1936 as "a rabbi representing the New York Live Poultry Dealers' Association" (the principal employer association) was the Amalgamated's choice to replace Herbert as the union's business agent. While Lederman was not in fact an ordained rabbi, he was the son of Rabbi Zudick Lederman and had undergone some rabbinic training. With his contacts among employers and rabbis, as well as connections with the city's political machine, he was an attractive person for the Amalgamated to recruit for the job even though he does not seem to have ever worked as a *shochet*.[38]

A testimonial dinner in Lederman's honor held immediately following World War II attests to the union's newfound clean image. Praise from prominent public officials filled the "10th anniversary jubilee" publication issued to commemorate the celebration. U.S. Secretary of Commerce Henry Wallace's accolade for Lederman's "devotion to the public ideal" was followed by similarly effusive praise from U.S. Senator Joseph A. Mead, Congressman Arthur G. Klein, and New York Mayor William O'Dwyer. Particularly notable in light of the union's previous notoriety were endorsements from leading jurists. New York State Supreme Court judge Henry Clay Greenberg promised to attend the dinner and praised Lederman's "rare leadership and a capacity for compromising differences." Moreover, 186 rabbis placed individual greetings in the program, an indication, along with an executive board that was entirely composed of rabbis, that Lederman had strong support from New York's rabbinic community. As one who, the program explained, "knew that it is much better to have peace in the industry than warfare," Lederman was well-positioned to incorporate the poultry *shochetim*—as well as the kosher cattle butchers, for whom he also served as business agent—into the sturdy unionism of New York's kosher meat trades.[39]

Unionization and collective bargaining, in conjunction with the Kosher Law Enforcement Division's activities, helped stabilize application of kosher standards. Unionized butchers, protected from arbitrary dismissals, were well-positioned to notice if meat passing through their shop did not have the required tags and could call on state regulators to act in the event their employer sought to cheat consumers in this manner. For the poultry *shochetim* in Amalgamated Local 370 and the kosher cattle slaughterers in Local 491, inclusion of kosher slaughtering rules under collective bargaining agreements gave these workers protection to take the time and care necessary for proper *shechita*. Even the *mashgihim* had a union. Kashrus Supervisors Local 621 drew 75 percent of its membership from rabbis, some who also headed Orthodox congregations.

Local 621, aptly termed a "Torah union" by one member, sought simultaneously to elevate the working conditions of its members and expand enforcement of kosher law. Chartered in 1939 and headed by Rabbi Chaim Hurwitz, one of the Local 621's early successes was relieving *mashgihim* stationed in delicatessens and restaurants from the actual tasks of food preparation. Rabbi Benzion Cohen, who described himself as "one of the old timers in the Union," recalled that before the *mashgihim* organized they "received $3.00 a day for peeling tomatoes and potatoes, wash the dishes and other menial chores." But now, he explained to a large gathering of union members and supporters in 1958, "one is no longer ashamed to be known as a Mashgiach." And, underscoring the link between the unionized rabbis and the Amalgamated Meat Cutters locals, he emphasized that "we must be appreciative for all of this to the Block Brothers."[40]

The union *mashgihim*'s enforcement of kosher standards depended on support from the Amalgamated and other New York–area labor organizations. They insisted, for example, that events sponsored by Jewish organizations observe kosher law and employ union *mashgihim*; the union would then picket functions that did not conform to these requirements. As it took the position its collective bargaining rights were at stake, Local 621 could secure agreement from the teamsters union (which delivered nonmeat food) and the waiters union to not cross its picket line, often forcing compliance. It also used contracts to advance other areas of Jewish law. In its 1959 negotiations with meat wholesalers, the union secured a clause banning work involving kosher meat on the Sabbath and Jewish holidays. Such a victory, Benzion Cohen proclaimed in a letter to the *Morning Journal*, "is a glory for the Torah and the Commandments."[41]

As the state Kosher Law Enforcement Division, unions, and employer associations brought order and predictability into kosher meat distribution throughout the New York area, rabbis remained in charge of *shechita* itself. Rabbi Pinchas Teitz, for example, exercised close control over kosher slaughtering in Elizabeth, New Jersey's three plants from the mid-1930s until the 1980s. He trained and appointed *shochetim* and *bodekim* from local synagogues who were union members, and frequently visited the slaughterhouses himself. Rabbi Teitz's supervision extended not only to practices in the factory but also to the degree of religious observance. "He would watch them *daven* [pray]," Rabbi Seth Mandel recalled, "does this guy come in late to davening, is he busy looking at a book during davening?" Through ongoing observation of their religious behavior, Rabbi Teitz knew "whether he could rely on them" to enforce kosher principles. While the men had to be Amalgamated members, union business agent George Lederman ultimately deferred to Rabbi Teitz to appoint the *shochetim* and *bodekim* in the Elizabeth plants.[42]

BEGISSING

The regulatory web of rabbis, state inspectors, unions, and butcher shop associations was sufficiently flexible to survive the shift in kosher meat production away from the greater New York area. Shortly after the war's end, creating space for the United Nation's East Side headquarters forced closure of several large kosher slaughtering establishments. Over the next twenty years, the remaining plants on Manhattan's West Side and in Brooklyn gradually closed along with the Jersey City stockyards and several large New Jersey slaughterhouses. With this change, more meat began coming to New York, and other East Coast cities with a strong Jewish market, from hundreds of miles away. Seeing the opportunity, the Big Four meatpacking companies (Armour, Cudady, Swift, and Wilson) expanded kosher operations in their Midwestern plants to replace product once generated by East Coast facilities. Cudahy, for example, centralized kosher meat production in Omaha, Nebraska, where Rabbi Arthur Gendler oversaw company operations substantial enough to supply kosher wholesalers as well as local butcher shops.[43]

The relocation of kosher meat production offered opportunities for Harry Kassel and his nascent wholesale business. After several years under his father-in-law's tutelage, Kassel founded Zeger Meats in the early 1950s (named for his partner, Mel Zeger) specializing in the distribution of prime meat to the hotel, restaurant, and institutional market. Although the firm did not initially service kosher retailers, Kassel found "the hindquarters we bought were from slaughterhouses that actually produced kosher meat." Since this meant that the same slaughterhouses were just "selling the forequarters to a different distributor," Kassel deduced that "it was a natural fit that we get into the business, and instead of just buying half of the animal, we could buy the whole animal, which made us a more desirable customer and of course gave us buying power." He had discovered that the dispersion of meat production created a new niche for wholesalers who could distribute both kosher and nonkosher meat. In 1959 Kassel took over a New Jersey slaughterhouse supervised by Rabbi Teitz to supplement supplies of Midwestern meat and then merged with the kosher Flushing Meats wholesaler in 1965 to create Flushing-Zeger Meats. The company grew by leaps and bounds; by the late 1960s, it handled five thousand kosher forequarters weekly, approximately half of New York City's kosher meat supply.[44]

Kassel's success rested on his ability to manage the flow of fresh-killed meat into both kosher and nonkosher channels. He could purchase all or a portion of a slaughterhouse's output, process it in his Brooklyn warehouse, and then distribute it to kosher and nonkosher customers. With this capacity, he was then able to broker the establishment or expansion

FIGURE 7.3 Flushing-Zeger Meat, with kosher forequarters on one side and non-kosher hindquarters on the other. Courtesy of Harry Kassel.

of kosher beef production at new plants. Doing this in Midwestern facilities, though, ran up against the traditional seventy-two-hour rule, which had, in the past, limited kosher meat production to locations near where it was consumed. For more distant sources of supply to be acceptable, rabbis had to permit a dramatic expansion of the practice known as *begissing*—literally the *washing* of meat.

While not widely used, *begissing* had an impeccable lineage in kosher law. The sixteenth-century *Shulchan Aruch* permitted this valuable leniency to the seventy-two-hour rule. By thoroughly washing the meat such that it remained moist enough for salt to extract the blood, the time between slaughter and kashering could be doubled—and even tripled if the meat was washed twice. The first indications of *begissing* New York's kosher meat appear in the late 1930s, but it was an occasional practice resorted to by local firms to extend the usable life of kosher-slaughtered beef when demand lagged behind supply.[45] By the 1950s *begissing* was widespread and used for a different purpose, to extend the geographic basin in which kosher meat could be produced. "In shipping across the country," the Cudahy meatpacking firm explained in 1954, "Cudahy regularly stops its refrigerated cars of kosher meat en route for such spraying."[46]

Indeed, it is likely that most kosher meat eaten in New York for a generation after World War II had been *begissed* during shipment at least once. *Begissed* meat was so prevalent in the 1950s that the Kosher Advisory Board of New York State's Kosher Law Enforcement Division began looking closely for ways to "improve the enforcement of laws and rules relating to the washing of kosher meats en route from distant points." Under its direction, Kosher Law Enforcement inspectors closely supervised *begissing* in the Buffalo and Syracuse railroad yards where beef carcasses came to the East Coast from Midwestern plants. Despite resistance from meatpacking firms, in 1958 New York State added specific rules governing *begissing* to its kosher regulations. These new requirements specified that *plumbas* on *begissed* meat had to include the date and time the meat was washed. No doubt influenced by the New York laws, Minnesota adopted a similar requirement for its meatpacking firms.[47]

While New York State inspectors monitored *begissing* upstate, Mashgihim Local 621 enforced kosher requirements for this practice in the greater New York City area. Reuben Levovitz, "the rabbi of the union" and vice president of the OU-affiliated Rabbinical Council of America, checked incoming cars in the New Jersey rail yards for proper kosher documentation. Once in the city, union *mashgihim* took on the responsibility of ensuring proper washing of meat waiting for processing. The union contract provided for *mashgihim* to wash five cars weekly as part of their regular wages, with charges of five dollars per car for amounts in excess of their standard stint. In the mid-1950s Rabbi Benzion Cohen, for example, washed eleven to twelve railcars weekly for local wholesale distributor Eastern Meats and an equivalent amount for the Sioux City Packing Company. In all likelihood thousands of rail cars were inspected and, if necessary, *begissed* by union *mashgihim*.[48]

Managing *begissing* was an integral part of Kassel's business. As his kosher operations in the 1960s relied on trucks rather than railroads to convey meat to his Brooklyn processing center, washing took place at "regular stations where the drivers would pull up to get a rabbi." As unpredictable road conditions meant that the trucks often arrived "at strange hours," Kassel had to place "rabbis on our payroll that they could count on." Using a portable unit with a "long nozzle" like "fire extinguishers," the rabbi would "spray the forequarters en route, and that made them kosher for another seventy-two hours." Severe delays could throw these arrangements into disarray. "If a truck broke down," Kassel recalled, he would have to find a rabbi and if necessary "fly him to the truckload of meat" before seventy-two hours elapsed.[49]

Sometimes efforts to save kosher meat seemed almost comic. One January morning at 5 AM, Sacramento, California rabbi George Wald was awakened by a frantic call from the California State Police. A truckload of kosher meat originating in Dubuque, Iowa, and destined for San Francisco had been delayed by a blizzard and could not reach its destination within the allotted seventy-two hours. The driver had desperately called the police to see if they could find a rabbi to *begiss* the meat. "Amid glaring lights and shrieking sirens," patrol cars escorted Rabbi Wald "at breakneck speed" to the police barracks where the truck was parked. With hoses already prepared for his use, Rabbi Wald *begissed* the meat in the trailer "with only minutes to spare."[50]

Rabbi Wald's heroic act took place in 1978; by then truckers driving "reefers" (refrigerated trucks) were familiar with this peculiar way to "bless the meat" and keep it kosher. But the lapses also indicate the fragility of kosher meat distribution, how easily it could be disrupted, and the ad hoc arrangements necessary to supply observant Jews with this necessary food. By the late 1970s, kosher meat was in crisis, as the arrangements that had served it so well at mid-century disintegrated under the pressure of dramatic changes in supply, distribution, and consumer demand.

THE NEW *GLATT*

My mother disliked shopping for meat beneath the disapproving gaze of her mother-in-law, and she chafed under the strong opinions of her mother while continuing to summer in Lake Placid in the late 1950s with her own children. She was a free spirit, an artist, and a serious student of philosophy, having completed all her Columbia University coursework for a doctorate. Tired of having to do what her mother and mother-in-law expected, she and my father began spending summers on Shelter Island, New York, a tiny, quiet town accessible only by ferry from eastern Long Island. Construction of the Long Island Expressway made the trips much easier, encouraging my parents to buy a tiny cottage there. I spent most of my childhood summers in this small waterfront house, and it remains a treasured place for our family to use.

FIGURE 7.4 Louise Horowitz, 1961, in front of her house on Shelter Island, New York. Personal collection of Roger Horowitz.

While my parents kept kosher in their city apartment, kosher food simply was not available on "the island." So, for the first time, my mother discovered the wonders of modern food shopping at Shelter Island's Bohack supermarket. Many years later she would recount her astonishment at the low prices for chicken and beef compared to New York's kosher butchers. For another few years or so my mother limited her meat purchases in the city to kosher products; but she had tasted the tempting apple of self-service meat. When her neighborhood kosher butcher shops began to close and the divorce with my father removed Florence's influence from the household, my mother made the transition to nonkosher supermarket beef and chicken without regret.

Tens of thousands of Jewish families followed a similar gradual path away from kosher meat. The gap between the price of kosher and nonkosher meat was a constant irritant to those who wanted to remain kosher; and as some, like my mother, experimented with supermarket meat, kosher butchers found it increasingly difficult to stay in business. As kosher shops closed, obtaining kosher meat became correspondingly more difficult. It was a short step for women to make supermarkets their regular source for meat and to reserve kosher beef purchases for special occasions like Jewish holidays.

Despite these competitive pressures, kosher meat consumption remained strong into the 1970s. As Jews moved to suburban areas following the war, stores that catered to them followed, especially butchers. Shopping plazas, such as West Hempstead's New Super Shopping Center, in "one of Long Island's Fastest Expanding Sections," aggressively recruited kosher butchers as tenants—and with success. Throughout Nassau County, where many city Jews decamped in the 1950s, the number of kosher butcher shops rose from thirteen in 1945 to seventy fifteen years later. For observant Jews moving out of the city and into suburbia, it was still quite easy to find meat, and for kosher butchers to find enough customers to stay in business.[51]

Kosher meat consumption, it seems, was the most intractable of the Jewish dietary customs in an era where observance was in decline. A 1957 study of an anonymous Jewish community, identified only as "Riverton," found that 31 percent still relied on kosher meat, but only 8 percent followed the kosher practice of maintaining separate dishes for milk and meat foods. Surveys by The Pulse, a New York market research firm, found a similar gap among New Yorkers, though overall observance was higher. In its 1957 study, 80 percent of New York Jews indicated they only purchased kosher meat, while 64 percent claimed to follow the dietary laws. Much as my mother dutifully went to kosher butcher shops in the 1950s under the guidance of her mother and mother-in-law, New York Jews obtaining kosher meat included many whose allegiance to other dietary laws was weaker than earlier generations.[52]

Lower meat prices in the self-serve supermarkets accentuated pressures on kosher meat. As early as 1948, Hyman Blum complained in the *Kosher Butcher News* that the new Grand Union store "gave me a worse headache" as there were "no butchers present to sell the meat." Shoppers could choose among precut pieces placed on "small cardboard plates" and "covered with cellophane paper." With prices and weight clearly displayed, he advised skeptical readers that "the meat was good. It was fresh. It was low priced." Seeking a shopper's perspective, Blum accosted an elderly Jewish woman to see why she had bought nonkosher meat. "I came to buy vegetables," she explained, but, "curious about the packaged meat," bought some lamb chops, too, as their price was "so reasonable." Since they turned out to be delicious, she told Blum that she would be a "fool no more" and buy all her meat at the Grand Union.[53]

By the 1950s, price competition with supermarket meat fueled endemic debates over why kosher meat was so expensive. While complaints about prices went back at least as far as the 1902 meat boycott, actual protests had been episodic and usually inspired by short-lived spikes in costs. But, following the Second World War, widely advertised conventional meat prices in local newspapers brought home to observant Jews the higher prices charged by kosher butcher shops. "The average Jewish consumer," concluded Rabbi Sol Friedman in 1961, "feels that he is being unnecessarily over-charged for Kosher meat in comparison with the same type and grade of non-Kosher meat."[54]

To mollify the widespread discontent over kosher meat prices, religious leaders initiated community-wide surveys in New York, Detroit, Los Angeles, and Minneapolis to determine why kosher meat was so expensive (the New York survey failed due to lack of funds). These studies did little to calm Jewish consumers and rabbinic leaders. In Minneapolis, local meat processors claimed kosher methods added only three cents per pound to the meats' cost. Yet some butchers priced kosher meat as much as forty cents per pound more than equivalent nonkosher cuts. No matter how the costs were calculated, one sympathetic author admitted that they "do not explain the entire difference in wholesale prices." It did not help when there were court cases, such as one in Newark, New Jersey, that confirmed kosher butchers colluded to maintain higher price levels.[55] In the absence of alternative explanations, consumers simply suspected kosher meat shops of gouging the observant public. Religious leaders openly worried that such practices would accelerate the drift away from kosher observance—as indeed was the case with my mother.

The sad truth was the kosher butchers simply could not afford to offer the same low prices as supermarkets. They began with an unambiguous disadvantage: the meat they received was more expensive than nonkosher meat. Moreover, they could not counter the common practice of self-service stores to use meat as a loss leader to attract customers, with advertised prices often below costs. In a diversified supermarket, meat department losses could be compensated by profits in produce, dairy, and other areas generated by increased traffic. Kosher butcher shops, since they did not carry other products, just did not have this option. They had to charge the full price for kosher meat, but in doing so they contributed to their own demise.

Placing competitively priced pre-packaged kosher meat in supermarket's self-serve meat departments might have helped to sustain consumer demand and stem the silent desertion of Jewish shoppers such as my mother. She preferred kosher meat, and if prices had been competitive perhaps she would have continued her purchases of it. But since the postwar regulatory system had been built around butcher shop distribution, and was designed in large part to limit competition, shifting to self-service faced intractable obstacles from all parties connected to that structure.

Philadelphia's Food Fair supermarkets, which operated a kosher slaughterhouse, did try to include self-serve kosher meat in their stores in the mid-1950s. The Philadelphia Vaad (council) of local rabbis objected on the basis that the store was open on Saturdays, when kosher meat sales were forbidden. The Orthodox Union tried to broker a compromise that required the store to place the kosher meats in a locked box during the

Sabbath, but Philadelphia's rabbis were unmoved. The Vaad continued to oppose Food Fair's plans, foiling the company's experiment by refusing to provide necessary kosher supervision.[56]

A similar experiment in New York never took place, as it would have broken the law. Rules originally intended to prevent fraudulent practices by butcher shops meant, as one industry expert explained, that "it was unlawful to sell prepackaged kosher meat products from the same display case as nonkosher product."[57] The very state laws intended to protect kosher meat's integrity prohibited integration of self-serve kosher products into supermarkets. For their part, Local 234 imposed a punitive pay scale on stores that shifted to a self-service format. Its 1964 contract established a base weekly wage of $110 for meat cutters in conventional kosher shops, but required a $150 rate at stores "that sell meat already packaged, weighed, and priced"—that is, self-service—clearly as an impediment to this new practice. And, even if kosher stores managed to circumvent these union requirements, the meat they offered ranged between 20 and 40 percent more expensive than equivalent nonkosher supermarket meat.[58]

Kosher butchers shops simply closed by the thousands in the face of such daunting challenges. New York's four thousand kosher butchers at the end of World War II dwindled to less than one thousand by 1964. Harry Kassel's father-in-law, along with his partner, sold their shops in the late 1950s, anticipating that declining demand for kosher meat would continue apace. Other butchers found work on Long Island as the urban business declined, but in a few years those too were affected. Kosher butcher Abraham Smith, for example, worked at a shop on the corner of 82nd Street and Columbus Avenue (where my mother may well have bought meat) from 1945 until its closure in 1961. He then found work in a growing Jewish neighborhood in Queens, even buying his employer's store in 1965, but having to close it eight years later because of declining sales. He then sought work in his old trade through Local 234, but learned "that they had no employment for me." His only choice was to find a job in a conventional food store. In the mid-1970s the once proud kosher butcher's union had to merge with its nonkosher counterpart as membership losses meant that it could no longer "stand on its own." Kosher butchers, once ubiquitous on Manhattan's Upper West Side where

I had grown up, had almost disappeared from the neighborhood by the early 1980s.[59]

Turmoil in the nation's meatpacking industry placed additional pressures on kosher meat. As trucks replaced trains as the main source for transporting meat, the established firms that had supplied most of the country's beef found themselves in an increasingly competitive industry. Insurgent companies such as Iowa Beef Packers (IBP) steadily eroded the market share of the old Big Four. Packinghouses built in rail hubs such as Chicago, Kansas City, and Omaha closed, as new plants, located deep in the countryside closer to cattle, took over as the principal locations for animal slaughter. As urban plants that had produced kosher meat closed, firms did not replace them with new sources of supply. Cudahy, for example, shuttered its Omaha plant in 1967, and with that withdrew from the kosher meat business altogether.

As established firms terminated kosher meat manufacturing, Kassel worked hard to encourage new producers to enter the field. "What we did was protect our supply by moving the source of supply to the people who were going to survive in the business," he recalled. He persuaded IBP to produce kosher beef at its plant in Luverne, Minnesota, and recruited a new independent company, Spencer Foods. By the mid-1970s Spencer kosher-slaughtered six thousand cattle weekly, and IBP's smaller plant three thousand, with Kassel's company handling Spencer's entire output and one-half of IBP's meat. Kassel also established a new plant in Omaha that emulated methods of the big firms by contracting for cattle from a feedlot, rather than obtain them through livestock auctions. With these steps, Kassel sought to integrate kosher meat production into the operations of the industry's new dynamic firms.[60]

As Kassel ramped up new sources for kosher meat, however, he discovered that the structure of demand was changing. Jewish families such as mine were moving away from kosher food entirely, while a new wave of Jewish immigrants demanded a stricter form of kosher, known as *glatt*. Serving this market complicated Kassel's efforts immensely.

Glatt—Yiddish for smooth—reflected a stringent standard for the postmortem inspection of kosher-killed cattle. "Smooth" referred to the condition of the animal's lungs and the absence of *sirchas*—adhesions. Many *glatt* consumers were Hasidim, from European sects such as the

Lubavitch or Satmar that had been devastated by the Holocaust. As their practices differed from those of the Modern Orthodox Jews that dominated organizations like the Orthodox Union, Hasidic rabbis would only authorize consumption of meat killed by *shochetim* under their direct supervision.

The disagreement concerned whether cattle with *sirchas* were acceptable under Jewish law. Established rabbinic practice in the United States was to accept kosher-slaughtered cattle with *sirchas* unless their removal revealed an actual lung perforation. This "regular" standard for kosher beef had impeccable *halachic* roots in the Ashkenazi world and was routinely observed by the Russian, Lithuania, Romanian, and Polish Jews before they migrated to America. Its lineage could be traced to the Talmud, in Chulin 46b, which specified the procedure of immersing a lung with *sirchas* to see if it leaked air; if the lung held air even after all were removed, "it is permitted." Following from the opinion of the Rama (Rabbi Asher ben Yehiel, c. 1250–1327), Ashkenazi *rabbonim* largely accepted this practice and the presence of *sirchas* known as *ririn* that were soft and easy to remove without damaging the underlying tissue.

Sephardic authorities, however, had long disagreed with the Ashkenazi on this practice, especially the Mechaber, Rabbi Joseph Caro, author of the *Shulchan Aruch*. When a *bodek* applied this standard, any *sircha* on an animal's lungs rendered it *treif*. Sephardim followed Caro's ruling and a very strict form of *glatt* that accepted no *sirchas* at all, known as Beis Joseph *glatt*. *Glatt* practices crossed over to Ashkenazi Jews with the spread of the Hasidic movement in central Europe (especially Hungary), and their close adherence to Jewish law, especially Caro's *Shulchan Aruch*. The Ashkenazi form of *glatt* was not quite as strict as the Sephardic, as cattle could be acceptable with two or three *ririn* on their lungs as long as they passed the immersion test. As tens of thousands of Hasidim migrated to the New York area following the Holocaust and World War II, they brought with them *glatt* kosher requirements that made New York's regular kosher meat unacceptable in their communities.[61]

Kassel's first contact with *glatt* consumers came when he was asked by the followers of German émigré Dr. Joseph Breuer to produce meat for them. Though not Hasidic, Breuer's German Jewish adherents would only eat beef that met the *glatt* standard. At first Kassel turned them down, worried that making *glatt* meat might result in his regular rabbis "adopting those rules for regular kosher meat." But after hearing a "sob story" from a Breuer representative that "broke me down," he figured out how accommodate the group in his Elizabeth, New Jersey slaughterhouse. "We had to create a separate section in this modern, efficient plant that was really designed not to have a separate section," he recalled with a rueful shake of his head, and "set aside one or two days a week to service them."[62]

His experience with the Breuer group opened Kassel's eyes to the potential of the *glatt* market. "I started seeing the growth of the Satmar, the Lubavitch, and three or four other groups," he recalled, and "because of the lack of beef produced for them, they primarily ate chicken and fish." Yet these same groups were becoming more prosperous, "moving up the economic ladder," and wanting, no different than other American immigrants, to obtain better access to beef. Once the Hasidim realized what Kassel had done for the Breuer group, they "came flocking to me." Seeing an opportunity, Kassel began using his connections within the meat industry to aggressively expand *glatt* production.[63]

Kassel faced an additional obstacle—the rabbis certifying *glatt* beef would not accept *begissing*. Curiously, there was no clear connection between the *glatt* standard and this new stringency—indeed, the *Shulchan Aruch* clearly permitted *begissing*. Instead, prohibiting *begissing* principally was a pragmatic strategy to keep close control over the meat. Requiring sale within seventy-two hours of slaughter ruled out using Midwestern plants supervised by non-Hasidic rabbis to supply East Coast consumers with *glatt* meat.

As a wholesaler familiar with the slaughterhouse business, Kassel knew where to locate alternative suppliers willing to kill cattle for Hasidic groups that could get the meat to the New York area in less than seventy-two hours. He approached small East Coast slaughterhouses "that were declining, dying if you will" to see if they would be willing to "slaughter for these people." Several agreed which, as Kassel recalled proudly, "really kept them in business." Kassel managed the process, arranging for meetings between the Hasidic groups and plant operators and, most important, directing the meat into separate distribution channels: selling

UTA
CITATION
PRESENTED TO

Harry S.
Kassel

This expression of gratitude
is awarded to a leader in
philanthropy whose selfless
devotion to the cause of
Jewish survival has helped
provide aid to impoverished,
oppressed, endangered men,
women and children throughout the world, and assured
them the blessings of life,
freedom and dignity in Israel,
the United States and other
free lands.

UNITED JEWISH APPEAL OF GREATER NEW YORK

Presented by the Meat and Allied Industries Division at a Dinner in his
honor at the Delmonico's Hotel.   June 22, 1967

FIGURE 7.5 United Jewish Appeal award citation for Harry Kassel. Courtesy of
Harry Kassel.

hindquarters and nonkosher forequarters through his company and deliv-
ering the *glatt* kosher meat to his Hasidic customers.

All did not go smoothly. As a Reform Jew deeply involved with support for Israel and Jewish philanthropic causes, Kassel knew enough about
Orthodox practices to serve as a cultural ambassador between his customers and the gentile world. To establish *glatt* production at a slaughterhouse in Rochester, New York, for example, Kassel brought a rabbi
from the Brooklyn-based Hasidic group to meet the plant's owner. Upon
boarding the plane together, however, the rabbi refused to take a seat when
the only one available was next to a woman who was in the middle of a
three-seat row. "I can't sit," he told the flight attendant, insisting, "you've
got to find me a seat all by myself." A standoff resulted. "He is a rabbi,
they can't get tough with him," recalled Kassel, "the plane is sitting there,
nobody wanted to talk to this woman." For the rabbi the problem was
gender propriety—he couldn't sit next to a woman in the absence of her
husband or male family member. That she also was African American

made the situation tenser. Little wonder the airline balked at asking her to move to accommodate the rabbi's objections. Finally Kassel intervened and explained the situation to her. "She was kind, she moved over," and Kassel took the seat next to her so the rabbi could sit down along the aisle. When the pair finally got to Rochester, the slaughterhouse owner was appalled at *glatt* kosher processing requirements and tried to argue with the rabbi about the terms of the agreement. Kassel had to intervene. "You can't bend these people," he explained to the owner. "They are not flexible. It's got to be exact." Since the owner saw "big bucks," he finally went along.[64]

With this agreement in place, Kassel arranged for the *shochetim* and *bodekim* from the Hasidic group to fly to Rochester the following Monday. They would perform *shechita* on the cattle while regular plant employees took care of other necessary tasks. Around 10:30 that morning he received two phone calls in rapid succession: first from the slaughterhouse owner demanding to know where the "rabbis" were and second, more troubling, from one of the rabbis at La Guardia Airport warning that "they" wanted to put them in jail. Their offense? Carrying large knives used for slaughtering through airport security, including the intimidating machete-sized *chalef*. When the police tried to disarm them, the rabbis refused to let go of their knives—as they felt their religion demanded. The police, naturally, would not back down. When Kassel arrived at the airport, the rabbis—still in possession of their knives—were "surrounded by cops and security people." Kassel was able to explain "the whole thing" to the police and get the rabbis released from custody. Thenceforth, one of the *shochetim* drove up to Rochester with the knives the night before slaughtering operations commenced.[65]

While the seventy-two-hour rule did not interfere with *glatt* production in small East Coast plants, Kassel also wanted to take advantage of the efficient Midwestern facilities he had recruited for regular kosher production. To do so, he linked the newest innovations in meatpacking technology with the demanding requirements of his *glatt* customers. He turned to the technique of sealing chilled, freshly killed meat in airtight plastic, known as "Cryovacing" in the industry after the firm that pioneered the technology, and adapted it to *glatt* kosher production.

Kassel had been one of the first in the meat industry to work with Cryovac in the 1950s to develop new meat packaging technology. Cryovac's innovative process vacuum-sealed PVC-based plastic around large cuts of meat; excluding oxygen allowed for a quick-chilling process that did not damage the surface. It was a difficult technology to control; Kassel joked that "Cryovac should have paid us a fortune" for all his work helping the company perfect its new methods.[66]

Cryovacing greatly extended meat's life along with the potential geographic reach of distribution companies. With this technology, Kassel could take 250-pound cattle quarters, cut them into distinct types of beef (e.g. chucks, tenderloins, porterhouse) weighing 20–40 pounds each (referred to as "primals"), and package them for shipment to restaurants, hotels, and other institutional consumers. In the 1950s, packing boned meat in airtight plastic bags allowed Kassel's company to ship meat economically all over the country and even overseas. The technology spread widely throughout the meat industry. In the 1970s IBP and other new packing firms depended on Cryovac packaging to develop boxed beef, a process that replaced the traditional shipments of "hanging beef" (cattle quarters) to supermarkets and butcher shops.

The Cryovac technology had facilitated Kassel's initial foray into kosher meat. Much as New York's interwar packinghouses directed the high-quality nonkosher product from its kosher plants to the local restaurant trade, Kassel could take kosher-slaughtered cattle, sell the kosher portions in the New York area, and dispatch conventional portions of the same animals to high-end customers anywhere in the United States. We "had no problem expanding our hindquarter sales and usage," he explained (referring to the nonkosher portions of kosher-killed cattle), "because of our leadership in the fabricating business and the Cryovacing."[67] Over a decade of experience with these methods served Kassel well when he had to grapple with the new challenges of seventy-two-hour *glatt* beef.

It was a short, logical step for Kassel to adapt Cryovac technology to *glatt* meat production so he could use Midwestern plants. He leased Spencer's slaughterhouse in Hartley, Iowa, for this purpose. The day shift workers kosher-killed cattle, while workers on night shift performed *nikur* (removal of veins and forbidden fats), soaked and salted the meat to kasher it, and then sealed it in Cryovac bags, all under OU supervision. "We had no seventy-two-hour problem," Kassel explained, "because we had deveined, salted it, and we Cryovaced it." As the meat had been kashered before freezing, the seventy-two-hour rule had been satisfied, even if several weeks passed before it reached *glatt* customers.

With this innovation, Kassel created *glatt* boxed beef, where tasks previously performed in butcher shops (such as *nikur*) and the home (salting and soaking) were brought back into the packinghouse. While the labor intensive *shechita* and *nikur* processes slowed kosher production compared to conventional methods, Kassel was able to automate the soaking and salting stages. Generally no more than 30 percent of the cattle met *glatt* standards; so Kassel secured OU permission (not without difficulty) to sell regular kosher meat as well. And, as before, the nonkosher portion similarly underwent sealing in Cryovac bags (albeit without the soaking and salting stages) and became one more source for Kassel to distribute to his institutional customers.

As the dominant certifying agency regulating *shechita*, the OU had to figure out how to accommodate the emerging *glatt* standard. Its 1983 *Kosher Products Directory* took note of *glatt* for the first time, albeit tentatively. "Though not all adhesions will necessarily render an animal 'treif,'" the OU explained in an elaboration on its "meat" section, "some Jewish communities or individuals only eat of an animal that has been found to be free of all adhesions." But, in the midst of other debates within the observant Jewish community over its certification practices, the OU was loath to cede *glatt* meat supervision to Breuer and Hasidic groups. Instead, it adopted *glatt* as its own preferred standard. Two years later, the kosher guide's section heading had changed from "Meat & Meat Products" to "Meat & Meat Products—Glatt," with a qualifying notation if slaughterhouses included in the list did not follow the *glatt* standard. By 1990 the OU would only certify meat producers if their meat was *glatt*. In so doing, meat administrator Rabbi Mandel explained, the OU created a consistent Ashkenazi *glatt* standard, which "represent what were done in all the kehillahs [Jewish communities] in Europe." Taking this step brought the Hasidic *shochetim* and *bodekim* into OU supervised slaughterhouses.[68]

During the 1980s the same stringencies became the new norm in most New York butcher shops. Many of the new stores that opened in the 1970s and 1980s were founded for the express purpose of serving *glatt* consumers,[69] while established kosher butcher shops found themselves under irresistible pressure to only sell *glatt* beef; this was the experience of Little Neck Meats at 254-51 Horace Harding Boulevard in Queens. For many years after its 1961 opening, it had received certification from the Long Island Commission of Rabbis, an organization encompassing several dozen Modern Orthodox congregations. It was the principal rabbinic association providing kosher supervision of Long Island butcher shops—until the Vaad Harabonim of Queens began challenging its authority in the late 1970s. Established for the express purpose of strengthening the "Torah community," the Queens Vaad reflected the influence of growing Hasidic groups that felt Modern Orthodox practices were too lax. Gradually the vaad attracted enough adherents to displace the Long Island Commission as the principal supervising agency and to enforce the new "seventy-two-hour *glatt*" standard that prohibited *begissing*. By 1990 the vaad could gloat that it had a "virtual monopoly on *kashrus* supervision" in this area. Butcher shops such as Little Neck Meats had no choice but to comply with these stricter standards and obtain meat from *glatt* slaughterhouses to keep their kosher certification.[70]

As the impact of these stringent practices reverberated back through the supply chain, Harry Kassel decided that he had had enough and made plans to close down his operations. Pivotal to Kassel's decision was a forecast he prepared for the American Meat Institute (the principal industry trade association) in 1977. In his study Kassel predicted that the high levels of beef consumption of the 1970s would not last and that poultry would, in time, become American's favorite meat. He deduced from this that the drop in aggregate demand for beef would permit only the most efficient firms to survive. "I actually believed what I wrote," he recalled. Financially secure in his late fifties and unwilling to risk the investments needed to compete with the mammoth meat producers, Kassel had sold all his assets by the summer of 1980.[71]

His foresight was remarkable. Within five years of Kassel's retirement, all the old Big Four firms were out of business, their assets acquired by other meatpackers. Similarly, many of the new companies were overwhelmed by a few rapidly-growing firms and disappeared. Within ten years a new oligopoly of three companies dominated the beef industry: IBP, Con-Agra, and Cargill, with the last two composed of reassembled fragments of the Big Four firms plus remnants of newer companies, such as Spencer Foods, which became part of ConAgra.

The meat industry's transformation in the 1980s is now well known; but its consequences for kosher meat are far less appreciated. By the 1970s Harry Kassel had become an indispensable bridge between the industry's main firms, located far from centers of kosher meat consumption, and the wholesalers and retailers who supplied kosher consumers. His ability to take kosher-slaughtered cattle and effectively divide the meat into first two, then three supply chains—conventional, kosher, and *glatt* kosher— kept kosher meat production part of the mainstream meat industry. He was a meat quarterback who knew where to pass particular varieties of beef into the hands of appropriate consumers. Midwestern firms that produced kosher meat in the 1970s relied on Kassel's knowledge, garnered through decades of experience as an East Coast wholesaler, to profitably distribute what they produced.

The shift in demand to *glatt* kosher made Kassel's connections as a wholesaler even more important, and his departure that much more catastrophic. After the retirement of the trade's most skilled wholesaler, firms evaluating whether to produce *glatt* meat encountered discouraging economics. Typically no more than 30 percent of cattle slaughtered in conformity with kosher requirements qualified as *glatt*, and of that only the forequarters could enter the kosher market. As a result, prospective *glatt* producers doubtless were disturbed to learn that at least 85 percent of its product would have to be sold as something other than that which the production methods employed were intended to create. Not surprisingly, the huge companies seeking to survive in the cutthroat competition of the 1980s did not find burdening themselves with higher processing costs very appealing and simply eschewed kosher meat production altogether. The *glatt* standard was the final blow to participation in kosher production by the country's dominant meatpacking companies.

The consequences for kosher beef were dramatic. Kassel was able to list eighteen slaughterhouses that produced kosher meat in the 1970s, including major older companies such as Swift and Wilson, and up-and-coming new firms including IBP, Excel, and Missouri Beef Packers. None appear in the OU listings of supervised meat plants in the mid-1980s. In their place, now producing almost exclusively *glatt* meat, was a coterie of small companies mostly on the East Coast, such as European Kosher Provisions in Baltimore, S. Lundy's and Sons in Philadelphia, and the Gartner-Hart plant in Erie, Pennsylvania. Kosher meat, once a central product of American's meatpacking industry, now survived tenuously on its fringes.[72]

KOSHER BEEF'S TROUBLES

Kassel's withdrawal from the marketplace marked the final eclipse of kosher beef's mid-century stability. The network of producers, wholesalers, and butcher shops that had once supplied it were gone or greatly diminished, leaving state inspectors and rabbis the job of managing a fluctuating and unstable supply chain. A tight, mutually reinforcing system where firms had benefited from rules inhibiting marginal operations from cutting into their business instead became porous, with allegedly kosher meat entering retail shops from ever changing (and hard to verify) sources.

The worries, indeed desperation of kosher meat regulators can be read through the expansion of legal requirements and the escalation of penalties. Aside from inclusion of language governing *begissing*, there had been no substantive changes to New York State's kosher regulations for three decades following World War II. But as the power of kosher butcher shop associations and labor unions faded, so too did the ability of state regulators to rely on their former institutional partners to enforce behavior in the marketplace. Simultaneously, the emerging *glatt* standard placed pressures on the Kosher Enforcement Division to alter its practices so as to protect the more stringent Orthodox requirements. The result was an increasingly punitive intervention by state regulators into meat distribution.

Creating ways to delineate between *glatt* and regular kosher meat was the most striking change among the fourteen amendments added to the kosher laws between 1977 and 1987. The new rules required all meat offered for sale to indicate prominently whether it had been salted and soaked; meat identified as "not soaked or salted" had to display a tag identifying the date and time of slaughter—if greater than three days, then obviously the meat had been washed. While the regulations still permitted *begissing* by an Orthodox rabbi or a person authorized by him, these labeling rules created a highly visible distinction between washed regular kosher meat and unwashed *glatt* kosher product.[73]

Punishments for violating the state's kosher laws increased drastically as well. Since the 1940s, the maximum fine for a first offense (a misdemeanor) had been $500. Regulations passed in 1984 made violations in excess of $5,000 a class E felony, permitting far higher penalties. Fines escalated further if a business had violated the kosher laws previously in the past ten years. In those instances, judgments could rise to $10,000 for each offense.[74]

These changes reflected a new strategy for the Kosher Law Enforcement Division. For a generation it had secured compliance by relying on systematic inspections of meat purveyors, rather than heavy penalties. "You could count on them coming around," Harry Kassel recalled, "to make sure that you were using the proper wires—*plumbas* if you will—and that your records were intact." A typical year for the division's staff involved around 15,000 inspections and aggregate fines of well under $10,000. In 1960, for example, the division conducted 14,625 inspections, pursued 82 prosecutions, and secured fines totaling $5,400. In one typical conviction, a Mineola judge fined Larry Shor $400 and levied a suspended sentence of 6 months for fraudulently attaching "kosher tags and *plumbas* to non-kosher meats" in his Long Island butcher shop. The relatively low fine and suspended sentence were stern warnings to observe the kosher laws while at the same time not harming the butcher shop's capacity to stay in business—so long as it followed the rules. Regulation, rather than prosecution, was the dominant enforcement mechanism.[75]

The balance between inspections and prosecutions began to change in the late 1970s, as the division increasingly relied on the threat of substantial fines to enforce its regulations. In 1977, with the passage of the new requirements for salting and soaking meat, prosecutions and penalties increased dramatically at the same time as the number of inspections actually declined. Annual fines rose steadily to $107,450 in 1983, and then over $500,000 by the late 1980s. In 1992 the division's staff conducted only 5,746 inspections (a new low) while levying fines of $1,970,375 for 288 violations of the kosher laws.[76]

Resorting to punitive measures reflected the dissipation of the private associations and established businesses that had cooperated with the kosher regulation, and the emergence of systematic fraud by new firms seeking to profit from the meat industry's chaos. With kosher meat supplies dependent on a patchwork of small plants, fraud inevitably returned on a scale not seen for decades.

The prosecution of Rachleff Kosher Provisions indicates what regulators were up against as the industry came unglued. In December 1984, state inspectors seized seven cartons of nonkosher briskets that the Brooklyn company had fraudulently labeled as kosher. When it balked at paying a $17,500 fine, the New York attorney general's office subpoenaed the firm's files and uncovered a startling pattern of systematic violation of the kosher laws. During 1984, Rachleff obtained more than thirty-three thousand pounds of tongues and fifteen thousand pounds of briskets from nonkosher suppliers and then, the owner admitted, sold them as kosher. The attorney general assessed an additional penalty of $996,600 for these violations. The company fought the fine, initially winning in the Kings County Supreme Court, but losing before the New York State Supreme Court in 1992. By that time, however, it had ceased operation; the fine was never paid.[77]

Such onerous penalties were meant undoubtedly to punish companies such as Rachleff Kosher Provisions by putting them out of business and in so doing intimidate others tempted to deliberately evade the kosher laws. But the new rules and penalties could serve another purpose—to compel butcher shops to follow rules intended to protect Orthodox supervision of kosher meat. The travail of Commack Self-Serve Kosher Meats, founded by brothers Brian and Jeffrey Yarmeisch in 1979, offers a sobering example of how the Kosher Law Enforcement Division could far exceed its official mandate to prevent fraud.

Located in the middle of Long Island, Commack Self-Serve Kosher Meats obtained kosher supervision from local Conservative rabbi William Berman, rather than the Queens Vaad. In doing so, they rejected the new *glatt* standard and the increasingly stringent Orthodox requirements. With a clientele drawn from observant Jews who trusted Rabbi Berman, the Yarmeischs were successful for a few years. Reliance on a local rabbi for supervision was, moreover, fully in keeping with Jewish law. But using a Conservative rabbi brought them to the attention of state kosher law enforcement officers who cited them repeatedly for dubious infractions of the kosher laws.

An inspection on July 6, 1986, returned the first violation. Kosher Law Enforcement staff seized two packages of beef and veal spare ribs and sent them to the state laboratory to test for salt content. As the analysis allegedly showed that "neither package of spare ribs was soaked and salted as mandated by Hebrew Orthodox religious requirements," the Yarmeisch brothers were fined $600. A brief letter from Jeffrey Yarmeisch accompanying payment of the fine requested that the state let them know "what the analysis was and what the standard should be." His note went unanswered.[78]

Barely six months later, the store received a second citation. On January 7, 1987, state inspectors removed two chuck steaks from the self-service case on suspicion that they were not salted as the label claimed. Based on findings from the state laboratory that the salt content inside the meat was no different from that on the surface, the Yarmeisch brothers were again fined $600. This time Jeffrey Yarmeisch sent a stronger protest, affirming that "we do everything according to Kasuruth Law." He explained that the interior and exterior salt content were the same because the soaked and salted meat had been "faced" (trimmed of the meat darkened through direct contact with salt) so it would look more attractive to consumers once packaged. Repeating his earlier request, Yarmeisch asked "that your department . . . notify me with the proper procedure." Once again, the state did not respond to his request for clarification.[79]

Commack Self-Service Kosher Meats received yet another fine the following year, this time $750 for having fifty lamb tongues (each weighing about seven pounds) soaking in a salt water solution that ostensibly rendered "the tongues irreversibly non kosher." This time the store fought the charges, supported by a letter from Rabbi Berman. The rabbi explained the tongues were soaking in water to draw out some of the salt "as some of the customers have been complaining that the meat is too salty" and that once "the meat is kashered, it cannot by unkashered by lying in salt water."

Rabbi Berman's irrefutable defense did not deflect the Kosher Enforcement Division from its preoccupation with the Yarmeischs' store. As an internal memorandum later revealed, its officials searched for other charges to make the fine stick. In 1989 the New York attorney general modified the complaint to charge Commack Meats with a completely different violation—failing to properly remove veins from the tongues. Now represented by an attorney, the Yarmeisch brothers spent much of 1989 and 1990 fighting the amended charges as well. Two years later the matter was still unresolved and the tongues remained quarantined in the store's freezer.[80]

Opposing the revised (and even more flimsy) citation for the lamb tongues doubtless cost the store more than the proposed $750 fine, but stymied the charges and thoroughly embarrassed the Kosher Enforcement Division within the state's government. The New York attorney general's office chided it for inadequate documentation of the initial inspection and failure to respond adequately to requests for a detailed bill of particulars. The clear implication of the review was that the division was engaging in harassment of a recalcitrant store, stepping beyond the boundaries of its proper regulatory function.

Undeterred, kosher inspectors once again entered Commack Self-Serve Kosher Meats on November 30, 1992, and charged it with not having the necessary *plumbas* on meat. Seeking to forestall additional fines, Brian Yarmeisch immediately responded that he had the tags in question and produced appropriate kosher documentation for the particular shipment; nonetheless the division assessed a fine of $1,000. A full-blown confrontation was brewing.[81]

Barely two months later, the same state inspector slapped the store with yet another violation, this time for allegedly offering poultry for sale that did not have the necessary labels identifying whether it had been soaked and salted. Among the borderline violations assessed against the store, the latest charges were especially flimsy. The chickens in question were found in a walk-in refrigerator located in a closed work area in the rear of the store that was off limits to shoppers and, aside from the one package opened by the inspectors, the remaining eighteen boxes were banded, vacuum-sealed containers that had been shipped to the store from the poultry company. Clearly, customers could neither see nor purchase this chicken in the form it was at the time of inspection. Since the labeling requirements of the law applied only to meat and poultry "offered for sale at retail," the inspectors had no basis for the charges.[82]

None of that mattered to the Kosher Law Enforcement Division—in short order it levied a damaging fine of $11,000, enough to seriously affect the store's profits. Moreover, notice of the violation appeared in publications that circulated widely in observant Jewish circles on Long Island, prompting a sharp decline in sales. Similar to the Rachleff Kosher Provision case, the hefty fine and detrimental public disclosure seemed intended to put Commack Self-Serve Kosher Meats out of business. Infuriated, and with their livelihood threatened, the Yarmeisch brothers filed suit in federal court contending that New York State's kosher laws violated the U.S. Constitution's separation of church and state.

The brothers pursued their litigation relentlessly even though the fines were not enforced once they filed the lawsuit. Six years of battling Kosher Law Enforcement inspectors had left them determined to take their case to the end. They doubtless were encouraged by the 1992 Ran-Dav's Kosher Kitchen ruling from the New Jersey Supreme Court that the state's kosher laws, similar in character to New York's, were unconstitutional. They secured a clear decision from the U.S. district court judge Nina Gershon in 2000, which found the New York State laws unconstitutional. A year later the second circuit of the U.S. Court of Appeals upheld Judge Gershon's ruling with even more robust language than her initial decision. The "challenged laws," they held, "produce an *actual* joint exercise of governmental and religious authority. United exercise of authority of this kind are prohibited by the Establishment Clause." Moreover, as this authority was exercised in favor of an Orthodox interpretation of kosher law and against views of the Conservative rabbi who supervised the Commack store, the appeals court concluded that "the State has effectively aligned itself with one side of an internal debate within Judaism. This it may not do." The U.S. Supreme Court declined to review the court's decision, firmly settling that the New York kosher laws, and other similar state laws, were not constitutional.[83]

A "HIGHER AUTHORITY"?

When the Commack decision came down, only the Orthodox protested, albeit vigorously. The Kosher Law Enforcement Division no longer had the support of the vast majority of New York's Jews who had once relied on it to ensure a reliable source of kosher meat. The improper pressure on the Commack store, and the division's efforts to advance the *glatt* standard, made it "political" in a way it had not been in Harry Kassel's heyday. It had come to represent a faction among Jews (and a small one at that) and thus when it lost the power to enforce kosher law only those with whom it was aligned mourned its passing. The loss of regulatory authority that would have, two generations before, disturbed Jews such as my Conservative grandmother Bertie Schwartz passed with scarcely a ripple outside Orthodox circles.

Kosher meat certainly had fallen a long way since the 1920s, when 25 percent of the country's steers were slaughtered in conformity with Jewish religious requirements. The *glatt* standard did not start kosher meat's decline, but it accentuated its isolation from the meat industry—and from observant Jews who felt that the standards observed by their parents and grandparents were good enough for them. And it created a chasm between what had once been the "paradigm of Kosher food" and the easily obtainable processed products bearing *heckshers* of rabbinic certification.

Indeed, by 1990 shopping for kosher food on the Upper West Side was utterly reversed from experiences of my grandmothers. Kosher meat, once easy to find at a number of competing shops, now was available only in a few scattered stores. In quiet contrast, reliably kosher cereals, canned soups, and other processed foods, once virtually absent from the marketplace, crowded the shelves and display cases of supermarkets there and throughout the United States.

Particularly striking is the way these new standards rendered a popular and easily obtained kosher beef product—Hebrew National hot dogs— unacceptable to the Orthodox. Here was a fine irony: the firm whose slogan used kosher certification to attest to its product's quality did not follow "a high enough authority" for those following the *glatt* standard.

For many decades Hebrew National had been an acceptable staple item in New York's kosher delicatessens. As I child I didn't eat hot dogs very often at home, but, when we did, Hebrew National would have been an acceptable brand even for Florence. Similar to Manischewitz and Rokeach, which concentrated on the Jewish market, Hebrew National had its own rabbis who made sure their hot dogs were kosher—and certainly Jewish consumers did not doubt Hebrew Nation's commitment to kosher standards.

Seeking to capitalize on American's growing interest in processed meat products, the firm began selling prepackaged corned beef in 1956, followed shortly thereafter by hot dogs. Sales skyrocketed, as its prepackaged kosher products did not face the same restrictions as fresh beef. Unlike kosher meat, which customers had to purchase in kosher butcher shops, Hebrew National was able "to put the food where they [consumers] could get it," company president Leonard Pines explained to the *New York Times* in 1960, "in the supermarket in which they buy other products." Just as Manischewitz chicken soup could go into a supermarket's conventional soup aisle, so too could Hebrew National's packaged hot dogs sit next to nonkosher Oscar Mayer wieners in the cold cuts case.[84]

Mainstreaming made it possible for Hebrew National to reach non-Jewish markets and vastly increase sales; but it also ruined its reputation among Orthodox Jews. Relying on Rabbi Tibor Stern, an independent rabbi not affiliated with the OU, OK, or other mainstream certification organization became more suspect in the 1960s and 1970s, especially after Hebrew National became part of large conglomerates. Even after control reverted to the Pines family who had started the business, Orthodox antipathy remained—especially as Hebrew National never turned to *glatt* meat, as the costs for doing so would have priced it too high compared to its competitors in the American mass market. It also used *begissed* meat, an additional violation of the new standard—even though washed meat had been fine for my devout grandparents. Supervision passed to the Triangle K agency in 2004 after Rabbi Tibor's death, mollifying Conservative Jews. But as Hebrew National continued to rely on regular kosher meat that was not *glatt*, the OU and other principal certification organizations would not endorse consumption of its products.[85]

As a result, Hebrew National's stimulus to kosher food did not translate into fresh kosher meat becoming more widely available. Without Orthodox demand for the regular kosher meat produced for Hebrew National, most if not all of it went into hot dogs and not into steaks, roasts, or stewing meat available for purchase. Indeed, Hebrew National's travails instead served as a warning to meatpacking companies of just how difficult it would be to satisfy the Orthodox rabbis who were the gatekeepers to the principal consumers of fresh kosher meat. Harry Kassel had known how to make money on *glatt* meat in the 1970s, but without his knowledge and connections, and perhaps also without the passion and sympathy that came from his deep Jewish roots, no one in the industry cared to try. Without fanfare, the observant Jewish consumer simply faded from the order books of America's principal meatpacking firms.

Kosher meat's marginal presence in the U.S. economy was an indication, similar to kosher wine, of the food industry's attenuated acceptance of production methods that incorporated Jewish ritual requirements. It was easy to produce kosher-certified processed foods when the ingredients and techniques so used entailed little additional cost. However, when generating kosher food required substantive changes in how firms made food, and measurably increased costs for doing so, large companies weren't interested. Much as kosher wine became the preserve of observant Jewish producers principally concerned with selling to other observant Jews, so too would it become necessary for Orthodox Jews to create meatpacking firms to supply their coreligionists. And, when those companies emerged, so too did older and deeper troubles, questions about the compatibility of Jewish religious slaughter with the ethical views of a predominantly Christian nation.

8

SHECHITA

THROUGHOUT THE research for this book, a day spent in New York City archives ended with a visit to my mother's Upper West Side apartment and a debriefing of my latest finds over sandwiches from Fine & Schapiro's kosher delicatessen on 72nd Street. My mother's sharp questions and incisive suggestions were punctuated with reminiscences of her encounters with kosher practices. Fine & Schapiro sandwiches were themselves an exercise in memory; it was the only West Side restaurant where we could eat with my father's Orthodox mother.

As my mother's chronic obstructive pulmonary disease progressed, her ability to talk, and even control her body, declined such that these visits, toward the end of her life, became monologues on my part punctuated by efforts from her caregivers to help her consume the traditional kosher tongue sandwich. The second to last time I saw her alive, I brought the biopic on Temple Grandin to watch with her, as she scarcely had enough breath left to speak and certainly could not engage in the conversations we had been able to hold even six months earlier.

As a great champion of animal rights (and a member of just about any animal rights organization that solicited her), she was an admirer of Grandin's efforts to improve treatment of animals meant for slaughter. What she didn't know, and enjoyed hearing me relate (even if she couldn't respond herself), was Temple Grandin's deep involvement with improving kosher slaughter and reconciling humane treatment of animals with Jewish religious requirements.

While we couldn't really have a conversation about the movie, watching it together brought full circle a conversation between us that stretched back thirty years, when I first began researching the meatpacking industry. She had always felt that I didn't pay as much attention as I should have to animal rights, and I would argue that understanding labor relations and consumer demand didn't have much to do with those issues. Showing her Grandin's movie, and telling her how important the humane slaughter issue was to kosher meat production, was a way to let her know about the latest stage of my current research—and also to communicate that I had in fact been listening to her all those years. She died about a week after we watched the movie together.

It was, after all, around the same time my uncle Stu challenged me to write about kosher food that the practices of the Agriprocessors slaughterhouse brought national attention to kosher food production—and not in a positive light. In 2004 clandestine videos released by PETA disclosed horrific treatment of cattle undergoing *shechita*. Then in 2008 a federal immigration raid on the Postville plant owned by the Rubashkin family again riveted attention on the firm's deplorable practices toward its employees, suppliers, and livestock. These episodes forcefully posed the relationship between ethical practices and kosher food production. From that watershed a new Jewish food movement has emerged, focused centrally on ethical issues involving food, much less concerned with traditional kosher standards—and, in so doing, creating much consternation among traditional observant consumers.

Yet, the closer I looked at the relationship between kosher food and "ethics," the more complicated it seemed, especially when it came to *shechita*, the religiously mandated slaughtering methods employed to make kosher meat. Indeed, concern over *shechita* was—and remains—a defining feature of many animal welfare societies, even with the efforts of sympathetic reformers such as Temple Grandin. As kosher slaughter shifted almost entirely to Jewish companies in the late 1980s and 1990s, the actions of those firms received heightened scrutiny, especially whether their actions and values were consonant with secular laws and mores. Inexorably questions over the compatibility of *shechita* with ethics reemerged once again in the early years of the twenty-first century.

HUMANE SLAUGHTER—AND THE JEWS

Organizations formed to advocate for the humane treatment of animals first emerged in the mid-nineteenth century. Inspired by Christian ethical concerns to aid those who could not help themselves (a category that included women and children), these organizations campaigned against a number of practices that they found objectionable. Many initiatives had unimpeachable objectives; in the U.S., activists secured humane regulations mandating provision of water and food for live animals conveyed on trains from the Midwest to East Coast slaughterhouses. But the same commitment to reduce animal's suffering often made these activists intransigent critics of kosher slaughtering methods—at the same time that they disclaimed any dislike of Jews as such.

In the United States, Massachusetts Humane Society president Francis H. Rowley captured the antipathy felt by some animal welfare advocates toward Judaism in his address to the national Humane Society's 1913 convention. Rowley's speech—later issued as a pamphlet—was infused with a Christian ethos that marginalized Judaism. He equated Christian ethics with the universal ethics that could support "a worthier civilization" and argued that the reform for which "there is no room for argument"—the stunning of all animals before slaughter—should be adopted without doubt by any "twentieth-century" land boasting a "Christian civilization." Yet abolishing nonstunned slaughter, "a remnant of our barbarous past," remained blocked by "bitter and persistent" resistance. While deploring the attitudes of packing companies, Rowley predicted that public opprobrium with their "brutality" could force them to change. Jews, however, presented a more "difficult" obstacle to this reform, with their specious "cry of religious persecution."

Reflecting Rowley's conclusion that Jews were the main obstacle to humane slaughter reform, three-quarters of his pamphlet was devoted to attacking *shechita*. Much as he might proclaim that on many occasions he had "stood alone in defense of his [Jews'] character," he nonetheless showed his prejudice by denouncing "the large and growing section of the population who will bar our way to reform in the name of their religion." Equating *shechita* with a "barbarous" past and praising reformers' efforts to create a "Christian civilization" certainly cast Jews, and their

FIGURE 8.1 *Shochet* performing *shechita*, Chicago, 1909. The animal's rear leg is elevated while its shoulders remain on the ground, its head restrained by a helper. LOT 11985–3, Library of Congress Prints and Photographs Division, Washington, DC.

religion, as outside of the ethical standards of a modern and "worthier civilization."[1]

Rowley's unequivocal praise for more successful efforts to mandate preslaughter stunning in European nations such as Germany reflected his indifference to the overt anti-Semitism influential in those campaigns. Most of his sources used to attack *shechita* were published by veterinarians in Germany after 1900, when anti-Semitic organizations became influential in humane slaughter efforts. Rowley's theme that *shechita* was uncivilized drew on their arguments. One German pamphlet declaimed against the "torment" experienced by animals undergoing *shechita*, while another called it "one of the most barbarous methods of slaughter." While framed in the language of science, these opinions were part of a general opprobrium towards kosher slaughter that linked its alleged brutality with Jewish hostility toward Christians and the blood libel claim that Jews killed Christian children to use their blood in Jewish rites.[2]

Not all opposition to *shechita* had anti-Semitic taproots. Nonetheless, agitation by animal welfare organizations against kosher slaughter created an opportunity for anti-Semitic organizations to operate in a seemingly respectable environment, and to grow. After his release from prison in 1924, Adolf Hitler reoriented the National Socialists to seek a national audience—and identified opposition to *shechita* as a way to achieve greater political legitimacy. Leadership of campaigns against it in Bavaria and especially Munich placed the National Socialists within a spectrum of organizations—including animal welfare societies—seeking to end Jewish slaughter. By the late 1920s these efforts became infused with "anti-Semitic vitriol" that allowed, as Robin Judt explains, "participants to revive radically anti-Semitic views within mainstream political arenas." Parallel right-wing movements in Norway succeeded in banning *shechita* in the mid-1920s; and when the Nazis came to power, prohibiting Jewish slaughter was one of their first acts in Germany and then in the other nations that they conquered. Kosher slaughter remained banned through much of continental Europe until the Allies destroyed Nazi rule and reestablished democratic governments.[3]

In the United States, efforts to restrict *shechita* lagged in comparison to other nations; and the sobering connection with anti-Semitism may well have dissuaded opponents from pressing this issue in the 1930s and 1940s. Contemporary efforts to restrict ritual slaughter can be traced to the 1954 American Humane Society's national meeting. Participants there were shocked by a film graphically depicting the shackling and killing of live hogs, the meatpacking industry's standard practice. Not only were delegates incensed at the pig's evident suffering, they had a positive alternative to point to—the Hormel Company's successful use of anesthetizing gas to stun animals prior to "sticking," the killing stroke wielded by a butcher.[4] Deeply disturbed by what they had seen, the society determined to pass legislation that would prevent pain and suffering among all animals prior to slaughter, whether pigs, cattle, chickens, or sheep.

With its origins in outrage over pig slaughter, postwar efforts in the U.S. to pass humane slaughter legislation clearly did not reflect anti-Semitic motivations on the part of the movement's organizations. But in their efforts the Humane Society and similar groups sought to require stunning of all animals, including cattle, placing Jewish religious slaughter practices again at odds with animal rights activists' agenda.

The Humane Society's widely circulated flyer, "Facts About Meat," for example, focused principally on the "intolerably, impermissibly cruel" live slaughter of hogs who slowly bled to death while hanging upside down. It also dwelled on the crude stunning of cattle with a sledgehammer that too often required several blows to subdue the "agonized animal." To these "routine" cruelties, the pamphlet noted in passing even worse cases where the animal, "struggling in agony, is jerked off the floor by a chain around one ankle," before being killed—an oblique but unmistakable reference to the absence of stunning in kosher slaughter. With its insistence that all animals should be unconscious at the time of death, the humane slaughter movement set itself against the observant Jewish community.[5] And, as in Rowley's day, and to the dismay and eventual fury of its backers, ritual slaughter proved the most intractable issue to address.

Using a cautious strategy perhaps informed by the recent chilling example of Nazi Germany, advocates avoided a direct attack on the kosher requirement that cattle had to be conscious when the *shochet* cut its throat. Instead, they concentrated on expanding slaughter restrictions to include handling methods prior to slaughter, and especially the prevalence of "shackle-and-hoist" methods that were not part of Jewish law. Publicly, humane slaughter leaders did not contest Jewish arguments that a correct cut by the *shochet* resulted in substantial bleeding and rapid loss of consciousness such that the animal did not feel pain prior to death, though they avoided going on record agreeing that it was humane. Instead, they emphasized the need to end the shackling and hoisting of conscious animals of all species prior to slaughter, regardless of whether doing so would interfere with *shechita*—which it would have.

Hormel's example demonstrated that it was feasible to end live shackling of hogs; similarly, replacing a sledgehammer with a more consistently effective captive bolt pistol in cattle killing operations did not involve major changes in slaughtering procedures. However, eliminating the objectionable shackle-and-hoist methods for kosher processing of cattle was far more difficult, and for reasons humane slaughter activists had trouble appreciating. The complicating factors were far from evident, hidden as they were in the economics of the meatpacking industry.

By the time of the mid-1950s debates, most kosher meat came from conventional slaughterhouses that followed kosher practices for only a portion of the cattle they processed. This was a relatively recent development, as earlier in the century the New York City area's beef plants had slaughtered all cattle in accordance with kosher requirements; the last remaining plants to do so closed in the mid-1950s. Indeed, its very integration into conventional operations drew Harry Kassel into kosher meat distribution, as the plants that produced the nonkosher meat he started handling were by the late 1950s also producing a great deal of kosher meat.

At the time, humane advocates alleged that adoption of shackle-and-hoist kosher slaughter stemmed from government regulation of meat production, commencing with the 1906 Meat Inspection Act and subsequent sanitary measures. They were mistaken; nothing in the 1906 act and subsequent regulations prohibited casting, the method employed by the early twentieth-century kosher plants of placing cattle on the ground for slaughter. Industry sources provide overwhelming evidence that casting continued well into the mid-twentieth century and that in nonkosher operations cattle were routinely dropped to the floor for hide removal procedures. Shackle-and-hoist methods, which undoubtedly caused cattle far more pain and anguish than casting, stemmed from the incorporation of kosher slaughtering into existing meatpacking plants in which kosher meat was a niche product.[6]

This integration of kosher processing into conventional plants following World War II in all likelihood expanded the use of shackle-and-hoist methods. These slaughterhouses strove to keep the animals moving continuously, attached to an overhead chain; shackling took place immediately after the animal was stunned and before it was killed. When

FIGURE 8.2 Cattle skinning operation, Waterloo, Iowa, 1930s. Once the animal's throat was cut, both kosher and nonkosher cattle were dropped back to the floor so that a team of butchers could carefully remove the valuable hide for use in leather products. In the 1950s new technology permitted development of "on the rail" dressing and eliminated this discontinuous stage in cattle processing. Shackle-and-hoist methods in kosher slaughter likely became more prevalent after the development of "on the rail dressing." HAER Iowa, 7-WATLO, 4U–24, Library of Congress Prints and Photographs Division, Washington, DC.

animals were kosher killed, companies simply omitted the stunning phase to comply with kosher requirements, shackling and hoisting the live animal, then bringing in a *shochet* to perform *shechita*. Banning live shackling altogether, however, would have precluded using the same facilities for kosher and nonkosher meat. Rabbi Pinchas Teitz tried to communicate this practical situation to the Senate Committee on Agriculture when he explained that in the Elizabeth, New Jersey plants he supervised "we have one slaughter floor and the same killing floor, and the one who desires kosher gets kosher." If live shackling of animals was banned, however, Rabbi Teitz warned that using the same plant "will be impossible, and Jewish slaughterhouses will have to be established."

Doing so would, he predicted, make kosher meat expensive and difficult to procure.[7]

This fear that humane slaughter rules would render kosher meat inaccessible lay behind the intransigent Orthodox opposition to the legislation. Hence they were unmoved with the alternative proposed by humane slaughter advocates, using the "Weinberg" pen (originally developed in the 1920s) as an alternative to live shackle-and-hoist methods. This technology used a heavy iron cage that rotated upside down to restrain cattle and expose their neck for the *shochet*'s blade. The minute it took to complete slaughter for each animal was, however, far slower than standard methods and also would have required an expensive restructuring of killing operations. At the time, requiring its use would have created just the outcome that Rabbi Teitz feared.

When legislation first came before Congress in 1956, the drafts compounded Jewish fears by simply exempting *shechita* from humane slaughter requirements—an enormous error that bespoke an underling view, identical to Rowley two generations before, that Jewish slaughtering methods were fundamentally inhumane.[8] Leo Pfeffer, representing over eighty Jewish organizations, testified at the Senate Committee on Agriculture and Forestry hearings that, in fact, "the Jewish method of slaughtering cattle is by far the most humane method that has yet been developed," as the swift stroke of the highly trained *shochet* "insures practically instantaneous unconsciousness." He also cited specific "commandments" in the Bible and Talmud that imposed "a high obligation upon all Jews to avoid unnecessary pain to any living thing." As a result, Pfeffer bluntly described the language exempting kosher slaughter as "defamatory" for it implied that "Jewish slaughtering is not a humane method." Newly elected Minnesota senator Hubert Humphrey, who had spearheaded the legislation, granted his point and apologized for the implication; henceforth, all drafts considered during the next two years contained some form of sections 2a and b, declaring "slaughtering in accordance with the requirements of any religious faith" one of the humane forms of slaughter.[9] Handling, however, remained outside this protection, inflaming Orthodox concerns that the net effect would be to make kosher meat virtually disappear.

Humane slaughter advocates, consumed with their objective of banning cruel and avoidable practices in the pork industry, elided the legitimate concerns of observant Jews that humane slaughter restrictions could damage their ability to procure kosher meat. They were determined to prohibit the shackling and hoisting of live animals regardless of the species, even over Jewish objections. Their position, articulated by John C. MacFarlane at 1957 House hearings, was that the live shackling and hoisting of cattle was "not a part of ritual slaughter techniques" and thus any exemption of these practices was not acceptable to the humane societies. And they continued to dismiss appeals, such as those from David Greenwald of the American Federation of Retail Kosher Butchers, that the blanket "prohibitions" against shacking and hoisting "would prohibit kosher slaughter."[10]

Hubert Humphrey used his considerable influence to engender a split among Jewish organizations and secure a compromise sufficient for passage. With the aid of the humane societies and Minnesota Jewish organizations, he was able to draft language acceptable to Reform and Conservative Jewish organizations, but not the Orthodox. Humphrey also limited the legislation's scope to require only those firms selling directly to the federal government to be in compliance with humane slaughter regulations. And he warned Jewish organizations that unless they accepted some limitations on preslaughter handling methods wider restrictions might be adopted. In retrospect, there was little basis for Humphrey's claim. Yet his threat was effective; early in 1958 Conservative and Reform Jewish organizations endorsed legislation they admitted "would empower the Department of Agriculture to restrict or prohibit shackling or hoisting of conscious animals in connection with slaughtering according to the ritual requirements of the Jewish faith."[11]

The measure quickly passed the House, and when it came to the Senate the only Jewish organizations testifying against it were those affiliated with the Orthodox. In so doing, they locked themselves into the untenable position of defending shackle-and-hoist slaughter methods as humane. Testifying at the 1958 Senate hearings that focused on the handling issue, Union of Orthodox Rabbis (the Agudath Harabonim) representative Isaac Lewin once again cited examples of Jewish religious law prohibiting cruelty to animals, such as the ban against hunting for sport. "The Jewish religion is in fact the oldest society for prevention of cruelty to animals," he told the senators: "2,500 years we are working in this direction." Sharp questioning from senators nonetheless threw the Orthodox on the defensive. Rabbi Solomon J. Sharfman, president of the Rabbinical Council of America, unpersuasively tried to dismiss the handling issue by minimizing its impact on cattle. Based on his experience, he asserted that hoisting and shackling lasted for but one minute, and "we could not consider that to be inhumane, no more than holding a giant dog on a leash and the dog straining on the leash." Little wonder that humane slaughter advocates remained unconvinced and dismissive of Rabbi Lewin's concern that passage of the legislation "would make the Jewish method of slaughtering animals virtually impossible in the United States."[12]

The pressure to pass humane legislation was unrelenting. "Humane Appeals Swamp Congress" reported the *New York Times*, adding that if the volume of "mail is an indicator" it was the "leading question" in the minds of voters. While the humane slaughter organizations avowed respect for Judaism and for religious slaughter (even as they dismissed Orthodox concerns), the struggle over the legislation generated letters that were far less tolerant. "Kosher slaughter is not humane slaughter," Mrs. Peder Schmidt flatly told the Senate committee. Others echoed this sentiment. "The closing testimony presented by the Rabbis this afternoon positively horrified and revolted me," Therese Ann Olson wrote committee chair Allen Ellender. In protesting against the humane slaughter legislation, she huffed that "they are imposing their religious beliefs on me and every Gentile American." And although relatively few made explicit anti-Semitic statements, proponents of the legislation echoed Rowley's 1913 pamphlet by emphasizing the Christian values they embodied and decrying the primitivism of those who opposed them. William Milligan's assurance to Senator Ellender that "St. Peter will give you a big A on your conduct chart" if he helped to end slaughtering practices that were a "throwback to the biblical days of Abraham" were more typical of popular sentiment that equated humane methods with Christian morals and linked Jewish ritual requirements with retrograde antimodernism and cruelty toward animals.[13]

Humphrey did not alter his bill to accommodate Orthodox Jew's complaints; however, during the legislation's turbulent passage through the Senate, ritual slaughter ended up receiving important protections. Reflecting staunch industry opposition to the House bill, the Senate Committee on Agriculture approved a measure for the full Senate's consideration that only mandated studying the humane slaughter issue for another two years. In a marathon debate, Humphrey persuaded the Senate to overturn the agriculture committee recommendation and to instead consider the House bill that required immediate action. But, just before it came up for a vote, Senators Jacob Javits and Clifford Case successfully amended the measure by adding the phrase, "the handling or other preparation of livestock for ritual slaughter" to the exemption from humane slaughter requirements. It was a major victory for the Orthodox critics of the legislation. Humane societies viewed the act as "weakened" by the Case-Javits amendment, as it would permit shackle-and-hoist methods to continue in kosher beef slaughter, but they still had achieved the objective that had spawned the push for legislation, restrictions on killing pigs that were still conscious. President Eisenhower signed the Humane Slaughter Act on August 27, 1958.[14]

This political process left a curious footprint in the new law. Section 2, which defined humane slaughter, included as one humane method the "ritual requirements . . . of a religious faith" that requires "loss of consciousness . . . by . . . severing the carotid arteries with a sharp instrument," along with the "handling in connection with such slaughter." Then, curiously, section 6 went on to say, "in order to protect religious freedom, ritual slaughter and the handling and other preparation of livestock for ritual slaughter are exempted from the terms of this Act." *Shechita*—and the handling of cattle associated with it—thus was simultaneously judged humane and exempt from humane requirements. The OU's parent organization, the Union of Orthodox Jewish Congregations, took notice of this "inconsistency" between sections 2 and 6 in its appeal to President Eisenhower to not sign the legislation and warned that the measure's "utter confusion" could create "serious difficulties" for kosher meat.[15]

The union's warning turned out to be prescient. In the aftermath of the law's passage, humane societies pressed for legislation in twenty-eight states to further tighten slaughtering requirements—especially to eliminate the loophole permitting shackle-and-hoist methods in kosher slaughter. The well-funded Friends of Animals organization that claimed Brigitte Bardot as its honorary chairman lead especially aggressive efforts in New York and New Jersey. The provocative phrases "The Meat You Eat Is Seared with Pain," and "This Is Slaughter of Conscious Animals" headlined a series of mid-1960s advertisements that advocated a complete ban on the sale of nonkosher meat produced with shackle-and-hoist methods—especially that which came from animals killed for the kosher market. "About 90% of all ritual slaughter is sold without kosher designation," one advertisement explained. "The cruelty, then, continues because the non-kosher consumer unknowingly pays for it through his meat purchases." Making it impossible to sell ritually slaughtered meat to the nonkosher market would, it claimed, force slaughterhouses "to modernize the ritual." What "modern ritual slaughter" meant, the advertisement explained, was what had happened in Sweden, where rabbis allegedly permitted preslaughter stunning. The Friends of Animals sought no less than changing Jewish ritual practices to comply with its vision of humane slaughter. Short of that, its proposal would have rendered kosher slaughter impossibly expensive.[16]

Despite their professed sympathy for Jews, the Friends of Animals shared Francis Rawley's early twentieth-century views that Jewish practices were backward and antimodern. The very text of their preferred legislation labeled kosher meat as "the product of a ritual method of slaughter," while emphasizing that it was "modern slaughter" that produced nonkosher meat. The opposition of ritual with modern, past with present, Jewish with Christian, had echoes elsewhere in the Friends' rhetoric. Under the banner "The compassionate civilization," the Friends declared that "civilized people" did not kill animals "without first making them insensible to pain." Jews, then, were neither modern nor civilized if they clung to an outdated belief that the animal needed to be conscious before undergoing *shechita*.[17]

Under this pressure, the Jewish community split along denominational lines, much as it had in 1958. Some Reform rabbis, such as Rabbi Eagan Kullman, endorsed the Friends of Animals campaign; other Reform and Conservative rabbis backed a more moderate bill endorsed by the ASPCA. The Orthodox were the most determined opponents, with Rabbi Pinchas Teitz as their leading spokesperson. In a competing advertisement (sponsored by the Greater New York Association of Meat and Poultry Dealers), he once again defended *shechita* as humane, much as he had done before the U.S. Senate, and branded efforts by the Friends to force changes in Jewish ritual practices "un-American." But he went further and mini-mized the problems of shackle-and-hoist methods (much as Rabbi Lewin had done in 1958), claiming that the animal was in the air no more than forty-five seconds and that any injuries suffered were far less than took place in hunting, an activity banned by Jewish law.[18] Since the Friends of Animals also opposed hunting, his latter contrast was little more than an effort to deflect attention from his weak position; no doubt Rabbi Teitz's dismissal of the pain endured by a one-thousand-pound animal hung upside down by one leg did little to placate ritual slaughter's critics.

Efforts to restrict kosher slaughter beyond the definitions of federal legislation consistently failed, in large part due to sustained Jewish oppo-sition. State measures that did pass followed the federal Humane Slaugh-ter Act's language but extended its requirement to all meat produced under a particular state's inspection system. In the late 1970s, humane organizations strengthened the act by mandating humane practices in all federally inspected plants, not only those seeking to do business with the government. The measure secured Jewish support by also strengthening protection of ritual slaughter with the addition of the phrase "handling in connection with such slaughter" to clause 2b that defined ritual slaughter as humane. With this step, the legislation took the peculiar form it still has, with ritual slaughter and the handling associated with it classified both as exempt and as humane.

ENTER TEMPLE GRANDIN

Grandin's personal campaign to improve treatment of animals bound for slaughter began in the shadow of these national debates over *shechita*. In 1977 she toured Spencer's main Iowa plant to observe how it han-dled kosher slaughter; the experience gave her nightmares for days. Many years later she could relate the horrific "frantic bellowing of cattle" that were shackled and hoisted while conscious, then stretched sideways by a rope secured with a clamp in the animal's nose to expose its neck for the *shochet*. Their terror "could be heard throughout the office and parking lot," she later recalled.[19]

Repelled as she was by this example of kosher slaughter, Grandin none-theless appreciated the economics behind such inhumane practices. This was the era when Harry Kassel was recruiting often marginal plants to produce kosher meat on an occasional basis to make up the loss of slaugh-tering facilities in the East. Viewing the industry in the late 1970s, Gran-din noted that "some plants jump in and out of the kosher market" and thus relied on shackle-and-hoist methods as those entailed "only minor modifications" of their killing floors. Even the plants that consistently killed for the kosher market also resisted the capital investment needed to end shackle-and-hoist methods, as much of the meat they produced entered the nonkosher market and had to compete on price with that produced in nonkosher facilities. Until plants found that "humaneness makes a profit," the economics of the industry hampered improvements to kosher slaughter.[20]

As Grandin toured the plants that killed for the kosher market in the late 1970s, she saw scattered examples of more humane practices. The small Sunflower Beef plant in York, Nebraska, used an upright restraining pen originally developed by the Jewish-owned Cross Broth-ers Company in 1963. The ASPCA purchased the patent shortly there-after and made it freely available, leading this device to become known as the ASPCA pen. It used a small enclosure to restrain the animal while a chin lift pulled its head up to expose the neck for the *shochet*. After his cut, a belly lift inside kept the animal from collapsing; only after it was unconscious would a chain attached to its hoof lift the animal out of the pen. The ASPCA pen was too slow for larger slaughterhouses, as it could handle no more than eighty animals per hour, but the oppor-tunity to closely observe kosher slaughtering methods on more placid creatures—even though they were conscious—persuaded Grandin that *shechita* was humane. "If the cut is made correctly and the knife has no nicks the animal feels little or no pain," she concluded in 1977. Seeing kosher slaughter as humane, indeed as more humane than some conven-tional stunning methods, made Grandin a remarkably effective advocate for improvements in its technology. Her commitment to better treatment of animals, and unequivocal endorsement of Jewish ritual practices, gave her the knowledge and the authority to initiate major changes in kosher slaughter.[21]

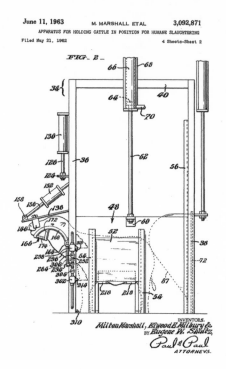

June 11, 1963   M. MARSHALL ETAL   3,092,871
APPARATUS FOR HOLDING CATTLE IN POSITION FOR HUMANE SLAUGHTERING
Filed May 21, 1962   4 Sheets-Sheet 2

FIGURE 8.3 ASPCA Humane Slaughter Pen patent, 1963.

Her initial breakthrough was at the same packinghouse in Spencer, Iowa, that had once given her nightmares. Acquisition of the plant by Land O'Lakes (a dairy farmers' cooperative seeking to expand into the meat business) allowed for an influx of capital to pay for redesign of its slaughtering process. Supervised by Grandin, the plant installed a curving no-slip walkway that guided cattle to a new automatic system, developed by the venerable Cincinnati Butchers equipment company with the intent of "eliminating agitation and bruising of the animals." Two "obliquely angled conveyors which form a V" gently restrained the animal such that it moved forward with its feet off the ground until reaching the slaughtering box. There a worker manipulated a clamshell device with precise hydraulic controls to hold the calm animal's head in the optimal position for the *shochet* to cut its throat. Only then was the shackled animal pulled to the overhead chain that moved it into the plant's conventional dressing operations. The new system could handle over two hundred cattle per hour, far faster than previous humane kosher slaughter technology and competitive with conventional packinghouse operations. A few years later Grandin modified this technology for calves and sheep by using parallel moving double rails to similarly convey smaller animals through the slaughtering process.[22]

Grandin's experience with this new technology (which she helped to develop) reinforced her belief that *shechita* was humane. Operating the restraint system herself in one plant, she observed that the animals "don't even feel the super-sharp blade as it touches their skin." If the *shochet* cuts properly, "the cattle do not realize what has happened" and stand quietly until they collapse into unconsciousness. And she contrasted the nightmares induced by the shackle-and-hoist methods with the sensations she experienced "operating the controls" that positioned each animal for slaughter. "I felt peaceful and calm," she explained to the industry readership of *Meat and Poultry* magazine.[23]

With this initial success, Grandin was able to persuade meatpacking companies to install her equipment in other kosher slaughter plants. Her technology replaced shackle-and-hoist methods in the John Morrell plant in Sioux Falls, South Dakota, the Utica Veal facility in Marcy, New York, and the packinghouses that supplied meat for Hebrew National hot dogs. Some of the small kosher beef slaughterhouses also moved in a more humane direction by installing the ASPCA restraining pen, since it was far less expensive that Grandin's conveyor systems. While Grandin remained concerned that the ASPCA pens permitted a greater margin for operator error, they were nonetheless a marked improvement from shackle-and-hoist methods.[24]

Grandin's endorsement of kosher slaughter won her the cooperation of the skeptical Orthodox community, especially the Orthodox Union. Rabbis were moved by her vigorous defense of *shechita* in journals oriented to both meatpacking companies and animal rights organizations, as well as her sustained efforts to persuade packing firms to accommodate kosher requirements. During the 1980s the OU worked closely with Grandin to end shackle-and-hoist methods, especially after Menachem Genack took over as its head and greatly expanded its kosher certification program. Rabbi Genack himself endorsed Grandin "as a very honest person" who "doesn't have an agenda against *shechita* in any way." Even Rabbi Teitz's Elizabeth plant installed the ASPCA pen, a development he endorsed even with his long resistance to humane slaughter legislation.[25]

"Why [do] the Rabbayim listen to a gentile, autistic woman?" Ben Wolfson asked rhetorically in the pages of the Hasidic Hebrew-language journal *Mishpacha*. He explained to readers that part of the answer is "she knows the laws of *shechita*" and the technology she developed "makes halachic sense." But he offered a more profound reason: her unequivocal public endorsement of the "sacred" approach of the Jews to animal slaughter in venues and to audiences that would be influenced by her views. He particularly credited Grandin for explaining to non-Jews that Judaism only permitted specially trained *shochetim* who lead a "blameless life" to kill animals and thus prevented those involved in *shechita* from becoming "numbed, callous, or cruel." Such a ringing endorsement in a book "written by a gentile for a gentile audience" meant a great deal to the observant and helped to create "a minor revolution in the way *shechita* is done."[26]

Grandin's successes, however, were built on the shifting sands of a meat industry undergoing a wrenching transformation. During the 1980s a new oligopoly of three firms—IBP, ConAgra, and Cargill—took control of American meat production. Armour, Swift, and Wilson, three of the oldest national meatpacking firms, all went bankrupt, as did many smaller companies, their plants sold and traded to the survivors—or closed entirely. Bitter strikes lost, causing union agreements to lapse and wages to plummet 30 percent between 1980 and 1990; these developments vitiated many of Grandin's accomplishments. One after another, the plants she persuaded to adopt her kosher slaughter technology went under.

The first fatality was Spencer, the plant brought into the kosher meat business by Harry Kassel, then made the showcase for Grandin's advanced humane slaughter conveyor system. Plant management had introduced the new technology under the shadow of litigation by former union members who had been laid off, and then not recalled, after Land O'Lakes bought the slaughterhouse in 1978. With the change of ownership, the company asserted that the union, the United Food and Commercial Workers, no longer had collective bargaining rights. While Land O'Lakes lawyers fended off union litigators, it shifted production from partially kosher to entirely kosher and decided to invest $1.3 million on plant improvements—funding the new kosher slaughter machinery.[27]

Land O'Lakes's timing couldn't have been worse. Shortly after the ownership change, Harry Kassel's retirement deprived the firm's management of a reliable broker for its kosher meat. Moreover, a conscious decision to avoid hiring former union members lead to employment of unreliable workers; to keep the plant's 220 production jobs fully staffed, the plant had to hire 525 people in the course of one year. Productivity suffered accordingly, at the same time that distribution of its main products became more challenging. In May 1982 local newspapers reported that "the Kosher market for Spencer is down" and that Land O'Lakes was trying to sell the plant. After limping along for two more years, the plant finally closed for good. In 1985 a U.S. district court finally ruled in favor of the union, but, as Land O'Lakes had left the meatpacking industry, there was no redress for the workers involved.[28] It was an ignominious end for Grandin's showcase kosher operation.

Her other major success stories also did not survive. Utica Veal closed, as its owners could make more money selling the land to developers than operating a slaughterhouse. John Morell shuttered its plant in Sioux Falls, South Dakota (once called "the most humane kosher facility in the United States"), as the company could not compete in the beef market against the new leading firms. By the early 1990s the only kosher plants using Grandin's high-speed kosher slaughtering technology were producing regular (not *glatt*) beef for Hebrew National hot dogs—meat that was not accepted as sufficiently kosher by any of the main certification agencies. The economics of the small facilities that used the ASPCA cage for kosher slaughtering remained precarious as well; even the plant in Elizabeth, New Jersey, once supervised by Rabbi Teitz closed in the early 1990s. Between the costs of installing special kosher meat–slaughtering technology and the vast amount of meat killed with kosher methods that could not be sold to *glatt* consumers, it was simply not worthwhile for mainstream meat producers to maintain a kosher line.[29]

With limited options in the United States, kosher meat distributors such as Alle Processing looked outside the country. *Kashrus Magazine* reported in December 1992 that, due to "supply shortages, the OU and others are currently obtaining meat from Central America" where, the magazine admitted, standards for humane slaughter "are not currently acceptable." Uruguay and Argentina emerged as important sources for *glatt* kosher meat by the end of the 1990s—and produced by aging plants using technology even worse than that decried by humane slaughter advocates in the 1950s.[30] Even as fewer and fewer American kosher meat producers used shackle-and-hoist methods, the difficulty of profitably producing *glatt* kosher beef forced suppliers to look to other nations where shackle-and-hoist methods remained in place. Cattle slaughter through this inhumane method remained essential for meeting domestic *glatt* meat demand, but would now come from outside the purview of U.S. slaughtering regulations.

Sadly, the outcome was exactly what Rabbi Teitz had prophesied in his 1958 testimony: the development of a separate Jewish meat industry. The higher requirement of *glatt* kosher contributed significantly to this development, as that made it even less desirable for large non-Jewish companies to enter the observant Jewish market. But abandonment of shackle-and-hoist mattered as well, as the alternative humane kosher slaughtering technology was sufficiently different from nonkosher operations to create a strong disincentive for the large meatpacking companies to invest in it. While some small companies continued to contract their facilities for kosher slaughter, these were marginal operations that did not attempt to compete with the dominant national firms and could not, on their own, generate a sufficient amount of *glatt* kosher meat.

Here was a troubling paradox. At the same time that processed kosher food was increasingly integrated into America's diet and its requirements observed by many of American's leading food companies, kosher beef intended for observant Jewish consumption was, in effect, expelled from mainstream meat production and distribution channels. And, to satisfy their observant customers, the most successful Jewish firm would play down ethical considerations including humane slaughter and find itself subject to much of the same moral opprobrium at the beginning of the new millennium that *shechita* had once earned at the turn of the twentieth century.

THE RISE AND FALL OF AGRIPROCESSORS

Harry Kassel had left the meat industry by the early 1980s, but his influence owed much to the entry of what would become a main supplier of kosher meat throughout the 1990s and early twenty-first century. Aaron Rubashkin, founder of the Agriprocessors meatpacking company, owned a successful butcher shop in Brooklyn and was an associate of Kassel's father-in-law. Rubashkin closely followed Kassel's success and even worked with a rendering company that Kassel established in the 1970s. "Rubashkin only wanted one thing," Kassel recalled. "He wanted me to come in with him as a partner. He was going to start this business out West if he could get a partner like me." Kassel wasn't interested—as he was a nonobservant Reform Jew, Rubashkin's affiliation with the Chabad Lubavitcher Hasidim made him wary of a partnership. "It couldn't lead to a good operation," he reflected.[31]

As butcher shop owner, Rubashkin was aware of Kassel's success at Spencer Foods industrializing *glatt* beef production. Using vacuum packaging for *glatt* meat that had been kashered—soaked and salted— allowed Kassel to escape the geographic boundaries imposed by the seventy-two-hour rule that had limited *glatt* production to the small packinghouses located in close proximity to consumers. Rubashkin saw an opportunity in Kassel's model, especially after Kassel himself left the business and the Midwestern packinghouses firms he had drawn into kosher meat production collapsed in the turmoil of the 1980s.

The plant closings of that decade gave Rubashkin his chance. In 1987 he acquired the shuttered Hygrade plant in Postville, Iowa (aided by a $20,000 grant from a town desperate to land a new employer), and opened a *glatt* kosher beef operation under his son Sholom's supervision. Learning from Kassel's late 1970s innovations, the Rubaskins installed a highly mechanized salting and soaking department to produce fully kashered meat that could be vacuum packed and frozen, eliminating pressures to get the meat to consumers within seventy-two hours. But they took Kassel's concept one step further by creating consumer-sized packages that were sealed and branded with the OU certification mark so they could be made available for sale without the need for additional processing and rabbinic supervision. Agriprocessors warehouses in New York City and Miami served as distribution hubs to local stores and regular deliveries to California and other Jewish communities served by Lubavitch *shluchim* gave Agriprocessors a national distribution network that connected directly with food stores wishing to sell kosher meat—even if they did not employ kosher butchers to prepare it.

Agriprocessors's approach made the company and the Rubashkin family heroes among observant Jews. Its sealed, shrink-wrapped Aaron's Best packages of *glatt* beef could be found throughout the United States in stores selling kosher products, and notably so in places with small Jewish populations that had particularly suffered during the decades of uncertain supply. Kashering and vacuum packaging of consumer cuts in Postville solved the uncertainties created by distribution and salved fears of fraudulent kosher meat. While the company did not emphasize its nonglatt regular kosher line, it sold profitably through private label arrangements with retail chains such as Trader Joe's. The company added a chicken processing operation and reportedly leveraged its market share by requiring retailers to obtain both beef and poultry from Agriprocessors distributors if they wanted either. Sales reached $80 million in 1997 after a decade of operation and more than doubled five years later to $180 million, aided by the opening of additional plants in Uruguay and Argentina and a small one not far away in Gordon, Nebraska. To maintain a sufficient supply of *shochetim*, Agriprocessors flew them in from the East Coast, and at times Israel, for six- to twelve-month stints. Kosher food stores such as Little Neck Meats on Long Island (renamed Mazur's Kosher Marketplace after the store's owner) could choose to get fresh beef from small Eastern packinghouses such as Star-K-supervised Trueth Packing in Baltimore since it had butchers on-site to create consumer-sized cuts. But outside urban centers with large observant populations, the Agriprocessors's Aaron Best brand became the principal means for obtaining *glatt* kosher meat.[32]

Such success depended on substantial investments in the salting and soaking, packaging, and distribution operations; similar improvements were not made to slaughtering. Rubashkin rebuffed entreaties by Grandin to use her double-rail technology and also rejected the OU-preferred alternative of the ASPCA restraint cage. The company instead installed an updated version of the Weinberg pen, a restraining cage that rotated

180 degrees so that the animal was upside down when the *shochet* cut its throat. Modern improvements provided for a hydraulic rotation mechanism, but in other respects this device, called the Facomia Pen, differed only marginally from the original early twentieth-century technology.[33]

Temple Grandin did not approve of this mechanism, even as she granted it was superior to shackle-and-hoist methods. Her objections were rooted in her career observing animal behavior in which she had noticed again and again that "animals resist being turned sideways or onto their backs." She also closely observed the pen's use and noted that its "disorienting" effects led cattle to hold their necks rigid while inverted, a reflection of their desire to return to an upright position. The time needed for the Facomia pen to rotate 180 degrees meant cattle had to be restrained almost twice as long as in the ASPCA pen, further increasing their discomfort. And, with unerring foresight, Grandin warned that use of this technology could weaken the defense of *shechita*, as "the average person on the street is more likely to dislike the idea of inverting an animal onto its back."[34]

Doubtless financial concerns were enough for the Rubashkin management to reject Grandin's double-rail conveyor system, as it cost $250,000 to install one that could handle a slaughtering pace of a hundred cattle per hour. Yet there was little difference in the price of the ASPCA and Facomia pens; new ones cost $35,000, while used versions could cost as little as $5,000. An important *halachic* dispute lay behind the Rubashkin's decision—a view that only *shechita munachas* (where the animal is on its back) was permissible for kosher slaughter. [35]

Shechita munachas was the traditional method for kosher slaughter. The age-old casting technique placed the animal's head on the ground while its hindquarters were elevated, allowing the *shochet's* killing stroke to proceed downward. The Weinberg pen allowed for similar movement, as the animals was inverted before *shechita*. The development of the ASPCA pen in the 1960s, and its dissemination in the 1970s, generated a debate among rabbinic authorities over whether the upward stroke it required violated *derasah*, the rule prohibiting placing pressure on the knife during *shechita*; Grandin's double-rail system posed the same *halachic* issue. The OU, with Rabbi Moshe Feinstein's encouragement, felt *derasah* could be avoided by using a head restraint (designed by Grandin) that restrained a steer's head with its jaw parallel to the floor. The Israeli chief rabbinate, however, insisted that it would only certify cattle slaughtered in an inverted position, and since Agriprocessors wanted access to the Israeli market, it would not install the ASPCA pen.[36]

Reliance on the Facomia device may have been an acceptable kosher practice that did not hurt it in the observant market, but it placed Agriprocessors in a weak competitive position within the meatpacking industry. A substantial majority of its meat went into the nonkosher market, including the nonkosher hindquarters and forequarters from cattle that failed the *bodek's* inspection. The company also had to find customers for the hides, intestines, and other animal parts—another 30 percent of the animal's total weight. Able to kill no more than fifty-five cattle per hour, and with costs well above those typical in meatpacking due to requirements of kosher slaughter, it was a challenge for Agriprocessors to compete in the nonkosher market with the giant firms whose plants could slaughter close to four hundred per hour. Even if it had employed the ASPCA pen, its competitive disadvantages would have remained.

Its vulnerable position in the meatpacking industry was invisible to writer Stephen Bloom when he visited the company in the late 1990s. The company was prosperous, "a dream come true for the locals." Even with the cultural conflicts between the effervescent Brooklyn Hasidim and reticent local Lutherans, the money it generated had kept Postville from turning into a town "of boarded-up shops on Main Street." Every week its refrigerated trucks delivered 1.85 million pounds of beef, lamb, and poultry throughout the country; in fact, "the meat was so prized that it was even flown to Jerusalem and Tel Aviv." The Rubashkin family and other Hasidim who moved there had scooped up the largest homes and turned them into mansions in the neighborhood Bloom termed "Kosher Hill." And in the aftermath of the annexation vote that formed the fulcrum to his book, and that added the company to the town's tax rolls, the Rubashkins remained despite earlier threats to leave. Even if the company now had to pay property taxes to Postville, business was just too good to change what they were doing.[37]

Unbeknownst to Bloom, and reporters fascinated by his story of cultural conflict, his book was a story of Agriprocessors at its peak. The company's underlying competitive weaknesses soon eroded the foundations for its success. The same year that Bloom's book came out,

Agriprocessors quietly established a $35 million line of credit from First
Bank Business Capital; it made heavy use of these funds as the company
"was always cash-starved." Three years later the cattle market turned
against meat processors, as prices rocketed upward, increasing 30 percent between 2002 and 2003 and then continuing to climb for the next
decade. As its cash needs became more severe, Agriprocessors began to
delay payments to its cattle suppliers, in violation of the federal Stockyards Act.[38]

The company suffered a more visible blow to its fortunes in December 2004, when investigators for the activist group PETA secretly filmed
gruesome footage of its slaughtering operations. People for the Ethical
Treatment of Animals had targeted mistreatment of animals in the meatpacking industry for many years; its clandestine investigation in Postville
followed a rebuff by Agriprocessors to initial inquiries in May 2003. In
nauseating detail the video showed cattle with slashed throats repeatedly
struggling to upright positions after being dumped from the Facomia
pen following *shechita*. One wandered around the filthy killing floor and
pathetically tried to hide behind the rotating pen, only to finally collapse
at the same time as another animal tumbled out of it. The footage also
showed workers removing the animals' trachea and esophagus following
the *shochet's* cut; some then struggled to their feet with long strips of
flesh dangling from open wounds. Deeply disturbing coverage in major
television news shows, the *New York Times*, and media throughout the
world once again placed kosher slaughter in uncomfortable juxtaposition
with cruelty toward animals—and put Orthodox Jewish organizations
in the untenable position of defending an obviously cruel slaughtering
process as kosher.[39]

Company attorney Nathan Lewin simply defended Agriprocessors
as a victim of anti-Semitism. Titling a December 15 opinion piece "The
Assault on *Shechita*" left little doubt as to his position. Denying that the
video showed anything improper, he alleged that forcing Agriprocessors
to change its "most traditional form of kosher slaughter" (a reference to
the Facomia pen) would be followed by efforts "to eliminate the kosher
slaughter practice in the plants that use the ASPCA restraining pen."
The Orthodox Union waffled under the pressure: vigorously defending the *kashrus* of the Agriprocessors slaughtering methods, but also

persuading the company to end the second cut and removal of the trachea and esophagus. The OU was in an especially vulnerable position, since it must have been aware for some time of company procedures, but remained silent.[40]

Temple Grandin did not equivocate. "This tape shows atrocious procedures that are NOT performed in any other kosher operation," she announced in a widely quoted statement posted on her website. Consistent with her practice over the previous quarter-century, she was careful to simultaneously defend *shechita* while decrying cruelty toward animals by distinguishing between Agriprocessors and other kosher beef plants. She pointed out that prior to *shechita* 50 percent of the animals in the video were "vocalizing"—bellowing—indicating that they were being shocked by electric prods to move them into the Facomia pen. Again separating out Agriprocessors as an aberrant case, she explained that "in a well-run kosher plant" no more than 5 percent of cattle should exhibit such behavior. Her major criticism, though, was the removal of the trachea when the cattle were "fully conscious," as "the pain of having their inner tissues cut and pulled" probably postponed a lapse into unconsciousness and prolonged the animal's agony.[41]

The disturbing second cut remained poorly justified. Menachem Genack explained it as a way to speed the drainage of blood, but did not add why this unusual procedure was necessary at all. The true explanation was all too simple: to increase the speed of the killing floor and permit more animals to be processed each day. Kosher plants that used the ASPCA pen followed Temple Grandin's recommendation that following *shechita* the animal remain in the head restraint for fifteen to thirty seconds so it would lapse into insensibility due to the massive drainage of blood and collapse; only then was it shackled for movement into the dressing operations. The Agriprocessors second cut, and the speedier drainage of blood it was intended to generate, was an effort to make this delay unnecessary. The PETA video showed the Facomia pen began rotating cattle back to an upright position immediately following *shechita* and the second cut, rather than wait the recommended time to permit blood loss to cause insensibility. This seemingly small increase in killing floor speed would have allowed the plant to expand production by sixty to a hundred more cattle each day.

Critics of Agriprocessors had the upper hand in the debate, but by viewing the case simply as a breakdown in ethics they did not appreciate that it also may have been a sign of the company's deteriorating financial position. Caught in a vise between its relatively inefficient slaughtering practices and steadily increasing cattle prices, the company was seeking to improve its income and reduce expenses by any means at its disposal. Increasing production speeds was only the most visible of a number of strategies.

Cutting cattle acquisition costs was another means to improve competitive position. Agriprocessors had neither the option available to New York's interwar beef plants to sell nonkosher meat to the city's white tablecloth steakhouses nor Harry Kassel's connections with high-end institutional customers willing to buy prime loin beef. The company instead went to the low end of the cattle market. It created a cut-rate nonkosher brand called Iowa Best Beef to distribute through food wholesalers and supermarkets such as Wal-Mart and Pathmark. For the 2005 Superbowl, for example, Wisconsin food distributor Family Farms Inc. promoted sales of discounted Iowa Best Beef rib eye and sirloin steaks, along with equivalent inexpensive options from other companies, such as Rochester Meat's "Miscut" pork chops and Abbyland's Beef Stick "Ends & Pieces." Much of Iowa Best Beef fell toward the bottom of the USDA's Select grade (itself the bottom third of all graded beef) with intramuscular fat scores (an indication of marbling or tenderness) beginning at the lower end of Slight, the seventh of nine rankings for meat quality. Since Iowa Best Beef came from the same animals as the company's kosher products, its place in federal grading standards is evidence of the cheaper cattle the company turned to in its difficulties.[42]

Securing labor for the lowest price was the other principal cost reduction strategy. Agriprocessors entered the meatpacking industry during a decade when union bargaining fell apart and real wages plummeted. Since its manufacturing operations were relatively inefficient, Agriprocessors needed to pay even less than the already depressed industry pay scale. When Stephen Bloom visited the plant in the late 1990s, the workers were refugees from the eastern European countries that had recently seen the collapse of communism: "Russians, Ukrainians, Kazakhstanians, Poles." Men just off the plane eagerly took jobs at $6.00 an hour in Postville.

"We couldn't believe our luck," one Ukrainian immigrant named Leonid told Bloom.[43]

The supply of European refugee labor soon dried up, as Leonid and his cohort secured legal status, learned English, and sought better opportunities. To replace them, Agriprocessors turned to the large Latino labor market that already was supplying much of the Midwestern meatpacking industry. Finding workers willing to work for starting pay of $6.25 an hour was still a challenge. The national hourly median wage for meatpackers was $10.43 in 2006; even the lowest tenth percentile earned $7.67. Immigrants with green cards or legal working papers could go two hours southwest to the plant in Marshalltown, Iowa, where experienced workers earned $13.35, or to another packing house four hours away in Worthington, Minnesota, that offered a starting pay of $11.50. The only workers Agriprocessors could recruit were those unable to get these better jobs—because they did not have legal immigration status.[44]

Hiring undocumented workers, and glossing over signs that they did not have a legal right to work, became company policy as early as spring 2002. The Rubashkin management ignored warnings from the company's human resources manager that more than two hundred workers had been mentioned in "no match" letters from the Social Security Administration, an indication that the social security numbers they had presented were fraudulent. The company also continued to hire applicants only able to present pink-colored Resident Alien Cards even after a warning from federal Immigration and Customs Enforcement agents that they were no longer valid. In the fall of 2007, the ICE documented that 735 of the company's 968 employees had "false or suspect" Social Security numbers.[45]

When Nathaniel Popper researched his 2006 exposé on Agriprocessors hiring practices, he found workers who were more refugee labor than immigrant. A worker using the name Manuel paid a smuggler $4,500 to get him across the border and then spent an additional $100 for a Social Security card; another going by the name Jaunita similarly had crossed the border a year ago and only found work in Postville. These recent arrivals with dubious credentials were shut out of the plants in Marshalltown and Worthington. Immigration raids in meatpacking plants in the mid-1990s, and prosecution of firms for employment of undocumented labor, had created an incentive for employers to cooperate with the federal E-verify program, which required them to check the citizenship status of job applicants. Too ready acceptance of clearly forged documents also incurred sanctions, so Latino workers with clean documentation were in the best position to find employment. Another round of immigration raids in 2006 and 2007 reminded firms of the penalties for hiring workers without legal status. With plenty of undocumented men and women from Mexico and Guatemala continuing to come into the United States looking for work, the lax controls at Postville were inviting, even if the pay was atrocious.[46]

With the company's financial position continuing to deteriorate in 2007 (perhaps exacerbated by cattle prices rising to over $90 per live hundredweight early that year), low wages and low-grade livestock purchases were no longer enough to keep cash flowing in and out. As court investigations would later find, the company turned to systematic fraud to raise money. Late payments to cattle suppliers, an infringement of federal law for which the company had been sanctioned in 2002, became a systematic practice. Between the fall of 2007 and April 2008, the court identified ninety-one instances of late payments—clearly an effort to hold on to cash.[47]

A more complex fraudulent scheme inflated the company's ability to draw on its lines of credit with local banks. Under these loan agreements, the amount available to borrow was proportional to the company's cash accounts and accounts receivable; the more money on hand and owed, the more the bank would lend, reassured that their short-term loans could be paid back. Again beginning in the fall of 2007, the company systematically inflated amounts owed—accounts payable—and concealed payments already received. Orchestrated by Sholom Rubashkin, the company created false invoices that vastly overstated amounts actually owed by regular customers. Genuine payments were routinely diverted into the accounts of two unrelated Rubashkin-controlled organizations, the Kosher Community Grocery and Torah Education of Northeast Iowa, which then wrote checks to Agriprocessors. This money laundering allowed the company to have both the cash from those payments (with their source concealed) and to claim them as accounts receivable, effectively doubling (on paper) their impact on the company's bottom line.

With its books showing fictitious levels of cash reserves, the chicanery allowed the company to extract almost $30 million from its revolving credit accounts.[48]

Critics did not detect Agripricessors's financial difficulties, hidden as they were behind the Rubashkin family's personal wealth and their extensive philanthropy in Lubavitch circles. "The company's business model has been economically successful," Nathaniel Popper allowed while citing many of its legal problems in clinical journalistic language. These were ethical and moral failings, a penchant for "violating every law that's out there," as one United Food and Commercial Union vice president contended. A disregard for the law had been evident in Bloom's late 1990s account; the Agriprocessors "computer guru" told him, "I get bills and I throw them away. . . . When *I'm* ready to pay them, I'll pay them." But the systematic nature of the fraudulent activity bespoke planning, not arrogance; desperation, not business as usual. Its business model was not proving successful, weighed down as it was by the unprofitable nonkosher products that in volume constituted three-quarters of its entire output.[49]

Agriprocessors finally crashed in 2008. In May the ICE conducted a draconian raid on the plant and arrested 398 workers as undocumented immigrants. They were charged with identity fraud for improper use of social security numbers, a federal offense far more severe than violating immigration laws. Many plead guilty to immigration violations to avoid the more severe identify fraud charges and were immediately deported, often with little opportunity for legal counsel. Deprived of much of its workforce, the plant was barely able to operate. It lost $5,699,000 in the fiscal year ending June 30, 2008, an amount no doubt impacted by the disruption caused by the ICE arrests but also reflecting losses prior to the raid which had helped incite the Rubashkin management to such extreme measures.[50]

More blows fell as the company struggled to recruit enough employees to survive. Jewish organizations outraged at its treatment of immigrant workers called for a boycott of Agriprocessors meat. The Iowa attorney general filed charges of over nine thousand child labor law violations. A new PETA video documented the company once again using a second cut on cattle that had undergone *shechita*. In November Agriprocessors finally filed for bankruptcy; the federal prosecutions that followed exposed the company's many tawdry practices. Plant executives pleaded guilty to a variety of charges—violation of immigration law, money laundering, etc.—and two years later Sholom Rubashkin received a twenty-seven-year sentence for orchestration of financial fraud. The Agriprocessors moment was over.

THE ETHICAL QUESTION

The company's collapse was an utter disaster. The massive deportations wiped out the gains, and the dreams, of hundreds of immigrant workers. Postville plunged into an economic and social crisis after two decades of recovery. Kosher meat became harder to find and more expensive. The Rubashkin personal fortune was destroyed, the family disgraced by Sholom's long prison sentence.

Temple Grandin deserves much of the credit for averting wide challenges to *shechita* in the United States after the Agriprocessors scandals—in part because she was so tough on the company. She had given the plant good marks when brought there in 2006 to observe its reformed slaughter practices, but waded back into the debate when a PETA film made in August 2008 showed a return of the second cuts that had taken place in 2004, which Grandin had thought were eliminated. "This gouging second cut would definitely cause the animal pain," she told PETA in 2008, in text superimposed on the video itself, and, outraged at the deception, she added in other media interviews that the plant's killing floor needed to be under twenty-four-hour video surveillance and audited by an independent third party. "They act good when you are there, and they don't act good when your back is turned," she told the *Jewish Journal*. Yet she continued to distinguish Agriprocessors' behavior from other kosher slaughterhouses "that do things right." Repeating her long-held opinion, she explained to another newspaper in September 2008, "I have no problem with ritual slaughter when it is done correctly." Her views clearly influenced PETA, an organization committed to ending use of animals for human food entirely. The organization did not use Agriprocessors to tout the need to end Jewish slaughter; instead it described the company (in terms echoing Grandin's) as an exception to the way "Kosher slaughter is intended to minimize animals' suffering." It even echoed Grandin's exact language when it concluded, "performed properly, *shechita* appears all but painless and quickly renders the animal unconscious." Thus after Agriprocessors's demise there was no campaign against *shechita* more generally, as some Orthodox Jews had predicted.[51]

A similar tolerance was not the case in Europe, where animal rights groups pressed relentlessly for legislation prohibiting ritual slaughter. Agriprocessors did not cause the new assault on Jewish practices, but its deplorable record, including mistreatment of animals, was a useful example to invoke for critics of *shechita*. These organizations fought *shechita* as well as *dhabihah*, Muslim religious slaughter, which similarly required animals to be conscious when their throats were cut. In a chilling reminder of the early twentieth century, animal rights groups aligned with conservative and far-right political movements to propose restrictions on Jewish and Muslim practices in national legislatures and to force a debate in the European Parliament.

Among Jews, the Agriprocessors wreckage gave them something domestic to argue about with an intensity ordinarily reserved for disagreements over Israel. The district court's severe twenty-seven-year sentence to Sholom Rubashkin for financial fraud was salt to this wound. Sentenced not long after the 2008 financial meltdown in which the bankers responsible mostly walked free, even his critics cringed at the disparity in treatment. The scarcity of previously easy-to-obtain kosher beef gave a sharp edge to competing assessments of Agriprocessors and Rubashkin since the consequences of its collapse were painfully evident.

At bottom were ethical questions: what behavior was permissible by Jews in seeking to fulfill the requirements of their religion? Was Agriprocessors a success because it made kosher meat so much more available than it had been for many years, or was it a stain on Jewish honor because of the methods it had used? What ethical constraints outside of kosher law limited pursuit of ritual observance of dietary requirements?

I wish I could have talked about all this with my mother, to bring her training in ethics and law to bear on these issues. She had always despaired at my lack of interest in the course work she had followed for her doctorate in philosophy; instead I had opted for history and the concrete. But it was too late for that conversation; she died shortly after we watched the Grandin biography together. Then again, sometimes there are no answers, only opinions. For Jews conscious of their identity as Jews, these questions—and the debates they provoked—would cast a new shadow over the procurement of kosher food.

CONCLUSION

KOSHER ETHICS/ETHICAL KOSHER?

THE COLLAPSE of Agriprocessors was a watershed for American Jews and kosher food. Guilty pleas by company administrators, the mountain of incriminating evidence produced in court proceedings, and the damning videos obtained by PETA irrefutably proved the company's guilt. While Orthodox organizations protested Sholom Rubashkin's long sentence, and the Lubavitch stubbornly insisted on his innocence, most Jews were appalled that the largest producer of kosher meat had followed such unethical business practices. The arguments over this issue grew to include Jews from all major denominations, including Reform Jews who had shown little interest in kosher food for a century. The debacle thus forced Jews to reexamine the relationship between ethics and kosher law.

Ethical concerns were central to Judaism from its inception. However, *defining* Judaism principally by its ethics emerged among the rabbis and religious leaders of the nineteenth century who would create Reform Judaism. They sought to minimize the religion's long preoccupation with ritual practices and to create a Judaism more compatible with secular society. In the late nineteenth century, American Jewish Reform leaders broke decisively with tradition in their Pittsburgh Platform, which, among other precepts, rejected dietary rules, as observance was "apt rather to obstruct than to further modern spiritual elevation." Instead, the platform emphasized that the principal "duty" of Jews was "to participate in the great task of modern times, to solve, on the basis of justice and righteousness, the problems presented by the contrasts and evils of the present organization of society."[1]

Even though we were raised within Conservative Judaism, I had some familiarity with the Reform approach through the Ethical Culture Society, whose schools I attended from fourth grade through high school. Founded by Felix Adler (whose father was an architect of American Reform Judaism), the Ethical Culture schools were nominally secular, but in fact saturated with a Jewish ethos. We had weekly ethics classes devoted to discussions of contemporary issues; and, as I attended these sessions between 1967 and 1975, this meant civil right, Vietnam, Israel, poverty—indeed, all the social issues of this turbulent period in American history. Kosher practices were, so far as I could tell, not followed; there was always milk to drink with our bologna sandwiches. Grapes, however, were available only episodically in high school due to the United Farm Workers boycotts.

Ethics also formed a central component of the Judaism I absorbed from my family. In their 1947 book *Faith Through Reason*, my mother's parents, Charlie and Bertie Schwartz, devoted an entire chapter to the "mission" of the Jews, which they defined as "adoption and practice by all peoples of the ethical principles revealed to the Jews by God at Mount Sinai through Moses." Although praising Jews for spreading monotheism and ethics throughout the world, my grandparents admonished readers that, until war, "the terrible scourge of mankind throughout all recorded history," was ended, and "justice, righteousness and peace . . . reign supreme," the Jews' mission was not fulfilled.[2] Unlike Reform Jews, however, they combined concern with ethics with adherence (as they saw it) to kosher law.

Agriprocessors ineluctably connected, through its misdeeds, ethics with kosher law—and with wide repercussions throughout American Judaism. Elements within each of the major Jewish denominations sought to link issues that had not previously found purchase in extended rabbinic debates about kosher food. Hasidic and mainstream Orthodox organizations pushed back, arguing that ethics were distinct from the requirements governing *kashrus*. Their major concern was to ensure kosher food's availability, regardless of what was necessary for that to take place. And, as many of the Jews concerned principally with ethical issues did not feel obliged to consume kosher food, the Orthodox organizations that had struggled to make it available felt betrayed.

Within Orthodox circles, the Uri L'Tzedek (Awaken to Justice) organization began by calling for a boycott of Agriprocessors products shortly after the 2008 immigration raid. Over the next four years it concentrated on persuading restaurant owners to display a Tav HaYosher (shield of justice) affirming their ethical treatment of employees. Among Conservative Jews, Minnesota rabbi Morris Allen launched a campaign for a Hecksher Tzedek (justice certification) after learning about the treatment of Agriprocessors workers; the Conservative Rabbinical Assembly endorsed the initiative and assumed leadership of the project. Over the next few years the initiative, renamed Magden Tzedek (to indicate it was not a rabbinic endorsement of a food's *kashrus*) asked food manufacturers already under conventional kosher certification to adhere to extensive environmental and labor standards. Both efforts sought to insert ethical considerations into kosher food provisioning.

For Reform Jews, unconcerned with kosher law as such, the Agriprocessors case intersected with widespread interest in developing alternatives to what they saw as a deeply flawed industrial food system. Hazon, founded in 1999, started as a Reform-based organization committed to organic products and local production whenever possible and framed within the rubric of Jewish ethics. Beginning with its 2008 conference, held in the midst of the Agriprocessors' collapse, Hazon added a "food justice" track; in the aftermath it sponsored practical workshops to stimulate emergence of small, local kosher meat and chicken producers who would only perform *shechita* on humanely raised animals. Eschewing the certification approach of Uri L'Tzedek and Magden Tzedek (though endorsing their efforts), Hazon sought to create Jewish initiatives around food that mirrored the activism of non-Jewish food activists. Its Community Supported Agriculture programs generated contact with local farmers and inspired new ones to begin planting crops, while its conferences sought to infuse Jewish food traditions with modern food ethics. While Hazon encouraged observance of kosher tradition, especially in animal slaughter, ecological and social justice practices received far more emphasis in its activities.

The multidenominational new Jewish food movement could draw on several evocative passages in the five books of Moses to claim a special Jewish lineage for its concerns. Leviticus 19:9 and 19:10 admonished Jews to leave the "edges of the field" and the "gleanings of your harvest" for the "poor and stranger," an admonition for charity and sharing the bounty of the land. Those angered by Agriprocessors' treatment of immigrants (and the low pay of food industry workers more generally) could cite Leviticus 19:13, "The wages of the laborer shall not remain with you until morning," and Deuteronomy 24:16, "You shall not abuse a needy and destitute laborer, whether a fellow countrymen or a stranger." Deuteronomy 22:1–22:10, especially its blunt prohibition "You shall not plow with an ox and ass together," allowed Jewish critics of industrial livestock production methods to claim the concept of *tza'ar ba'alei chayim* obligated Jews to oppose unnecessary pain and suffering of animals—such as took place at Agriprocessors.

Mainstream Orthodox organizations and the Hasidim would have none of this. In their view, ethical concerns were not pertinent to determination of a food's *kashrus*; concepts such as *tza'ar ba'alei chayim* had never been part of the rabbinic debates over kosher law. In the extended arguments over the *kashrus* of animal products such as glycerin and gelatin, for example, rabbinic and lay discussions never touched on the treatment of workers or livestock—only on whether the animals had been slaughtered in accordance with the requirements of the *Shulchan Aruch*. Rabbi Moshe Feinstein had raised an objection to the methods of raising veal as unnecessarily cruel, but still held that such an animal could produce kosher meat if it passed the inspections dictated under traditional Jewish law.[3] The Orthodox had over a millennium of tradition on their side to support their position.

Orthodox opposition to the ethical challenge was vocal and sustained. "The 'Whatever Tzedek' is simply the latest manifestation of Conservative leaders' tradition of exchanging Divine mandates for contemporary constructs," wrote Agudath Israel spokesperson Avi Safran in a blistering, sarcastic critique. "Its seal is a trained one, and its neat trick isn't balancing a ball on its nose but leading people to confuse kashrut with contemporary issues."[4] The Tav HaYosher, though originated by Orthodox rabbis and rabbinic students, fared little better. In the spring of 2012 restaurants displaying this mark found themselves threatened with a boycott; the Lubavitch seemed the source for much of this pressure. Anger at Uri L'Tzedek's 2008 call to not buy Agriprocessors products motivated many so involved. "It's time for the frum community to boycott any restaurant with this unethical Heksher," one wrote to the Orthodox e-journal *Vis Iz Neias*. "They acted unethically creating a boycott against Rubashkin." The author then included a link to a list of restaurants endorsing Tav HaYosher, appending the advice "Tell them that unless they remove it you will take your business elsewhere."[5]

Five years after the Agriprocessors debacle, both ethical seal initiatives had stalled. Not one firm signed up for a Magden Tzedek, and the number of restaurants accepting the Tav HaYosher declined following the Lubavitch boycott. Determined opposition from Orthodox organizations explains much of this outcome; producers and purveyors of kosher food naturally were loath to offend their principal market and the agencies that certified their products. But the explanations offered by these Orthodox organizations for the failure of ethical initiatives eschewed acknowledgment of their own role; instead, they claimed such add-ons to kosher certification were unnecessary and perhaps even improper. Orthodox spokesperson Menahem Lubinksy (creator of the Kosherfest trade show) alleged that firms currently under kosher certification simply were not interested, as they felt consumers only cared about "the product and the price" and not whether they "treat their workers properly." Other Orthodox critics objected to asking rabbis to rule on issues for which they were not trained. "Rabbis specialize in making decisions about law," rabbis Michael Broyde and Yitzchok Adlerstein explained in a typical comment, "not in creating new systems of rules to enforce ethical principles."[6]

The Orthodox position that ethical issues lay outside kosher law was indeed consistent with Jewish tradition. Such a recourse to tradition was, however, at odds with the celebration by industry stalwarts of the non-Jewish consumers of kosher food who did so in the belief that rabbinic endorsement meant the food was somehow better, even if they cared not a whit about Jewish religious requirements. Indeed, if much of kosher food's wider availability depended on consumers unconcerned with Jewish law, how could factors outside this legal tradition remain irrelevant? Might in time non-Jewish consumers develop doubts about kosher food's value if they learned that certification did not include consideration of ethics, environment, workers' health, and other so-called "contemporary constructs" that mattered to them?

Certainly there was plenty of evidence of consumer demand for products certified to comply with a variety of practices. After 2000, third-party audits spread in the food industry as a variety of organizations offered to certify that products were organic, GMO-free, vegan, gluten-free, made from humanely raised animals, etc. Highly profitable niche businesses emerged to take advantage of this interest, using chains such as Trader Joe's and Whole Foods to reach consumers inspecting shelves for such products or selling directly to homes through express mail services. In the 1980s socially conscious if nonobservant consumers had little more than the U or K in a circle to serve as a proxy for a product's quality; but by the twenty-first century a far greater number of symbols provided equivalent assurances—and with far more specific information.

Firms seeking a range of certifications to satisfy particular consumer preferences could consolidate compliance by signing on to Quality Assurance International's multiple audit program (MAP). Through MAP firms could secure certifications to fit almost any market niche: organic, non-GMO, gluten-free, local food sourcing, "and even social justice." Instead of firms having to arrange "separate days, separate times" for inspectors, a common record-keeping structure created a "one-stop shop" to secure permission to adorn packages with symbols that reassured consumers it met their exact preferences. Quality Assurance International contracted with the Star-K agency to assess a product's compliance with kosher law, but other symbols documented the virtues that consumers had once sought indirectly through reliance on rabbinic *heckshers*.[7]

Many of these new marks countered misunderstandings about kosher certification's reach, and in so doing reduced its implied value. Parallel certification implicitly communicated what kosher food was not—it was not GMO-free, sustainably caught, humanely raised, locally sourced, etc. Halal consumers might realize that kosher products could have been manufactured with alcohol, incompatible with their religious requirements but not a concern for observant Jews as long as its source was acceptable. Vegetarians could learn that unless a dairy symbol accompanied the kosher mark on a product it could contain fish, vegans that eggs were parve and thus could be in any type of kosher food, and GMO-free advocates that kosher certifiers had no objection to genetically modified ingredients. In a world of very specific dietary preferences, kosher was not as special as it once had been. If kosher food's nonobservant consumers learned more about the limits of kosher standards, its future might not be as promising as its proponents had claimed.

The strongest arguments from Magen Tzedek supporters stressed the benefit of strengthening kosher food's association with the values and practices signified by the new certification marks. Noting that many food processors "are adding socially responsible practices to help differentiate their brands in the marketplace," Magen Tzedek adopted principles that encompassed ethical treatment of workers and animals, improved workplace safety, and environmentally sound manufacturing practices. "Creating such standards is a win-win for the kosher food industry," Rabbi Morris Allen explained, as it would increase sales of kosher food among those who wanted to see food produced "in an ethically appropriate manner." Taking these steps would make kosher-certified more attractive, especially among the nonobservant who were the largest group of consumers purchasing kosher food.[8]

Magen Tzedek's supporters made few converts among the Orthodox. Much as the Orthodox certification organizations celebrated kosher food's attractiveness to nonobservant consumers, their very existence came from a devout commitment to facilitate religious observance by Jews by making sure kosher food was widely available. It was one thing to rhetorically invoke non-Jewish demand to persuade firms that kosher certification would be profitable; it was quite another to allow the preferences of non-Jews to influence their decisions.

Orthodox leaders focused instead on the continuing challenge of generating sufficient supply at affordable prices. Their agenda was consistent with Abraham Goldstein's concern that difficulties obtaining kosher food could lead Jews away from religious observance. The durable relationships of certification agencies with major food companies rested on their commitment to accept those firms' priorities—not to challenge them beyond what was necessary to make products kosher. Layering new and potentially burdensome requirements (e.g., higher pay for workers) atop already complex religious rules could, they feared, weaken those partnerships, make rabbinic certification less appealing, and in the end reduce access to kosher food. These were steps they would not take.

Since they didn't use kosher food in their daily diet, nonobservant Jews were not touched by anxiety over adequate supply. It was all too easy for them to turn a deaf ear to the worries of Orthodox Jews. But concerns over supply and price were legitimate. While Jews living in the dense Orthodox neighborhoods had a wide range of kosher food options, obtaining items such as meat outside those areas were challenging, especially after the demise of Agriprocessors. The vigorous discussions among observant Jews on Internet food sites offer a window into these real concerns. One participant in a spirited exchange on *chowhound.chow.com* complained that it was hard to find kosher meat other than frozen chicken as she lived near the Maryland state line in "treyf PA." And she told those living in New York that they should be "grateful for the ability to live a kosher life without going on expeditions." New Yorkers in this forum could get *glatt* kosher meat, but if they shopped at supermarkets acceptable to the local rabbis, prices were double those for equivalent nonkosher cuts—a greater disparity than in the 1950s. Daily discussions of price variations between stores, revelations of great bargains, debates over whether a store's lower prices reflected an unreliable certification, complaints that high prices at rabbinically endorsed stores reflected a kosher monopoly, celebration when the Five Towns Costco began carrying kosher meat: all reflected intense anxiety over access to adequate and affordable kosher supplies.[9]

The Orthodox Jewish press also closely followed worrying challenges to *shechita's* very legality in other nations—efforts to ban it outright in places such as Poland, France, and New Zealand, and debates in the United Kingdom and European Union over whether all meat slaughtered through kosher methods should be identified as such, even if not sold as kosher (a new Jewish star, some called it). All too often the advocates of these restrictions reprised the troubling alliances between animal rights activists and anti-Semites of varying stripes of the early twentieth century who helped lead to the Nazi triumph. The mobilization of "ethics" to support restrictions on Jewish ritual slaughter only reinforced Orthodox rabbis' antipathy toward alignment of ethics with kosher requirements.

Attacks on kosher slaughter even surfaced in the United States—and against Jews with the most sympathy for ethical concerns. In Berkeley the Hazon-affiliated Urban Adamah group encountered intransigent protests from local animal rights activists when they tried to organize a *shechita* training workshop, using hens that could no longer lay eggs. To avoid a confrontation, Urban Adamah held it secretly; when news leaked out, animal rights activists vented their anger with chilling language. One deplored the use of "tradition and culture . . . to excuse violence"; another decried these "bullies who tried to justify their depraved acts"; the participants were "no better," to another commentator, than "anyone who needlessly kills another innocent." "Chickenadvocate" attacked the "psychopathic" defense of the religious ceremony by Jewish participants and disturbingly speculated that "maybe one day such a person will be the helpless victim of some other 'pious' group." Another was even blunter that, with this act, the Jews so involved could be subject to retaliation: "I hope these humans [who] are participated in needless killing will remember that mercy rightfully should be denied to them as well."[10] While none of these animal rights activists engaged in any violent acts, their intolerant, intemperate vitriol contained disturbing echoes of the attacks on Jews a century earlier for following practices that diverged from their Christian neighbors.

Most unsettling was their focus on Urban Adamah, a group associated with Hazon, the most successful effort in Jewish circles to treat ethical issues in food production on the same level as kosher requirements. "While kosher is important," the organization explained in its 2011 Food Guide, Hazon sought to expand the definition of what was "fit" for Jews to eat to include "how and where it was grown, and the effects of its production on the people who do the work and the land where it is produced." Even its slaughtering initiative, decried by Berkeley's animal rights activists, was a local food riff on Jewish traditions, as Urban Adamah sought to teach lay Jews *shechita* without rabbinic oversight, an approach at odds with Jewish law.[11]

Even with all its accomplishments, Jewish food traditions remained, in some indissoluble way, *different*, and their admittedly incomplete absorption by the modern food industry a signal achievement. Success rested above all on the pioneering efforts of Abraham Goldstein and Rabbi Tobias Geffen to inject science into kosher law; the expansion of kosher certification organizations following World War II with the OK Laboratories, Orthodox Union, Star-K, and other agencies; the accomplishments of entrepreneurs such as Meyer Robinson, Harry Kassel, and

David Herzog to make their kosher products widely available; and the efforts, throughout, of Orthodox Jews to take non-Jewish food professionals by the hand and explain the whats, whys, and hows of kosher law. It was a tremendous accomplishment of American democracy reflecting, as Tobias Geffen's grandson David emphasized to me, the legal basis of complete separation of church and state and the ability of the Jews to live their culture in a land dominated by the Christian faith.

Kosher food's success also, inadvertently, generated what might be called an argumentative convergence among American Jews in the early twenty-first century, perhaps not dissimilar from my family's Yom Kippur argument over sturgeon. Kosher food's presence in the American food system has made it a source of debate among Jews—whether they should be kosher; whether kosher by itself is enough; whether some of the methods used to produce kosher food actually contradict Jewish ethics.

Calls to add ethics and other contemporary considerations to kosher certification built on top of the innovations introduced by the Orthodox that allowed kosher food to penetrate the heart of America's secular food industries; such pressure was in fact an inevitable consequence of such integration. By the twenty-first century kosher food was embedded in an industrial food system structured by rules and practices developed outside Jewish law and with the principal intent of satisfying a non-Jewish market. Much as kosher law sought to remain aloof, it could not, as implementation of kosher requirements rested in part upon these rules, practices, bureaucratic hierarchies, and market imperatives. Much as the Orthodox insisted that considerations outside of kosher law were not pertinent to creating kosher food, the very integration of kosher requirements within modern food production made it impossible to firmly shut the door on those issues. Kosher food was implicated in the enormously broad range of issues surrounding our food system.

Thus we return to Uncle Stu's question, which incited this journey, and to my friend Arwen Mohun's trenchant emendation that his question really was about the integration into modernity of religious practices rooted in the ancient world. Selectively appropriating modernity in kosher food production—management hierarchy, scientific knowledge, computer control systems, etc.—meant accepting many of its imperatives, as well as those of the secular world. Yet kosher food's partisans also sought to deny other integral elements of modernity—the ethics and other "contemporary issues" decried by Avi Safran—drawing lines of demarcation indecipherable to Jews who have incorporated these modern issues into their belief systems and, yes, into their very notion of what it means to be a Jew.

Modernism cut another way, though. If 40 percent of the items in a typical early twenty-first-century supermarket were kosher, that left the remaining 60 percent *treif*. Kosher food's limits and the challenges procuring products whose requirements often are at odds with industrial food manufacturing methods indicate the persistence of significant obstacles to Jewish ritual practices. Secular America remains saturated by a Christian culture, perhaps debased with the consumerism of Christmas and Easter, but still marked by the temporal cycles and religiously informed practices of its Catholics and Protestants. For all their great success, Jews remain in an attenuated relationship with that culture, certainly free to pursue their hopes and dreams untrammeled in most respects by anti-Semitism, but still oddities at best and outsiders at worst, with their peculiar holidays, sayings—and foods. Try as they might, Jews remain an *Other*, seeking ever to pass yet never quite managing to do so. Indeed, much Jewish wariness comes from a deep cultural memory that acceptance can be fleeting and that all the talk of ethics could turn into a coda for suppressing the difference that Judaism embodies.

I have a memory, perhaps when I was ten years old, of my grandmother Bertie Schwartz lecturing me about Jewish history. The occasion is gone, but her words remain. We lived in the Middle East, she said, for hundreds of years and then we were told to leave. We lived in Spain for hundreds of years and then we were expelled. We lived in Russia for hundreds of years and still we were forced to flee. "How long can we count on being able to stay in America?" she asked rhetorically.

Ridiculous, I thought then; and perhaps I was right. But her cautionary history lesson bears more reflection than I could give it as a child. The history of Jews is a deeply troubled saga, long stays in one place have again and again been followed by expulsion after regime change, after economic collapse, after political turmoil—many reasons leading to a similar end, proscribing of Jews as different, as outsiders, and getting rid of them. This history too lives inside my family: Bertie's grandmother who fled

FIGURE 9.1 Stuart Schwartz and David Horowitz, Columbia University, late 1940s. Personal collection of Roger Horowitz.

the late-nineteenth-century Cossack pogroms and would never speak her memories, my Uncle Stu ostracized in his Army unit in 1946 when his Jewish identity was discovered, my son Jason harassed by white eighth-grade students in 1999 when they figured out he was Jewish because of his last name. "I was the only Jewish enlisted man in the company, and I felt it," Stu told me once. While most called each other by their first name, "I was always called Schwartz." Our degree of observance, or denomination, or appearance, did not matter; all that did was a Schwartz or Horowitz name saying, unmistakably, this is a Jew.

My grandparents, parents, aunts, and uncles might smile if they could hear me say this and the following: Kosher food, its triumphs and its limitations, our decision to observe or not, forces Jews to remember that even if we feel rived by differences, we remain connected, bound together by a history that we have never fully controlled and that we have managed as best we could, often magnificently, thrown into the air and landed in places where we found sanctuary and opportunity. Whether we like it or not, we are still family, crowded around a table and arguing whether the food upon it is fit and proper for us to eat.

EPILOGUE

REMEMBERING, DISCOVERING, THANKING

THROUGHOUT THIS book, family has been both a metaphor and source, a way to imagine a highly diverse American Jewish population and a reservoir of experiences to help me explore kosher food's journey since the 1930s. Family also pushes us to try to understand people with whom we strongly disagree, as we have no choice but to encounter and talk with seemingly odd and perhaps quite different relatives at the bar and bat mitzvah celebrations, marriages, and funerals that are the great meeting grounds for extended Jewish families. In a serendipitous manner my family captures much of this diversity: my Orthodox paternal grandparents, my Conservative maternal grandparents, and my parents who became nonobservant in middle age yet specified in their wills burial in accordance with traditional Jewish practices. As I have sought to present the competing Jewish approaches to kosher food, I often have thought of individual family members (even if not introducing such thoughts into the text) and felt that it was my duty to be as generous as possible to their views, to present these opinions and outlooks as fairly and as understandably as possible, without letting my own choice of words interfere with giving grandmothers Florence and Bertie, or my mother, Louise, a chance to have their say.

I believe strongly that such generosity toward historical subjects is one of the quintessential tasks of the historian; as E. P. Thompson wrote, it is our job to not allow the "condescension of posterity" to obscure our understanding of actors in the past.[1] The desire to take this approach is, however, not enough; appropriate sources are needed to let us perceive what our protagonists saw, and did, in their day. It is tempting, and deceptively reassuring, to start research on a project such as this from the end, by talking to the people who are visible today about how it was that they came to do what they did. Oral history, a research method I have used for thirty years, offers insights into the pitfalls of such an approach. Interviews conducted about events many years before that conversation are not only a documentary source but narratives as well, in which the events of the past are selected and arranged in such a manner as to make sense of the interviewee's passage through time. Perhaps, being Jewish, I think this problem is magnified for this project, as so many Jews are storytellers whose anecdotes about past experiences are marshaled to make a point. So I decided early on that recording stories of the past with leading figures of the present was a fraught methodology; instead, I needed sources created contemporaneous with the events they described and the opinions they conveyed.

The search for sources took me first to the New York Public Library and its remarkable Dorot Jewish Division. There I discovered the *Kosher Food Guide*, the quarterly journal created by Abraham Goldstein, and continued by his son George, which forms a major source for chapters 2 and 3 and influences the entire book. I read it from its start in 1935 to ending in 1969, aided by the NYPL's willingness to send the microfilm to the Hagley Library, and the tolerance of my peers at Hagley who allowed me to spend untold hours, reading it during working hours and making abundant copies. The Dorot division provided other key sources as well: *Ha-Pardes,* kosher food guides published by the Orthodox Union, and a number of key imprints that to my knowledge are unique. Through its good offices the New York State library in Albany sent the annual reports of the state Department of Agriculture down to the city, allowing me to access the annual reports of the Kosher Law Enforcement Division contained therein. These reports form the only source on that division, as the state archives responded to my Freedom of Information Act request by saying the division's records had been destroyed in accordance with standard state "retention" policies—a statement I am not sure I believe, but was not in a position to challenge.

The other pillar of my research was the American Jewish Historical Society. There I found the papers of Rabbi Tobias Geffen and the records of the Orthodox Union; the former opened up to me issues developed in chapter 2 and indeed throughout the book, and the latter generating the main sources for chapter 4 and key evidence elsewhere. Similar to the NYPL, the AJHS also had a number of key imprints and journals not otherwise available. Its staff tolerated my massive copying requests and went above and beyond the call of duty to make available to me the marvelous poster of Molly Picon selling Rokeach food that appears in chapter 4.

Other New York libraries formed key sources at well. At Yeshiva University I found the rich Benjamin Koenigsberg papers, which in many respects are a portion of the OU archives. The New York Municipal Library has the extraordinary "Food in the City" archive of the Federal Writers Project, as well as important city reports and publications on its own kosher supervision program. The Federal District Court of Lower Manhattan arranged for the court files of *Commack Self-Serve Meats vs. State of New York* to be transported from the court repository in Kansas City, and its staff tolerated my presence in its small waiting room while I copied copious amounts. In Washington, D.C., the staff of the Legislative Reference Service of the National Archives helped me locate the files of the House and Senate committees that oversaw adoption of humane slaughter legislation in the 1950s.

These New York research visits were all day trips that ended with a stop at my mother Louise Horowitz's Upper West Side apartment. In addition to discussing my discoveries, my mother used her access as an attorney to legal databases to explore court decision pertaining to kosher food issues. She located many of the decisions cited throughout this book, though the references are to the formal legal location and not to how some came to me, as e-mails from her with the downloaded documents.

With children and a full-time administrative job, traveling more distant than a day's train ride was more challenging than it might have been for a professor or journalist. So I am especially thankful to the librarians who responded so helpfully to my requests to send copies of material that I was able to identify through perusal of finding aides. The University of Buffalo provided key documents from the Rabbi Isaac Klein papers, enormously aiding my determination to include the perspectives of

Conservative Judaism on kosher food. The Minnesota Historical Society sent insightful material from the Hubert H. Humphrey papers pertaining to humane slaughter; the University of Connecticut copied a remarkable market research report on Manischewitz wine; the Wisconsin Historical Society helpfully dispatched microfilm reels of the Amalgamated Meat Cutters and Butcher Workmen records, which offered novel insights into the post-1945 meat distribution system in New York City. To those reading this book who wish I had said more about places like Boston, Chicago, Miami, and Los Angeles, I can only explain that on a journey one cannot go everywhere and still make it home in a reasonable time. I hope others will explore these very important histories.

These sources answered many questions, but more remained. With the larger parameters of kosher food's journey falling into place, I felt comfortable turning to oral history to fill in gaps and silences, now in a position to critically evaluate those sources. Mordy and David Herzog responded favorably early on, taking time from the demanding schedules of running Kedem to answer historical questions. Avi Goldstein invited me to his parents' house where his father, Arthur, told me about his father, George, and grandfather, Abraham. Gale Robinson and her husband Marshall Goldberg welcomed me into their home, fed me coffee and cake, and told me about Meyer Robinson (Gale's father) and Monarch wine. Harry Kassel took a cold call from someone he didn't know and said sure, come to the house and let's talk; with his wife, Zeena, we held two long interviews that opened up the dynamics of kosher meat provisioning during a period when little was known. Ernie Weir responded warmly to an e-mail and over the phone explained his role in the California wine industry and the development of advanced *mevushal* technology. Joe Regenstein spent a precious day with me, consenting to a long, detailed interview as well as opening many windows and doors on kosher law. Gerry Kean explained the dynamics of industrial kosher practices, arranged for the tour of Ventura Food's Chambersburg plant that forms a central part of chapter 6, and managed the internal approval process that allowed me to publish this information. Len Mazur, of Mazur Foods on Long Island, put down his butcher knife during a busy day to tell me about the history of his store. More informally, I spent many hours at the Kosherfest food expos, attending yearly between 2006 and 2014 and absorbing an enormous amount from conversations with the vendors and the literature so freely distributed. The food was excellent, too!

These interviews also generated some of the amazing pictures that are in *Kosher USA*. Avi Goldstein found that a relative living in Israel, Ezra Friedman, had a rare picture of Abraham Goldstein; Gale Robinson and Harry Kassel dug into their personal files for pictures that are in chapters 6 and 7, respectively. Shulamith Berger allowed me to peruse her unique collection of advertising images in Yiddish newspapers, and the director of the LeRoy Historical Society, Lynne Belluscio, graciously arranged for scanning the Yiddish Jell-O booklet that appears in chapter 3. The pictures of my family are from my personal files, those contents themselves a legacy of my grandparents and parents.

Throughout these many personal meetings I took care to present myself as I am—a Jew for whom history and family defines my Judaism. I only wore a *kippah* if I went into an Orthodox person's house, out of respect for their beliefs. In public settings I did not. Communicating honestly through my appearance was, I felt, the way to begin the conversation of how and why I was writing a book about kosher food. Not speaking Hebrew or Yiddish also created challenges, especially when I came across key documents that I could not read. For translations I turned to Daniel Bugel-Shunra and Dena Shunra of Shunra Media, both certified court interpreters and familiar with Judaism and Jewish practices, whose interest was evident in the speed and skill of their translations.

Many people believed in this project and helped keep me going for almost a decade. Very early on I had the incredible good fortune to be introduced to literary agent John A. Ware though the intercession of Judith Dobrzynski and Leah Spiro; for some reason John took me on as a client when he was in his mid-sixties and busy with his other authors who doubtless promised a better financial return on time invested. To me John was from a different world, a place where agents hunted for large advances and editors competed for authors. Without him this book probably would not have come together as it has. He liked the project immediately, taught me how to put my best writing forward, and never doubted the book's prospects even when rejection letters came rolling in. I remain sad that John was not able to see it to completion, as he died of leukemia in 2014.

Rabbi David Geffen also believed in this project, and helped throughout. The grandson of Rabbi Tobias Geffen and a historian in his own
right, I met David through a circuitous means. In 2009 I was fortunate to
receive appointment as Cain Postdoctoral Fellow at the Chemical Heritage Foundation, giving me nine months away from my regular job to
focus on *Kosher USA* and the opportunity to benefit from conversations
with Ronald Brashear and the many talented scholars at the CHF. The
wonderful support came with a lecture that the CHF avidly promoted,
attracting a large crowd that included Toby Holtz, a professor of chemistry at Barnard College. Toby helped me with the scientific elements of
kosher certification and one day e-mailed from Israel to say she knew
David Geffen and that he was interested in my work. David went on to
open many doors, supplying unpublished materials from Rabbi Tobias
Geffen and giving permission to use his papers at the American Jewish Historical Society—and, above all, sending an unending stream of
e-mails encouraging my efforts. Through his good offices I met many,
many people, including his very kind family members, Rela Geffen, Stanley Raskas, and Peter Geffen, who shared their own insights on their
family's patriarch.

Joe Regenstein saw this project through with encouragement and keen
insight. A distinguished professor of food science at Cornell University,
and one of the nation's leading authorities on kosher food, Joe was an
active figure in many of the post-1980 events described in this book. He
too encouraged me early in the process, engaged in a lengthy oral interview, participated in several panels at academic meetings, and read the
entire manuscript, correcting not only various errors of fact and judgment
but also fixing my comma usage in many places. One day perhaps he will
write his own memoir on kosher food's history, and we will all be the
wiser for it.

Support from my own employer, the Hagley Museum and Library, was
strong and unstinting from the outset. My day job is running Hagley's
Center for the History of Business, Technology, and Society, the library's
programming and scholarly division, as well as managing the affairs of
the Business History Conference, the largest academic association of
business historians in the world. Hagley has consistently supported my
scholarship, and *Kosher USA* was no exception. Center director Philip

Scranton, a friend and also a tough critic, endorsed it throughout and helped to ensure that Hagley provided the time and flexibility I needed over many years to research and write. It was at Hagley that I had the germinative conversation with University of Delaware faculty member Arwen Mohun about modernism and also received generous support from library directors Terry Snyder and Erik Rau. Many scholars come to Hagley to do their own research, and often the conversations turned to my project, a wonderful opportunity for me to learn from the best and brightest in historical scholarship.

At a very early stage I received strong encouragement from an enthusiastic audience at the Tasting Histories conference organized at the University of California-Davis by Carolyn de la Pena. Useful feedback also came from attendees and commentators hearing papers delivered at meetings of the American Historical Association, Association for Jewish Studies, Association for the Study of Food and Society, Business History Conference, German Historical Institute, Labor and Working Class History Association, and especially from Elizabeth Higgenbotham, who responded to a paper I gave in the Hagley Research Seminar series. Columbia University Press editor Philip Leventhal has patiently encouraged me through the extended process of finishing the manuscript; he has my deepest thanks for arranging for the publishing contract just months before both my parents passed away.

Librarians are a researchers' best friend. I want to note the assistance from Deena Schwimmer and Shulamith Z. Berger at Yeshiva University, Tanya Elder and Boni J. Koelliker at the American Jewish Historical Society, Philip Mooney in the Coca-Cola archives, Vital Zajka at the YIVO Institute for Jewish Research, Betsy Pittman in Archives and Special Collections at the University of Connecticut, Sara J. Logue in the manuscripts and photographs library division at Emory University, and the very patient staff at the Dorot Jewish Division of the New York Public Library who kept me fully supplied on my special research days. Hagley staff also made it possible for me to research kosher food at an archive not associated with that topic. Chris Baer made me aware of the Rokeach market research report in the Ernest Dichter collection and also pointed me to materials in the Pennsylvania Railroad collection on the Jersey City stockyards. Many other materials came to me at Hagley via interlibrary loan through the careful efforts of Linda Gross and Max Moeller in the Published Collections Department.

Many "civilians" helped me locate people and sources. Rabbi Yisroel Selwyn put me in contact with Ari Goldstein and also arranged for me to meet other leaders of the OK certification organization for informal discussions about kosher food. Rabbi Menachem Genack asked OU staff to cooperate with my sometimes annoying research requests, which they always did. Todd Menacker introduced me to Gerry Kean and opened the door for my research on Ventura Foods. Nachman Frost and then Debbie Cohen at Kedem made it possible for me to meet and interview Mordy and David Herzog. Jenny Woods at PETA provided access to the now famous Agriprocessors videos. The fine culinary historian Laura Shapiro told me about the Rosemarie Dorothy Bria thesis on Jell-O. Michaela Rodeno, now an active wine commentator and author, took time to share with me her experience as CEO of St. Supery winery. Robin Shulman was especially helpful, publishing enlightening information on the Monarch Wine Company in her insightful 2012 book, *Eat the City*, and then having the generosity to put me in touch with Gale Robinson.

This book has grown into my family in the long time it has been underway. My wife, Jessica Payne, and my children have had it around for so long that it will seem odd when it is just ninety thousand words of text and twenty-seven pictures between covers; I am sure, though, that they will be relieved it is finally done! Celebrating Hanukkah and Passover with them has allowed keeping these family traditions alive. Uncles Ernest Schwartz and Gedale Horowitz shared their own memories and family stories with me as they patiently awaited the project's completion. My grandparents are of course long gone, but this book has allowed me to revisit them, spend time in their world, and to understand them better as an adult than I was able to as a child. My parents—well, I miss them all the time and wish they could have seen the final product, but writing this book has kept them with me even as they are gone. And to Uncle Stu: all I can say is thank you for the idea and for being all that you were, as an example to us all.

NOTES

1. MY FAMILY'S STURGEON

1. Charles and Bertie G. Schwartz, *Faith Through Reason* (New York: Macmillan, 1947), 7.
2. Quotations and references are all from the Jewish Publication Society edition of *Tanakh: The Holy Scriptures* (Philadelphia: Jewish Publication Society, 1985).
3. http://www.chabad.org/library/article_cdo/aid/968257/jewish/Maachalot-Assurot-Chapter-1.htm; Michael Miller, *Rabbis and Revolution: Jews of Moravia in the Age of Emancipation* (Stanford: Stanford University Press, 2010), 67; Aryeh Shore, "Halacha and Habitat," April 22, 2012, http://aryeh-shore.blogspot.com/2012/04/halacha-and-habitat.html.
4. http://www.chabad.org/library/article_cdo/aid/901656/jewish/Introduction-to-Mishneh-Torah.htm.
5. See, for example, http://www.torah.org/advanced/shulchan-aruch/archives.html.
6. Quotes are in Rabbi Isaac Klein, "Swordfish," *Proceedings of the Rabbinical Assembly* 30 (1966): 111–15. The full Yoreh De'ah has not been translated; online summaries of this section 83: 1 do not distinguish between the opinions of Caro and Isserles. See, for example, http://torah.org/advanced/shulchan-aruch/classes/chapter1.html.
7. Jay Berkowitz, "Historicizing Orthodoxy," *AJS Perspectives* (Spring 2008): 12–13; Shore, "Halacha and Habitat"; Seth Mandel, http://www.aishdas.org/avodah/vol09/v09n057.shtml#22, July 3, 2002.
8. Miller, *Rabbis and Revolution*, 68; Marc B. Shapiro, "Forgery and the Halakhic Process, part 3," January 11, 2008, http://seforim.blogspot.com/2008/01/forgery-and-halakhic-process-part-3-by.html; "Rabbi Aron Chorin pt. 1—The Great Fish Controversy," January 6, 2011, http://onthemainline.blogspot.com/2011/01/rabbi-aron-chorin-pt-1-great-fish.html.
9. *Kosher Food Guide* (July 1965), 20–22, reprints statements by Rabbi Tendler that first appeared in *Young Israel* (April 20, 1964); Klein, "Swordfish."

10. M. D. Tendler to Wolfe Kelman, August 15, 1968 and Kelman to Tendler, August 20, 1968, 6, 21, Rabbi Isaac Klein Papers, 1925–1979, MS 149, University Archives, State University of New York, Buffalo.

2. KOSHER COKE, KOSHER SCIENCE

1. Marcie Cohen Ferris, *Matzoh Ball Gumbo: Culinary Tales of the Jewish South* (Chapel Hill: University of North Carolina Press, 2005), 165. The *New York Times* reprinted her story in its food section, September 28, 2005, F4.
2. Rabbi Tobias Geffen, "A Teshuva Concerning Coke," Tobias Geffen papers, 15;1, American Jewish Historical Society, New York and Boston.
3. C. L. Alsberg and A. E. Taylor, *The Fats and Oils: A General View* (Palo Alto: Food Research Institute, 1928); G .M. Weber and C. L. Alsberg, *The American Vegetable-Shortening Industry* (Palo Alto: Food Research Institute, 1934); Georgia Leffingwell and Milton Lesser, *Glycerin: It's Industrial and Commercial Applications* (New York: Chemical, 1945).
4. Saul Blumenthal, *Food Manufacturing* (New York: Chemical, 1942), 17.
5. Roy Gentry to L. F. Montgomery, July 17, 1934, and Affidavit by S. p. McCalmont, January 23, 1940, both Tobias Geffen Papers, 15;1, AJHS.
6. Interview by author with Arthur Goldstein (grandson of Abraham), February 9, 2009; *New York Times,* January 8, 1925; President Herbert S. Goldstein message to Union of Orthodox Jewish Congregations of America annual meeting, March 16–18, 1929, Benjamin and Pearl Koenigsberg papers 9;1, Yeshiva University Archives, Mendel Gottesman Library, New York, NY (henceforth Benjamin and Pearl Koenigsberg Papers, YU); *Kosher Food Guide*, July 1935, 6 (quote), July 1939, 38.
7. Saul Bernstein, *The Orthodox Union: A Centenary Portrait* (Northvale, NJ: Jason Aronson, 1997).
8. *Orthodox Union,* September 1935, 9.
9. *Kosher Food Guide* (henceforth *KFG*), March 1935, 4–6.
10. Simpson: *KFG,* April 1936, 25; Kalfen: *KFG,* July 1937, 29; Appelbaum, *KFG,* January 1940, 36.
11. Finkelstein, *KFG,* July 1942, 39; Packer, *KFG,* April 1942, 45.
12. *KFG,* October 1937, 42, January 1939, 28, April 1939, January 1940, 35, April 1941, 4.
13. Ackerman: *KFG,* April 1938, 43, Neauman: *KFG,* January 1939, 30; Klein: *KFG,* January 1938, 26; Feier: *KFG,* October 1941, 46.
14. *KFG,* July 1935, 17.
15. Weiss: *KFG,* July 1943, 30.
16. Appel: *KFG,* January 1938, 28; Goldstein: *KFG,* January 1941, 35. Copies of the affidavits are in Tobias Geffen papers, 15;1, AJHS.
17. Pardes affidavit is from the Coca-Cola Company archives.
18. Abraham Nachman Schwartz to Rabbi Tobias Geffen, February 8, 1927 [translated from the Hebrew] and Dr. Edgar Everhart to Rabbi Tobias Geffen, May 13, 1927, Tobias Geffen papers 15:1, AJHS; information on David Chertkoff from the *Jewish*

Floridian, February 13, 1933, 2; Adam Mintz, "Is Coca-Cola Kosher?" in *Rav Chesed: Essays in Honor of Rabbi Dr. Haskel Lookstein,* vols. II (Jersey City: KTAV, 2009), 2:75–90.

19. Coca-Cola archives; Hersch Kohn to Rabbi Tobias Geffen, January 29, 1935 [translated from the Hebrew], Tobias Geffen papers 15;1, AJHS.

20. Rabbi Shmuel Pardes to Tobias Geffen, February 21, 1931 [translated from the Hebrew], Tobias Geffen papers, AJHS.

21. Hersch Kohn to Rabbi Tobias Geffen, January 29, 1935 [translated from the Hebrew]; Pardes to Geffen, February 21, 1931 [translated from the Hebrew]; typescript of Tobias Geffen *teshuva;* all in Tobias Geffen papers 15;1, AJHS.

22. *KFG,* July 1939, 6.

23. *KFG,* January 1936, 6–10; *Ha-Pardes,* August 1933, inside back cover.

24. *KFG,* July 1936, 14 and January 1937, 40.

25. Rabbi Samuel Aaron Halevi Pardes, "Questions and Answers Regarding 'Junket' Rennet Products" (New York, 1938); *KFG,* July 1936, 15 and January 1937, 30.

26. Rabbi Zushe Yosef Blech, *Kosher Food Production* (Ames, IA: Blackwell, 2009), 43.

27. Pardes, "Questions and Answers Regarding 'Junket' Rennet"; Rudolf A. Clemen, *By-Products in the Packing Industry* (Chicago: University of Chicago Press: 1927), 366; *KFG,* January 1937, 28–34.

28. *KFG,* July 1936, 20 and July 1937, 16; Minutes of Executive Committee meeting March 26, 1936, Union of Orthodox Jewish Congregations of America Records, 3;12, American Jewish Historical Society (henceforth UOJCA Records, AJHS).

29. Benjamin and Pearl Koenigsberg Papers, 11; 3, YU; *KFG,* October 1939, 4.

30. *KFG,* January 1953, 3–5 (quote 3), and April 1953, 3.

31. *National Jewish Post and Opinion,* November 18, 1957.

32. For production methods see T. W. Chalmers, *The Production and Treatment of Vegetable Oils* (New York: Van Nostrand, 1919), 143–47; M. K. Schweitzer, *Margarine and Other Food Fats* (New York: Interscience, 1956), especially chapter 4, "Processing Fats for Margarine and Cooking Fats," 139–219; Truman M. Godfrey, "Methods of Production," in Carl S. Miner and N. N. Dalton, eds., *Glycerol* (New York: Reinhold, 1953), 33–40.

33. Rabbi Silver was respected for many deeds, above all for his role rescuing European Jews during and immediately after the Second World War. See Aaron Rakeffect-Rothkoff, *The Silver Era: Rabbi Eliezer Silver and His Generation* (New York: Yeshiva University Press, 1981).

3. THE GREAT JELL-O CONTROVERSY

1. Carolyn Wyman, *Jell-O: A Biography* (New York: Harcourt, 2001), 14–22, illustration on 22.

2. Carole B. Balin, "'Good to the Last Drop': The Proliferation of the Maxwell House Haggadah," in Rabbi Lawrence A Hoffman and David Arnow, eds., *My People's*

Haggadah (Woodstock, NY: Jewish Lights, 2008), 1:86. *New York Times,* October 18, 1926, 16.

3. *Kosher Food Guide* (henceforth *KFG*), January 1936, 36.

4. *KFG,* January 1938, 16.

5. G. Stainsby, "The Physical Chemistry of Gelatin in Solution," in A. G. Ward and A. Courts, ed., *The Science and Technology of Gelatin* (New York: Academic, 1977), esp. 125–26.

6. Rudolf A. Clemen, *By-Products in the Packing Industry* (Chicago: University of Chicago Press, 1927), 280–95.

7. Ibid., 296.

8. Opening Goldstein quote *KFG,* July 1939, 28.

9. *KFG,* April 1936, 24, July 1936, 41, July 1937, 29, October 1938, 46, October 1939, 44, July 1939, 48, July 1940, 46, July 1941, 40, January 1940, 36.

10. *KFG,* October 1936, 28, January 1938, 34, October 38, 47, April 1939, 41, January 1942, 43.

11. *KFG,* July 1940, 28, April 37, 30, October 1941, 41, April 1937, 44, January 1936, 47, January 1939, 34.

12. *KFG,* July 1941, 43, April 1938, 39, July 1941, 42, October 1941, 38.

13. *KFG,* January 1942, 32.

14. *KFG,* October 1942, 4, 6.

15. *KFG,* July 1944, 22, April 1944, 23, July 1946, 22.

16. Rabbi David L. Sheinkopf, *Gelatin in Jewish Law* (New York: Block, 1982), 10–11.

17. Rabbi Zushe Yosef Blech, "Will These Bones Live?" *Montreal Vaad News and Views* 2, no. 4, #9 (January/February 2001), rpt. in *Kosher Food Production* (Ames: Blackwell, 2004), 369–75.

18. Sheinkopf, *Gelatin in Jewish Law,* 30–31, 111; Rabbi Howard Jachter, "Taking Medicine in a Gel-Cap," *Journal of Halacha and Contemporary Society* 30 (Fall 1995): 66–80.

19. Sheinkopf, *Gelatin in Jewish Law,* 65.

20. Jachter, "Taking Medicine in a Gel-Cap," 71–73.

21. Sheinkopf, *Gelatin in Jewish Law,* 68–72, 91.

22. Ibid., 113.

23. *KFG,* January 1948, 6, 8.

24. "Kosher Products Guide," *Jewish Life* (Summer 1950): 77.

25. *New York Times,* April 15, 1952, 44 and April 29, 1952, 38; *KFG,* July 1951, 3.

26. *KFG,* July 1947, 3–4 and October 1947, 3.

27. W. F. Bronson, "Technology and Utilization of Gelatin," *Food Technology* 5, no. 2 (February 1951): 55.

28. American Meat Institute, *The Significant Sixty* (Chicago, 1952), 31; *National Provisioner,* February 24, 1951, 100; P. Johns and A. Courts, "Relationship Between Collagen and Gelatin," in A. G. Ward and A. Courts, eds., *The Science and Technology of Gelatin* (New York: Academic, 1977), 158; "Profits in Pig Skins," *National Provisioner,* October 11, 1951.

29. Samuel Baskin and Simon Winograd, "Atlantic Gelatin Is Kosher and Parve," *Jewish Morning Journal,* July 27, 1951, Rabbi Isaac Klein Papers, 6; 2, University Archives, State University of New York at Buffalo (henceforth Rabbi Isaac Klein Papers, SUNY-Buffalo); *KFG,* January 1952, 3, 14, and April 1952, 26 (quote).

30. Baskin and Winograd, "Atlantic Gelatin Is Kosher and Parve"; *KFG,* January 1952, 14.

31. *KFG,* January 1952, 5–6; Sheinkopf, *Gelatin in Jewish Law,* 12–13. *KFG,* April 1952, 3, and July 1952, 4–6. The withdrawal of the certification appeared in the February 15, 1952, issue of *Jewish Opinion* and is reprinted in the April 1952 *Kosher Food Guide.*

32. *KFG,* January 1954, 8, October 1954, 4–6. Certification by Rabbi David Telsner, December 19, 1960, Rabbi Isaac Klein Papers, 6; 2, SUNY-Buffalo.

33. Rosemarie Dorothy Bria, "How Jell-O Molds Society and How Society Molds Jell-O: A Case Study of an American Food Industry Product" (PhD diss., Teachers College, Columbia University, 1991), 172–73.

34. General Foods Kitchen, "Jell-O Information," May 1962, Rabbi Isaac Klein Papers, 6;2 SUNY-Buffalo.

35. Chaim Bloch, *Der Prager Golem* (1919), trans. Harry Schneiderman as *The Golem: Legends of the Ghetto of Prague* (Vienna, 1925).

36. Rabbi Chaim Bloch, "A Clarifying Statement Concerning Gelatine," *KFG,* April 1952, 6–16, quote 10.

37. Blech, "Will These Bones Live?"

38. Michael Kaufman, "The Orthodox Renaissance: Crisis and Challenge," *Jewish Life* (September-October 1966): 10.

39. Jonathan D. Sarna, *American Judaism: A History* (New Haven: Yale University Press, 2004), quote 285; Jeffrey S. Gurock, *Orthodox Jews in America* (Bloomington: Indiana University Press, 2009), 203–9.

40. "Gelatin," manuscript in Rabbi Isaac Klein Papers, 6; 2, SUNY-Buffalo.

41. Isaac Klein to *Kosher Food Guide,* November 2, 1962; Alexander Rosenberg to Klein, November 12, 1962; Robert Hammer to Klein, March 16, 1964; Sanford Shanblatt to Klein, March 20, 1964; J. Leonard Azneer to Klein, March 24, 1965; Arnold A. Lasker to Klein, November 9, 1965; Rabbi Isaac Klein Papers, 6; 2, SUNY-Buffalo. Klein to David Telsner, August 14, 1962; Rabbi Isaac Klein Papers, 5; 37, SUNY-Buffalo.

42. Klein to Hammer, March 24, 1964; Klein to Shanblatt, March 24, 1964; Klein to Lasker, November 17, 1965; all Isaac Klein papers 6; 2, SUNY-Buffalo.

43. Rabbi Isaac Klein, "Is Gelatin Kosher?" *1969 Proceedings of the Rabbinical Assembly, United Synagogues of America,* 216 and 217.

44. Ibid., 216.

45. Ibid., 218; Klein to Sylvan D. Kamens, March 25, 1975; Isaac Klein papers 6; 2, SUNY-Buffalo; Isaac Klein, *Responsa and Halakhic Studies* (New York: KTAV, 1975), 59–74.

46. Oscar J. Albert to Isaac Klein, Dec. 13, 1968, Isaac Klein papers 5;37, SUNY-Buffalo.

47. Mordecai Levy to Isaac Klein, January 23, 1968, Isaac Klein papers 6; 2, Arthur Oleisky to Isaac Klein, February 28, 1972, Isaac Klein papers 6; 1, SUNY-Buffalo.

48. Daniel A. Jezer to Isaac Klein, January 9, 1968, Isaac Klein papers 5;37, SUNY-Buffalo.

49. *KFG*, April 1967, 4.

50. General Foods Consumer Center, "JELL-O GELATION DESSERTS," December 1973, Isaac Klein papers 6; 2, SUNY-Buffalo.

51. *Kashrus Newsletter* (September 1985): 12 and (January 1987): 10 and 24–25. Tzipo-rah Spear, *Kosher Calories* (New York: Mesorah, 1985), 334–40.

52. *Prepared Foods* (August 1992): 15–16.

4. WHO SAYS IT'S KOSHER?

1. *KFG*, January 1938, 44–51.

2. *KFG*, January 1948, 34–42.

3. Minutes, Kashruth Committee of Rabbinic Council and Union, June 27, 1940, Union of Orthodox Jewish Congregations of America Records 4; 1, American Jewish Historical Society (henceforth UOJCA Records, AJHS); Kashruth Division Report, 1950, 2, UOJCA Records, 4; 5, AJHS.

4. Trudy Weiss-Rosmarin, "Making Sport of Kashruth," *Jewish Spectator* 27, no. 10 (November 1952): 5.

5. Benjamin Koenigsberg to Rabbi Samuel Levy, December 12, 1940, Benjamin and Pearl Koenigsberg Papers, 9; 2, Yeshiva University Archives, Mendel Gottesman Library, New York, NY (henceforth Benjamin and Pearl Koenigsberg Papers, YU).

6. Minutes, Kashruth Committee of Rabbinic Council and Union, June 27, 1940; Minutes, Joint Kashruth Committee of the UOJCA and Rabbinical Council of America, August 26, 1942; both UOJCA Records, 4; 1, AJHS.

7. Rabbi Israel Tabak to Samuel Nirenstein, September 16, 1948, Benjamin and Pearl Koenigsberg Papers, 9; 2, YU; "Kashruth Division, Report on Activities—1950," UOJCA Records, 4; 5; "Union Creates New Departments in Major Expansion," *Synagogue Guide*, April 1950; Agreement Between Union of Orthodox Jewish Congregations of America and Rabbinical Council of America, January 19, 1954; both Benjamin and Pearl Koenigsberg Papers, 9; 3, YU; Saul Bernstein, *The Ortho-dox Union: A Centenary Portrait* (Northvale, NJ: Jason Aronson, 1997), 292.

8. "Kashruth Division, Report on Activities—1950," UOJCA Records, 4;5, AJHS.

9. Kashruth Division report of activities—1950; Kasruth Division report for the year 1951; both UOJCA Records, 4; 5, AJHS; "Kosher Products Directory," *Jewish Life* (July-August 1955): 52–63.

10. Kashruth Division report of activities—1950; UOJCA Records, 4, 5; *KFG*, January 1955, 16; *New York Times,* March 10, 1956, 14.

11. *Kosher Food Guide* (henceforth *KFG*), January 1955, 34–47.

12. Peter Barton Hutt and Peter Barton Hutt II, "A History of Government Regulation of Adulteration and Misbranding of Food," *Food, Drug, Cosmetic Law Journal* 39 (1973): 64.

13. *KFG,* January 1950, 3 and July 1956, 6.

14. Ernest Dichter, *A Motivational Research Study of the Major Problem Areas for Rokeach Within the Kosher Food Market* (New York: Institute for Motivational Research, 1961), 112–13. Ernest Dichter Papers, Report 1368C, Hagley Museum and Library.

15. Leah W. Leonard, *Jewish Cookery* (New York: Crown, 1949), viii.

16. Ibid., 24, 38, 232–33.

17. Ibid., 461.

18. Leah Gross, ed., *The Ballabustas' Best* (New York: Judea, 1955), 2, endpiece.

19. Ibid., 2, 10.

20. *New York Times,* March 27, 1967, 33, October 18, 1926, 16, October 15, 1945, 26, October 6, 1937, 23, December 12, 1947, 14; Carole B. Balin, "'Good to the Last Drop': The Proliferation of the Maxwell House Haggadah," in Rabbi Lawrence Hoffman and David Arnow, eds., *My People's Passover Haggadah* (Woodstock, VT: 2008), 1:85–90; Kerri P. Steinberg, *Jewish Mad Men: Advertising and the Design of the American Jewish Experience* (New Brunswick: Rutgers University Press, 2015), 81–109.

21. Joseph Jacobs, *The Jewish Culture—and What It Means to the American Manufacturer in His Marketing of His Products* (New York, 1941), 19–20; Balin, "'Good to the Last Drop,'" 86.

22. Jacobs, *The Jewish Culture,* 20–21; Joseph Jacobs, *The Jewish Dietary Laws in the Day-to-Day Life of the Jew* (New York, 1949), 9, 10. The latter address was to the New York sections of the Institute of Food Technologists and American Association of Cereal Chemists.

23. Jacobs, *The Jewish Dietary Laws,* 10–11; *New York Times,* April 29, 1952, 38 and June 23, 1954, 36.

24. Susan Jacobs, "Ben Gallob, Assistant Editor at JTA for 30 years, dies at 83," *Jewish Telegraph Agency,* September 11, 1997.

25. Trademark Registration Number 0636593; Paul Duguid, "A Case of Prejudice? That Uncertain Development of Collective and Certification Marks," *Business History Review* 86 (2012): 311–33, Patent Office quote 316; 15 U.S. Code 1054.

26. *OU News Reporter,* May 1956; "Summary of Public Relations Highlights," April 1, 1963; both Benjamin and Pearl Koenigsberg Papers, 9; 5, YU.

27. "Report to members of the Joint Kashruth Commission," June 25, 1956; Arthur Wayne to Ben Gallob, May 4, 1956; both Benjamin and Pearl Koenigsberg Papers, 9; 3, YU.

28. Summary of Highlights of the Public Relations Program," April 1, 1963; Benjamin and Pearl Koenigsberg Papers, 9; 5, YU.

29. "Report to members of the JKCU," March 28, 1963; "Report to Members of the Joint Kashruth Commission," October 24, 1963; Summary of Highlights of the

Public Relations Program," April 1, 1963; all Benjamin and Pearl Koenigsberg Papers, 9; 5, YU.

30. Summary of Highlights of the Public Relations Program," April 1, 1963, Benjamin and Pearl Koenigsberg Papers, 9; 5, YU; *Chemical Week* July 18, 1959.

31. Report to the Joint Kashruth Commission, June 25, 1956, Benjamin and Pearl Koenigsberg Papers, 9; 3, YU.

32. Orthodox Union, *The Key to the Kosher Market* (1967), 29, UOJCA Records, 15; 3, AJHS.

33. Summary of Highlights of the Public Relations Program," April 1, 1963, Benjamin and Pearl Koenigsberg Papers, 9; 5, YU.

34. "Report of the Joint Kashruth Commission" (1966), K-3, UOJCA Records, 8; 9, AJHS.

35. *KFG,* October 1966, 8.

36. *KFG,* January 1968, 35–40.

37. Last five paragraphs rely on *Kosher Products and Services Directory* (Union of Orthodox Jewish Congregations of America, 1970–1971).

38. "Report of the Joint Kashruth Commission," (1966), K-8, UOJCA Records, 8; 9, AJHS; Rabbi Eliezer Gevirtz, "An Interview with Rabbi Moshe Heineman," *Kashrus Newsletter* (May-June 1982): 1–3. Rabbi Eliezer Gewirtz, "Inside the Cof K," *Kashrus Newsletter* (September 1983): 13–14.

39. *Kashrus Magazine* (Summer 1987): 15.

40. Arthur Goldstein interview by Roger Horowitz.

41. Dianne Feldman, "In Memorium—Rabbi Berel Levy, z"l," *Kashrus Magazine* (Summer 1987): 15. Rabbi Don Yoel Levy, "How Oil Stays Kosher in Transit," *Jewish Homemaker* (Fall 1998).

42. "Report of the Joint Kashruth Commission of the Union," 1958, UOJCA Records, 5; 10, AJHS; "Report of the Joint Kashruth Commission, 1966, UOJCA Records, 8; 9, AJHS; unsigned memo in UOJCA Records, box 47, folder marked "1978," AJHS.

43. Quote from Michael Kaufman, "The Orthodox Renaissance: Crisis and Challenge," *Jewish Life* (September-October 1966): 15; Jeffrey S. Gurock, *Orthodox Jews in America* (Bloomington: Indiana University Press, 2009), 209.

44. Kaufman, "The Orthodox Renaissance," 23.

45. The report is contained in *Madrich Lakashrus* 22 (November-December 1977), and is in UOJCA Records, 26; 11, AJHS.

46. Anonymous letter, "Ladies and Gentlemen of the Convention," UOJCA Records, 47; 7, AJHS. Although the letter is undated, it is filed in the folder labeled "Kashruth Division, 1978."

47. Rabbi Eliezer Gevirtz, "Inside the OU—An Interview with Menechem Genack," *Kashrus Newsletter* (March 1983): 7–8; Rabbi Yosef Wikler, "Inside the OU," *Kashrus Magazine* (December 1989): 34–35; Bernstein, *The Orthodox Union Story,* 328–29.

48. Orthodox Union client list, October 29, 1986, UOJCA Records, 26; 10, AJHS.

49. Financial information draw from UOJCA Records, boxes 16 and 47, AJHS.

50. Bonne Rae London, *Modern Jewish Cooking* (New York: Crown, 1980), 365–67; Helen Nash, *Kosher Cuisine* (New York: Random House, 1984), xv; Anita Hirsch, *Our Food—the Kosher Kitchen Updated* (New York: Doubleday, 1992), 124–25.

5. INDUSTRIAL KASHRUS

1. Joshua J. Hammerman, "The Forbidden Oreo," *New York Times Sunday Magazine*, January 11, 1998, 66; Natalie K. quote from http://stuffjewishyoungadultslike .wordpress.com/2008/04/02/11-taking-sides-on-the-hydroxoreo-conflict (accessed May 8, 2010); *Jewish World Review*, June 26, 2003; "The Oreo Has Arrived," Orthodox Union press release at www.ou.org/oupr/1997/nabisco97.htm (accessed May 18, 2010); Stephanie Thompson, "Nabisco Keeps Kosher in New Ad Push," *Advertising Age*, September 25, 2000, 58.

2. Tziporah Spear, *Kosher Calories* (Brooklyn: Mesorah, 1985), lists over ten thousand certified products in 1985.

3. Packaged Facts, *The Kosher Foods Market* (New York, 1988), 38.

4. Ben Sauer, Elaine Asp, and Jean Kinsey, *Food Trends and the Changing Consumer* (St. Paul: Eagan, 1991), 253.

5. Packaged Facts, *The Kosher Foods Market*, 38, 46, 55.

6. *Kashrus Newsletter* (June 1986): 17.

7. Ibid., 3.

8. Gershon Monk, "The Nine Days—My Introduction to Industrial Kashrus," *Jewish Observer* 20 (September 1987): 8–19.

9. *Kashrus Newsletter* (June 1986): 18.

10. Timothy D. Lytton, *Kosher: Private Regulation in the Age of Industrial Food* (Cambridge: Harvard University Press, 2013), 91–98.

11. "Inside the OU," *Kashrus Magazine* (December 1989): 34–35.

12. Bruce W. Marion, "Changing Power Relationships in the U.S. Food Industry," Working Paper 108, June 1995, https://www.aae.wisc.edu/fsrg/publications/ Archived/wp-108.pdf.

13. Stephen J. Hoch and Shumeet Banerji, "When Do Private Labels Succeed?" *MIT-Sloan Management Review* (Summer 1993); Kara Gruver, Matthew Meacham, and Suzanne Tager, "Deciding to Fight or Play in the Private-Label Arena," *Bain Insights*, June 1, 2011, www.bain.com/publications/articles/deciding-to-fight-or -play-in-the-private-label-arena-bain-brief.aspx.

14. Interview with Gerry Kean et al. by Roger Horowitz, May 11, 2010; the description of the Chambersburg plant is based on extended plant tour and discussions with plant officials on May 11, 2010, and is used with the approval of Ventura Foods.

15. Rabbi Zushe Yosef Blech, *Kosher Food Production* (Ames, IA: Blackwell, 2004), 44–47.

16. Ibid., 58–59.

17. http://www.ou.org/general_article/ou_direct_adds_enhanced_online_ingredient, accessed October 1, 2013.

18. "Software Aid Product Development," *Food Technology* (February 2006): 60.

19. Joe Regenstein interview with Roger Horowitz; Regenstein to Horowitz, April 29, 2015, in author's possession.
20. Lytton, *Kosher*, 117.
21. Blech, *Kosher Food Production*, 58; Joe Regenstein interview with Roger Horowitz, April 22, 2010.
22. Packaged Facts, *The U.S. Market for Kosher Foods* (New York: 1998), 4–6, 60.

6. MAN-O-MANISCHEWITZ

1. William Chazanof, *Welch's Grape Juice* (Syracuse: Syracuse University Press, 1977), 51.
2. Rabbi Israel Poleyeff, "Stam Yeinom," *Journal of Halacha and Contemporary Society* 14 (Fall 1987/Succot 5748): 67–78.
3. Ibid., 78–79; *Mishneh Torah,* book 5, The Book of Holiness, *Sefer Kedushah*; "Treatise 2 on Forbidden Foods," in *Maachalot Assurot* (New Haven: Yale University Press, 1961), chapter 11, sec. 9, p. 209, http://www.religiousrules.com/Judaismfood 13idols.htm (accessed March 5, 2013).
4. Information from the Rabbi Tobias Geffen diary, from David Geffen e-mail to Roger Horowitz, May 1, 2013; Jenna Weissman Joselit, *Our Gang: Jewish Crime and the New York Jewish Community, 1900–1940* (Bloomington: Indiana University Press, 1983), 89.
5. Joselit, *Our Gang*, 99, 105.
6. *New York Times,* June 13, 1992; Gale Robinson and Marshall Goldberg interview with Roger Horowitz, April 1, 2013.
7. Label from a bottle of Monarch's Manischewitz New York State Sacramental Concord Grape Wine, Kosher for Passover, from the Archives of the YIVO Institute for Jewish Research, New York.
8. Hearns's advertisements, *New York Times,* April 13, 1938, 19, March 28, 1939, 11, March 26, 1942, 17, April 3, 1944, 13 (quote). Macy's advertisements, *New York Times,* March 25, 1934, 19, March 26, 1942, 14, March 15, 1945, 15, April 3, 1946, 10. Gimbel's advertisements, April 8, 1938, 10, March 19, 1945, 12.
9. *Kosher Food Guide* (henceforth *KFG*), January 1946, 42; Monarch Wine company advertisements, *New York Times,* March 20, 1947, 22; April 10, 1949, SM39; *New Yorker,* April 21, 1951, 45.
10. Morris Freedman, "Wine Like Mother Used to Make," *Commentary* (May 1954): 481–89.
11. Ibid., 481.
12. Ibid., 488.
13. Mrs. [Maria Massey] Barrington, *Dixie Cookery: Or How I Managed My Table for Twelve Years* (Boston: Loring, 1867), 104; Martha McCulloch-Williams, *Dishes and Beverages of the Old South* (New York: McBride Nast, 1913), 87–88.
14. Leah Leonard, *Jewish Cookery* (New York: Crown, 1951), 75–76; Anne London and Bertha Kahn Bishov, *The Complete American-Jewish Cookbook* (New York: World, 1951), 23.

15. http://southernfoodways.org/documentary/oh/wine_in_the_south/georgia/tilford_slideshow/tilford.shtml (accessed April 8, 2013); http://homepages.rootsweb.ancestry.com/~cmddlton/famdox8.html#anchor236316 (accessed April 8, 2013).

16. *Pittsburgh Courier,* April 8, 1950, 10; *Ebony,* January 1954, 13.

17. *Broadcasting,* October 14, 1957, 35; Freedman, "Wine Like Mother Used to Make," 483, 487; *Sponsor,* September 15, 1955, 133; *Billboard,* March 3, 1956, 50.

18. *New York Times,* March 19, 1956; *New York Times,* April 9, 1957.

19. *Broadcasting,* October 14, 1957, 35; see, for example, advertisement in *Look,* January 27, 1958, 117; *New York Times,* October 22, 1958; *New York Times,* July 14, 1960, 34; *New York Times,* March 23, 1961; *New York Times,* April 16, 1965.

20. *New York Times,* July 19, 1956, 44; Gale Robinson and Marshall Goldberg interview, April 1, 2013; *New Yorker,* "American Champagne & Wine Advertising Pages and Expenditures by Brands, 1973," Records of the Seagram Company Ltd., Box 778, Hagley Museum and Library; Manischewitz Almonetta Wine with Sammy Davis," https://www.youtube.com/watch?v=cwsmJX-5yKc.

21. *Ebony* (April 1972): 110.

22. *New York Times,* February 3, 1974, 245.

23. Robinson and Goldberg interview; Steven Flax, "'Let Them Keep Laughing,'" *Forbes* September 28, 1981, 85.

24. Robinson and Goldberg interview.

25. Ibid.

26. Israel Silverman, "Are All Wines Kosher?" (1964), in Seymour Siegel, ed., *Conservative Judaism and Jewish Law* (New York: Rabbinical Assembly, 1977), 307–16; Meyer Hager, "Meyer H. Robinson—Kosher in Every Respect," *Synagogue Light* 44, no. 4 (March-April 1978): 3–6.

27. H. S. Adams, *Milk and Food Sanitation Practice* (New York: Commonwealth Fund, 1947), 84–86; Freedman, "Wine Like Mother Used to Make," 487, 485.

28. Rabbi Moshe Feinstein, *Igros Moshe,* Yore De'ah, part 3, sec. 31 (17 Elul 5726/ September 2, 1966); Rabbi Zushe Yosef Blech, "The Story of Wine, Beer, and Alcohol," in *Kosher Food Production* (Ames, IA: Blackwell, 2004), 528.

29. Robinson and Goldberg interview; Orthodox rabbis Joseph I. Singer and Solomon B. Shapiro were still certifying Manischewitz in 1980, *New York Times* March 23, 1980, Sunday Magazine 21.

30. "Dynasty," *New Yorker,* 2, 2981, 32; Robinson and Goldberg interview; Flax, "'Let Them Keep Laughing,'" 88.

31. Flax, "'Let Them Keep Laughing,'" 84; Paul Lukacs, *American Vintage: The Rise of American Wine* (New York: Norton, 2000), 203; John Henry, "Wine Firm's Problem Is, Namely, Its Name," *New York Post,* February 2, 1984, 66.

32. *KFG,* January 1949, 43, January 1954, 43.

33. David Herzog interview with Roger Horowitz, December 22, 2009.

34. Ibid.

35. Orthodox Union, *1970/1971 Kosher Products and Services Directory,* 57, Union of Orthodox Jewish Congregations of America Records, 14; 10, American

Jewish Historical Society (henceforth UOJCA Records, AJHS); Orthodox Union, *1974/1975 Kosher Products and Services Directory*, 50, UOJCA Records, 14; 11, AJHS.

36. Frank J. Prial, "Wine Talk," *New York Times*, April 5, 1978, C19.

37. *Jewish Courier of Pittsburgh*, n.p., March 25, 1982; *Kashrus Newsletter* (Summer 1982): 9; *New York Times*, February 24, 1983, C21; *New York Times*, March 23, 1983, C18.

38. Bill Zacharkiw, "Pass Me Over, 'Cause I'm Kosher?" *Montreal Gazette*, March 30, 2009; *Jewish Living Magazine* (May 2008); *Crain's New York Business*, September 23, 1991, 17.

39. Frank J. Prial, "Wine Talk," March 21, 1984, *New York Times*, C13; *Newsday*, March 17, 1986, 7; *Marketing News*, May 11, 1992, 10.

40. Victor F. Zonana, "Manischewitz Says Rival's Ads Are Not Kosher," *Los Angeles Times* March 28, 1991, n.p.

41. Michael Dresser, "Royal Kedem Has Kosher Wines with Fine Spirit," *Baltimore Sun*, March 13, 1994, n.p.; *New York Times*, March 13, 1991, C10.

42. "Report # 32: The New Wines of Israel," *International Wine Review* (July-August 2012): 4.

43. Ernest Weir interview by Roger Horowitz, November 20, 2012; *Time*, April 1, 1991, 11.

44. *The Wine Press* (published by Golden Medal Wine Club), November 1994, 1–7.

45. Dee Coutelle, "Quality Is Kosher in Passover Wines," *Chicago Sun-Times*, March 21, 1991, 19.

46. F. Fiene and Saul Blumenthal, *Handbook of Food Manufacturers* (New York: Chemical, 1938), 253–54; Peter Fellows, *Food Processing Technology* (Cambridge: Woodhead, 2009), 381–95.

47. Michaela Rodeno to Roger Horowitz, December 7, 2012; Joseph Berkofsky, "Beyond Passover: California Kosher Wines Come of Age," *jweekly.com*, April 18, 1997.

48. Zacharkiw, "Pass Me Over."

49. Jay McInerey, *A Hedonist in the Cellar* (New York: Knopf, 2006), 200; Daniel Rogov, *Rogov's Guide to Israeli Wines* (Tel Aviv: Toby, 2000).

50. Sidney Retsky, "Kosher, Mevushal, and Israeli Wines? Not What You Think," *American Thinker*, December 17, 2005, http://www.americanthinker.com/2005/12/kosher_mevushal_and_israeli_wi.html; Bill Strubbe, "From Vine to Vat to Bottle; the Journey of Kosher Wine," *Jewish Telegraph Agency*, June 21, 2001, 13.

51. Rogov from www.mykerem.com/blogs/doctordog/drink-or-not-drinkmevushal; McInerey, *A Hedonist in the Cellar*, 201–2.

52. Michael Stenberger, "Goodbye My Sweet: Kosher Wine Comes of Age," *Jewish Living Magazine* (May 2008).

53. *Modern Materials Handling*, October 2, 2009, 22; Freedman, "Wine Like Mother Used to Make," 481; Flax, "Let Them Keep Laughing," 84; Martha McKay, "No More Whining," *Record (Bergen County, NJ)*, October 14, 2005, B1.

54. James M. Vicary Company, "Major Factors Relating to the Marketing of Manischewitz Wine," May 1957, part 5, #9, James M. Vicary Papers, Thomas J. Dodd Research Center, University of Connecticut Libraries.

7. HARRY KASSEL'S MEAT

1. Rabbi Zushe Yosef Blech, *Kosher Food Production* (Ames, IA: Blackwell, 2004), 187.
2. Rudolf A. Clemen, "What 'Kosher' Means to the Meat Industry," *Monthly Letter to Animal Husbandman* 10, no. 3 (June 1929): 11; Elliott Ross Heisman, "The Actualization of the Jewish Dietary Laws in the Meat Industry" (master's thesis, Ohio State University, 1982), 5.
3. *New York Times*, August 1, 1973, 81.
4. Harry Kassel interview by Roger Horowitz, August 17, 2010.
5. U.S. Bureau of the Census, *Census of Business: Retail Trade, 1939*, 5 vols. (Washington, DC: 1941–43), vol. 1, part 2, 729.
6. Faith W. Williams, "The Food Manufacturing Industries," included in *Regional Survey of New York and Its Environs*, vol. 1B, *Food, Clothing and Textile Industries, Wholesale Market and Retail Shopping and Financial Districts* (New York, 1928), 17; *Kosher Food Guide* (henceforth *KFG*), July 1941, 58–58; Thomas F. Dwyer to Benjamin Koenigsberg, June 16, 1931, Benjamin and Pearl Koenigsberg Papers, 11; 1, Yeshiva University Archives, Mendel Gottesman Library, New York, NY (henceforth Benjamin and Pearl Koenigsberg Papers, YU).
7. British Board of Trade, *Report of an Inquiry Into Working Class Rents, Housing and Retail Prices in the Principal Industrial Towns of the United States of America* (London, 1911), 418.
8. The Shulchan Aruch has not been translated into English in its entirety. A partial translation that focuses on *shechita* is S.I. Levin and Edward A. Boyden, *The Kosher Code of the Orthodox Jew* (New York: Hermon, 1940).
9. Clemen, "What 'Kosher' Means to the Meat Industry," 3–5; Jeremiah J. Berman, *Shehitah: A Study in the Cultural and Social Life of the Jewish People* (New York: Bloch, 1941), 6–7.
10. Williams, "The Food Manufacturing Industries," 60; Berman, *Shehitah*, 8.
11. Zev Farber, "The Development of the Three-Day Limit for Salting," *Beloved Words (Milin Havinin): An Annual Devoted to Torah, Society, and the Rabbinate* (New York: Yeshivat Chovevai Torah Rabbinical School, 2005), 38–72.
12. Williams, "The Food Manufacturing Industries," 21; "Trade in Kosher Meats of Great Importance," *Market Reporter* 3, no. 13 (March 26, 1921): 193; *Report of the Federal Trade Commission on the Meat-Packing Industry*, Summary and Part I (Washington: Government Printing Office, 1919), 122.
13. Clemen, "What 'Kosher' Means to the Meat Industry," 6.
14. Florence Kreisler Greenbaum, *Jewish Cook Book* (New York: Bloch, 1918), 77; Leah W. Leonard, *Jewish Cookery* (New York: Crown, 1949), 191, preface; Anne

London and Bertha Kahn Bishov, eds., *The Complete American Jewish Cookbook* (New York: World, 1952), 312.

15. Leonard, *Jewish Cookery,* 197–98.

16. Clemen, "What 'Kosher' Means to the Meat Industry," 9.

17. Unprocessed records, Department of Public Markets, Kosher Division, New York City Municipal Archives; Harold P. Gastwirt, *Fraud, Corruption, and Holiness: The Controversy Over the Supervision of Jewish Dietary Practice in New York City, 1881–1941* (Port Washington, NY: Kennikat, 1974).

18. *State of New York v. Jacob Branfman & Son Inc.* 263 N.Y.S. 629.

19. Gastwirt, *Fraud, Corruption, and Holiness,* 157–67.

20. *KFG,* January 1940, 45.

21. *Hygrade Provision v. Sherman,* 266 U.S. 497.

22. *New York Times,* January 8, 1925, 29.

23. Holton V. Hoyes to Nathan Sobel, March 20, 1942, *Commack Self-Serve Kosher Meats v. New York State,* Joint Appendix, vol. 1, JA 81.

24. Isaac Lewin, "Legal Protection for the Kosher Consumer in America: A Historical Perspective," *Governor's Conference for the Kosher Food Industry* (Albany: 1988); Sol Bezalel Friedman, "Kashruth and Civil Law Enforcement in the United States, Canada, South America, Parts of the British Empire and Israel" (PhD diss., Yeshiva University, 1961), 76–97; Sidney Michaelson, *Digest of the "Kosher" Laws of the Various States* (New York, 1934).

25. Department of Public Markets, City of New York, Annual Report—1927 (New York: 1928), 37.

26. David Goldiss, "The New Kosher Meat Plumba," *Kosher Butcher News,* April 17, 1941, 17; Charles E. Hughes, "Kosher Meat Processing—Its Significance to the Livestock Industry," *Armour's Analysis* 2, no. 1 (April–May 1953): 5–6; State of New York, *Annual Report of the Department of Agriculture and Markets* (New York, 1954), 50.

27. *Annual Report of the Department of Agriculture and Markets* (1959), 59.

28. *Schoen v. Bernstein,* 95 N.Y.S. 2d 696.

29. Harry Kassel interview by Roger Horowitz, August 17, 2010; Press Release, Department of Agriculture and Markets, January 12, 1961, in Friedman, "Kashruth and Civil Law Enforcement," 160–62; Morris Katz, *Deception and Fraud* (Endicott, NY, 1968), 46–47.

30. Friedman, "Kashruth and Civil Law Enforcement," 123; Harry Kassel interview by Roger Horowitz, August 21, 2010.

31. *Kosher Butcher News,* January 7, 1941, 4; Joseph Belsky, *I, The Union* (New York: Raddock, 1952); 128–29.

32. *New York Times,* February 4, 1930, 10.

33. Gastwirt, *Fraud, Corruption, and Holiness,* 147–51; National Recovery Administration, "Supplementary Code of Fair Competition for the Retail Kosher Meat Trade of the United States," *Codes of Fair Competition* 2, nos. 539–43 (Washington, DC: 1935), 35–37; *National Provisioner,* January 5, 1935, 41.

34. Harry Kassel interview by Roger Horowitz, September 29, 2010.

35. Gastwirt, *Fraud, Corruption, and Holiness,* 49–54; Jeremiah J. Berman, *Shehitah: A Study in the Cultural and Social Life of the Jewish People* (New York: Bloch, 1941), 322–26.

36. Max Block and Ron Kenner, *Max the Butcher* (Lyle Stuart: Secacus, 1982), 84; Jonathan Kwitney, *Vicious Circles: The Mafia in the Workplace* (New York: Norton, 1979).

37. Harry Kassel interview by Roger Horowitz, September 29, 2012; Belsky, *I, The Union,* 127–28.

38. *New York Times,* December 5, 1936, 7; Friedman, "Kashruth and Civil Law Enforcement," 62; Amalgamated Meat Cutters, *In Honor of George Lederman* (New York, 1946), n.p.

39. Amalgamated Meat Cutters, *In Honor of George Lederman.*

40. Amalgamated Meat Cutters, "Investigation of Complaint by Members," 7 and 15, Amalgamated Meat Cutters and Butcher Workmen of North America Records, microfilm reel 502, Wisconsin Historical Society, Library-Archives Division, (henceforth Amalgamated Meat Cutters Records, WHS).

41. Seymour E. Freedman, *The Book of Kashruth* (New York: Block, 1970), 87–94; Ibid., 13.

42. Rivkay Blau, *Learn Torah, Love Torah, Live Torah: Harav Mordechai Pinchas Teitz, the Quintessential Rabbi* (Hoboken, NJ: Ktav, 2001), 208–9; *Humane Slaughtering of Livestock and Poultry: Hearings on S. 1231, S. 1497, and H.R. 8308 Before the Senate Committee on Agriculture and Forestry,* 85th Congress, 2d Sess. (1958), 346; Rabbi Seth Mandel, "A Behind the Scenes Look at the Kosher Slaughterhouse," http://program .ouradio.org/kosher/askoutreach_mandel_2_16_08.mp3 (accessed June 17, 2012).

43. Agenda, Board of Directors, Jersey City Stockyards Company, October 13, 1961, Pennsylvania Railroad Accession 18110, 292; 22, Hagley Museum and Library; "Swift to Close an Abbatoir Here in '65, Leaving Only One in City," *New York Times,* November 18, 1964; "Kosher Kill," *Cudahy Force* (July-August 1954): 2–5.

44. Harry Kassel interview by Roger Horowitz, August 17, 2010; "Zeger Applies Supermarket Methods to Wholesale Marketing," *Meat* (June 1958): 58–59.

45. *KFG,* July 1939, 12, and October 1939, 12; Federal Writers Project, "Beef in New York City," reel 137 in *Feeding the City* (1939), New York City Municipal Archives.

46. "Kosher Kill," *Cudahy Force* (July-August 1954): 3.

47. State of New York, *Annual Report of the Department of Agriculture and Markets* (New York, 1952), 55–57 [illustration 56]; State of New York, *Annual Report of the Department of Agriculture and Markets* (New York: 1956), 50–52 [illustration 50]; State of New York, Department of Agriculture and Markets, *Provisions of the Agriculture and Markets Law Relating to Sale of Kosher Meat and Foods,* 1959, circular 780; Friedman, "Kashrus and Civil Law Enforcement," 87.

48. H. Judah Hurwitz to Thomas J. Lloyd, October 3, 1960; Eliot Bernard Lloyd to Thomas J. Lloyd, June 24, 1959; Frank Davis to Patrick Gorman, September 16, 1960; all Amalgamated Meat Cutters Records, Reel 502, WHS.

49. Harry Kassel interview by Roger Horowitz, August 17, 2010.

50. *Connecticut Jewish Ledger*, January 12, 1978, 1.

51. *New York Times*, September 9, 1951, R10 and May 3, 1953, F8; Aleisa Fishman, "Keeping up with the Goldbergs: Gender, Consumer Culture, and Jewish Identity in Suburban New York, 1946–1960" (PhD diss., American University, 2004), 34.

52. Marshall Sklare and Marc Vosk, *The Riverton Study: How Jews Looks at Themselves and Their Neighbors* (New York: American Jewish Committee, 1957), 11; Stanley J. Shapiro, "Marketing of Kosher Meat," *Jewish Social Studies* 23, no. 2 (April 1961): 93.

53. Hyman Blum, "Problems of the Kosher Butcher—What Are They?" *Kosher Butcher News*, June 30, 1948, 15.

54. Friedman, "Kashruth and Civil Law Enforcement," 125.

55. Robert J. Holloway, "Kosher Meat Prices in Minneapolis," *Journal of Marketing* 18 (July 1953): 288; Shapiro, "Marketing of Kosher Meat," 99; Friedman, "Kashruth and Civil Law Enforcement," 125–26.

56. Shapiro, "Marketing of Kosher Meat," 105.

57. Jerome Luks, "Industry Support of Kashruth," *New York Governor's Conference for the Kosher Food Industry* (New York, 1988), 92.

58. *New York Times*, December 28, 1964, 39; King Kullen advertisement, *New York Times*, June 28, 1981, L19; Value-Plus Self-Service Kosher Meats advertisement, *New York Times*, May 27, 1981, C8.

59. Abraham W. Smith to Joseph Belsky, August 28, 1973, Amalgamated Meat Cutters Records, Reel 455, WHS; *New York Times*, December 28, 1964, 39; I. A. Fogel, "Amalgamated Butcher Union on the Threshold of Total Re-Structuring," *Jewish Daily Forward*, November 10, 1977, in Amalgamated Meat Cutters Records, Reel 315, WHS.

60. George Getschow, "Strictly Kosher," *Wall Street Journal*, May 11, 1976; Temple Grandin, "Kosher Beef Kill," *Meat Industry* (May 1977): 36–38; Harry Kassel interview by Roger Horowitz, August 17, 2010.

61. Rabbi H. M. Plottzky, "The True Meaning of Glatt Kosher," *Kashrus Newsletter* (April 1981): 5–7; Rabbi Ari Z. Zivotsky, *Jewish Action* (Winter 1990); "What Makes Meat Kosher," http://rabbikaganoff.com/archivres/18; Mandel, "A Behind the Scenes Look at the Kosher Slaughterhouse."

62. Harry Kassel interview by Roger Horowitz, August 17, 2010.

63. Harry Kassel interview by Roger Horowitz, August 17, 2010.

64. Harry Kassel interview by Roger Horowitz, September 29, 2010.

65. Harry Kassel interview by Roger Horowitz, September 29, 2010.

66. Harry Kassel interview by Roger Horowitz, August 17, 2010.

67. Harry Kassel interview by Roger Horowitz, August 17, 2010.

68. Orthodox Union, *Kosher Products Directory* (New York, 1983), 40–2; Orthodox Union, *Kosher Products Directory* (New York: 1984), 5; Orthodox Union, *Kosher For Passover Products Directory* (New York: 1990), 58; Mandel, "A Behind the Scenes Look at the Kosher Slaughterhouse."

69. In 1972, for example, the Satmar Hasidim built a new two-thousand-square-foot butcher shop on Williamsburg Street West in Brooklyn to supply members of its group with Beis Joseph glatt. Gerald Lieberman, "Kosher Food Gets Boost from Zoning Action," *New York Times*, September 24, 1972, 135.

70. Advertisement, "Little Neck Meats 21st Anniversary Sale," *New York Times*, May 29, 1981; "Rabbis Suing Times on Kosher-Bill Ad," *New York Times*, March 16, 1966, 5; Rachel Benzwanger, "Inside the Vaad: The Vaad Harabonim of Queens," *Kashrus Magazine* (September 1990): 24.

71. Harry Kassel interviews by Roger Horowitz, August 17, 2010, and September 29, 2010.

72. Orthodox Union, *Kosher for Passover Products Directory* (New York, 1982) 28–29; Orthodox Union, *Kosher Products Directory* (New York: 1983), 40–42.

73. State of New York, Department of Agriculture and Markets, Circular 811, *Provisions of Agriculture and Market Law Relative to Sale of Kosher Meat and Foods* (Albany, 1988).

74. Circular 811; Remarks by Robert Abrams, attorney general, *Governor's Conference for the Kosher Food Industry*.

75. State of New York, Department of Agriculture and Markets, *Annual Report—1959* (Albany, 1961), 24; Press Release, Department of Agriculture and Markets, August 8, 1960, in Friedman, "Kashruth and Civil Law Enforcement," 160–62; Harry Kassel interview by Roger Horowitz, August 17, 2010.

76. State of New York, Department of Agriculture and Markets, *Annual Report—1976* (Albany, 1977), 11; State of New York, Department of Agriculture and Markets, *Annual Report—1977* (Albany, 1978), 7; State of New York, Department of Agriculture and Markets, *Annual Report—1983* (Albany, 1984), 29; State of New York, Department of Agriculture and Markets, *Annual Report—1992* (Albany, 1993), 28; averages computed from State of New York, Department of Agriculture and Markets annual reports, 1946–2002.

77. Ben Gallob, "Intensive Probe Underway in N.Y. Against Kosher Food Fraud," *Jewish Telegraph Agency*, December 24, 1984; "N.Y.C. Firm Fined over $1 Million for Mislabelling Non-kosher Meat as Kosher, *Jewish Telegraph Agency*, April 17, 1986; *State of New York v. Rachleff Kosher Provisions*, 188 A.D, 2d 458 [2d Department 1992].

78. Deborah M. D'Agostino to Commack Self-Service Kosher Meats Inc. September 29, 1986; Jeffrey Yarmeisch to Department of Agriculture and Markets, October 6, 1986. Documents pertaining to *State of New York v. Commack Self-Service Kosher Meats, Inc.* are from the case file held by the U.S. Circuit Court of Appeals, Docket Nos. 00–9116 and 00–9118.

79. Deborah M. D'Agostino to Commack Self-Service Kosher Meats Inc. March 27, 1987; Verified Complaint; Jeff Yarmeisch to Legal Bureau, Department of Agriculture and Markets, April 29, 1987.

80. Deborah M. D'Agostino to Commack Self-Service Kosher Meats Inc. October 26, 1988; Rabi William Berman to Deborah M. D'Agostino, November 3, 1988;

Rabbi Rubin to Michael McCormick, August 3, 1989; Earl S. Roberts to Michael McComick, November 24, 1989; *People v. Commack Self-Service Kosher Meats, Inc.* Verified Complaint, December 12, 1989; *State of New York Against Commack Self Service Kosher Meats, Inc.* Demand for Bill of Particulars," May 3, 1990; Brian Yarmeisch to Department of Agriculture Kosher Law Enforcement, December 1, 1992.

81. Earl S. Roberts to Michael McCormick, November 24, 1989, and August 15, 1990; Brian Yarmeisch to Department of Agriculture Kosher Law Enforcement, December 1, 1992; *Commack Self-Service Kosher Meats, Inc. vs. Rabbi Schulem Rubin et al*, CV 96–0179, Amended Complaint, 20.

82. Kosher Food Inspection Report, February 23, 1993, for Commack Self Service Kosher Mts Inc.; Floor Plan, Commack Kosher Meats, April 14, 1999; State of New York, Department of Agriculture and Markets, Circular 811 *Provisions of Agriculture and Market Law Relative to Sale of Kosher Meat and Foods* (Albany, 1988), 201-a; Commack Self-Service Kosher Meats, Inc. vs. Rabbi Schulem Rubin et al., CV 96–0179, Amended Complaint, 11–14.

83. *Ran-Dav's Kosher Kitchen v. State of New Jersey,* 129 N.J. 141; *Commack Self-Service Kosher Meats Inc. v. Rabbi Shulem Rubin,* 106 F. Supp. 2d 445, 2000 U.S. Dist.; *Commack Self-Service Kosher Meats Inc. v. Rabbi Luzer Weiss* 294 F. 3d 415, 2002 U.S. App.; *Rabbi Luzer Weiss v. Commack Self-Service Kosher Meats, Inc.* 537 U.S. 1187.

84. *National Provisioner,* October 25, 1952, 31; James J. Nagle, "Tastes Widening for Kosher Food," *New York Times,* November 6, 1960, F10.

85. Yosef Wikler, "Inside Hebrew National," *Kashrus Newsletter,* December 1984, 1, 39; *New York Times,* August 5, 1968, 58; *New York Times,* February 13, 1976, 59; *New York Times,* December 18, 1979, D2; Miriam Colton and Steven I. Weiss, "Hebrew National Certified Kosher—But Not Kosher Enough for Some," *Forward,* June 11, 2004.

8. *SHECHITA*

1. Francis H. Rowley, *Slaughter-House Reform in the United States and the Opposing Forces* (Boston: Massachusetts Society for the Prevention of Cruelty to Animals, 1913).

2. Ibid., 13; Robin Judd, "The Politics of Beef: Animal Advocacy and the Kosher Butchering Debates in Germany, *Jewish Society Studies,* n.s., 10, no. 1 (Fall 2003): 117–50.

3. Robin Judd, *Contested Rituals: Circumcision, Kosher Butchering, and Jewish Political Life in Germany, 1843–1833* (Ithaca: Cornell University Press, 2007), 202–10, quotes 205.

4. Emily Stewart Leavitt et al., *Animals and Their Legal Rights* (New York: Animal Welfare Institute, 1968), 34–35; "Look, No Shackles, No Bruised Hams," *National Provisioner* April 14, 1956.

5. Many letters to the Senate and House committees considering humane slaughter legislation simply attached copies of this flyer. "Facts About Your Meat," Humane Society of the United States (n.d.), NARA RG 46, Sen. 84-E1, S. 1497, 60, 1.

6. Leavitt et al., *Animals and Their Legal Rights,* 39; see, for example, *Regulations Governing Meat Inspection of the United States Department of Agriculture* (May 1, 1908), https://archive.org/details/regulationsgovero3unit; *Regulations Governing the Meat Inspection of the United States Department of Agriculture* (November 1, 1922), http://ufdc.ufl.edu/AA00019023/00001; *Regulations Governing the Meat Inspection of the United States Department of Agriculture* (January 1947), http://babel.hathitrust.org/cgi/pt?id=mdp.39015004973494;view=1up;seq=5 (accessed May 17, 2013).

7. *Humane Slaughtering of Livestock and Poultry: Hearings on S. 1231, S. 1497, and H.R. 8308 Before the Senate Comm. on Agriculture and Forestry,* 85th Congress, 2d Sess. (1958), 348.

8. *S. 1497, A Bill to require the use of humane methods in the slaughter of livestock and poultry in interstate and foreign commerce, and for other purposes,* introduced March 5, 1957, Hubert H. Humphrey Papers—Senate Correspondence, 150.B.9.4F, box 46, MHS.

9. *Humane Slaughtering of Livestock and Poultry: Hearings on S. 1636 Before a Sub-comm. of the Comm. on Agriculture and Forestry,* 84th Congress, 2d Sess. 138 (1956), 141, 144, 143.

10. *Humane Slaughter: Hearings Before the Subcommittee on Livestock and Grains of the House Comm. on Agriculture,* 85th Congress, 1st Sess. (1957), 28, 109.

11. Leo Pfeffer to Congressman W. R. Poage, January 29, 1958, Hubert H. Humphrey Papers—Senate Correspondence, 150.B.9.4F, box 46, Minnesota Historical Society. In this letter Pfeffer stated he was representing the positions of the Rabbinical Assembly of America, the United Synagogues of America (both Conservative), the Central Conference of American Rabbis, and the American Hebrew Congregations (both Reform).

12. New York Times, May 4, 1958, 84; *Humane Slaughtering of Livestock and Poultry: Hearings on S. 1231, S. 1497, and H.R. 8308 Before the Senate Comm. on Agriculture and Forestry,* 85th Congress, 2d Sess. (1958), 156, 200, 149.

13. New York Times, May 4, 1958, 84; *Humane Slaughtering of Livestock and Poultry: Hearings on S. 1231, S. 1497, and H.R. 8308 Before the Senate Comm. on Agriculture and Forestry,* 85th Congress, 2d Sess. (1958), 223. Therese Ann Olson to Allen J. Ellender, May 5, 1958, NARA RG 46, Sen. 84-E1, 64; 2. William E. Milligan to Allen Ellender, July 9, 1956, NARA RG 46, Sen. 84-E1, 61, 6.

14. Emily Steward Leavitt, *Animals and Their Legal Rights* (New York: Animal Welfare Institute: 1970), 36–37, vii; R. L. Farrington to Allen Ellender, May 13, 1958, NARA RG 46, Sen. 85-E1, S. 1497 64, 2.

15. Moses I. Feuerstein to President Eisenhower, August 20, 1958, UOJCA Records, 2; 1, AJHS.

16. "The Meat You Eat Is Seared with Pain," *New York Times*, December 27, 1965, 12 and January 8, 1966; "This Is Slaughter of Conscious Animals," *New York Times*, March 17, 1967, 29.

17. "This Is Slaughter of Conscious Animals."

18. "I Was Shocked . . . " *New York Times*, January 21, 1966, 14; "Two Slaughter Bills Stir Controversy," *New York Times*, January 18, 1967, 26.

19. Temple Grandin, "Kosher Beef Kill," *Meat Industry* (May 1977): 36–38; Temple Grandin, "Humanitarian Aspects of *Shehitah* in the United States," *Judaism* 39 (1990): 438.

20. Temple Grandin, "Problems with Kosher Slaughter," *International Journal for the Study of Animal Problems* 1, no. 6 (1980): 383–84.

21. Grandin, "Kosher Beef Kill," 36, and "Humanitarian Aspects of *Shehitah*," 439–40.

22. "Spencer Smoothes Kosher Kill with 200 Hear per Hour System," *Meat Industry* (August 1980): 54; U.S. Patent 3,657,767 51, Apr, 25, 1972 CATTLE HANDLING APPARATUS, inventor: Carl Oscar Schmidt, Jr., Cincinnati, Ohio. Assignee: The Cincinnati Butchers Supply Company, Cincinnati, Ohio; Temple Grandin, "Double Rail Restrainer Conveyor for Livestock Handling," *Journal of Agriculture and Engineering Research* 41 (1988): 327–38, quote 327.

23. Temple Grandin, "The Way It's Meant to Be," *Meat and Poultry* (September 1991): 107; "Humane Methods of Kosher Slaughter," with Joe Regenstein, *Kashrus Magazine* (June 1992): 32.

24. Grandin, "Humanitarian Aspects of *Shehitah*," 441; Joe M. and Carrie E. Regenstein, "Looking In," *Kashrus Magazine* (December 1992): 34; Rabbi Moshe Edelstein, "Shehita Pens," *Kashrus Magazine* (September 1992): 52.

25. Genack quote from *JewishJournal.com*, September 17, 2008, http://www.jewish journal.com/food/article/peta_hidden_camera_expose_costs_agriprocessors _support_of_key_expert_video (accessed November 13, 2014); Michael Lesy, *The Forbidden Zone* (New York: Farrar, Straus and Giroux, 1987), 127–28.

26. Ben Wolfson, "Kosher Slaughter," *Mishpaha* 364:16–17, from http://www.grandin .com/ritual/kosher.slaughter.html.

27. 768 Federal 2nd District 1463, decided July 26, 1985, as amended August 15, 1985.

28. 768 Federal 2nd District 1463; *Daily Reporter* (Spencer, IA), March 3, 1982, 1 and May 3, 1984, 1.

29. *Kashrus Magazine* (December 1992): 35 and (November 1993): 44; Joe Regenstein interview by Roger Horowitz.

30. *Kashrus Magazine* (December 1992): 35; Yossie Bar-Moha, "Onward Conquistadors," *Ha'aretz Magazine*, September 25, 1998, translation available at http://www .grandin.com/ritual/kosher.meat.uruguay.html.

31. Harry Kassel interview by Roger Horowitz, August 17, 2010.

32. Nathaniel Popper, "How the Rubashkins Changed the Way Jews Eat in America," *Jewish Forward,* December 12, 2008; Stephen G. Bloom, *Postville: A Clash of Cultures in Heartland America* (New York: Harcourt, 2000), 254.

33. *Kashrus Magazine* (September 1992): 52.

34. *Kashrus Magazine* (June 1992): 33.

35. Grandin, "Humanitarian Aspects of *Shehitah*," 442–43.

36. Rabbi Moshe Edelstein, "*Shechita* Pens: The Self-Perpetuating Controversy," *Kashrus Magazine* (September 1992): 52–53; Temple Grandin and Joe Regenstein, "Religious Slaughter and Animal Welfare: A Discussion for Meat Scientists," *Meat Focus International* (March 1994): 115–23; I. M. Levinger, *Shechita in the Light of the Year 2000* (Jerusalem: Maskil L'David, 1995), 26–28.

37. Bloom, *Postville*, xi–xii.

38. *United States of America, plaintiff, vs. Sholom Rubashkin, defendant,* Sentencing Memorandum by Judge Linda R. Reade, 718 Federal Supp. 2d District 953, also 2010 U.S. District Lexis 61996; "Historic Cattle Prices," *Ag Decision Maker* (Iowa State University Extension and Outreach, March 2013), table 1, www.extension .iastate.edu/agdm; *United States of America, plaintiff, vs. Sholom Rubashkin, defendant,* Opinion by Judge Linda R. Reade, 2010 U.S. District LEXIS 18709.

39. http://www.foxnews.com/story/2004/12/01/peta-kosher-slaughterhouse-abusing-animals (accessed October 13, 2014).

40. http://www.jewishpress.com/indepth/the-assault-on-*shechita*/2004/12/15/ (accessed October 15, 2014); *Daily Forward*, December 4, 2004; Rabbi Menachem Genack, "Setting the Record Straight on Kosher Slaughter," *Daf HaKashrus* (January 2005): 7–9.

41. http://www.grandin.com/ritual/qa.cattle.insensibility.html (accessed November 3, 2014).

42. Jane A. Parish, Justin D. Rhinehard, and James M. Martin, *Beef Grades and Carcass Information, Mississippi Extension Service Publication 2522* (Mississippi State University, 2009); G. C. Lamb and L. Schott, "Targeting a Branded Beef Program," www.mmbeef.umn/edu/cow-calf/2007/pl.pdf (accessed October 27, 2014).

43. Roger Horowitz, *"Negro and White, Unite and Fight": A Social History of Industrial Unionism in Meatpacking, 1930–1990* (Urbana: University of Illinois Press, 1997), 274; Bloom, *Postville*, 134, 141.

44. Jerry Kammer, *The 2006 Swift Raids: Assessing the Impact of Immigration Enforcement Actions at Six Facilities* (Washington, DC: Center for Immigration Studies, March 2009), 15–19; Bureau of Labor Statistics, *Occupational Employment and Wages, May 2006: 51–3023 Slaughters and Meatpackers.*

45. *United States of America, plaintiff, vs. Sholom Rubashkin, defendant,* Sentencing Memorandum by Judge Linda R. Reade, 718 Federal Supp. 2d District 953, also 2010 U.S. District Lexis 61996; *Washington Post* May 18, 2008, 1.

46. Nathaniel Popper, "In Iowa Meat Plant, Kosher 'Jungle' Breeds Fear, Injury, Short Pay," *Daily Forward*, May 26, 2006; Kammer, *2006 Swift Raids*; Jerry Kammer, *Immigration Raids at Smithfield* (Washington, DC: Center for Immigration Studies, July 2009).

47. *United States of America, plaintiff, vs. Sholom Rubashkin, defendant,* opinion by Judge Linda R. Reade, 2010 U.S. District LEXIS 18709.

48. *United States of America, plaintiff, vs. Sholom Rubashkin, defendant,* Order for Detention by Judge Jon Stuart Scoles, 2008 U.S. District Lexis 96569.

49. *Washington Post,* May 18, 2008, 1; Popper, "In Iowa Meat Plant"; Bloom, *Postville,* 233.

50. Case No. 09-CV-1013-Lrr, 691 F. Supp. 2nd District 932; 2010 U.S. Dist. LEXIS 20483, decided March 8, 2010.

51. http://www.youtube.com/watch?v=VAU9DD24uUk (accessed November 10, 2014); Ben Harris, "PETA Hidden Camera expose costs Agriprocessor Support of Key Expert," *Jewish Journal.com,* September 17, 2008, http://www.jewishjournal.com /food/article/peta_hidden_camera_expose_costs_agriprocessors_support_of_key _expert_video (accessed November 13, 2014); Lynda Waddington, "Slaughter Expert Calls Agriprocessor's 'Sloppy.'" *Iowa Independent,* September 11, 2008, http://www .peta.org/features/agriprocessors?#ixzz32BuwhJe9 (accessed November 13, 2014).

CONCLUSION

1. http://www.jewishvirtuallibrary.org/jsource/Judaism/pittsburgh_program.html (accessed January 13, 2015).

2. Charles and Bertie G. Schwartz, *Faith Through Reason* (New York: Macmillan, 1947), 143, 148.

3. Jody Myers, "Orthodox Rabbinic Discourse on Kosher Meat Slaughtering," paper delivered at the 2014 Association for Jewish Studies conference, citing Moshe Feinstein, *Igrot Moshe, Even Ha-ezer,* vol. 4, no. 92.

4. Avi Shafran, "Magen Tzedek Seal Engaging in a Kashrut Cover-up," *Jewish Telegraph Agency,* May 12, 2011.

5. http://www.vosizneias.com/110717/2012/07/26/new-york-report-kosher -restaurants-threatened-because-of-ethical-certification/.

6. Julie Wiener, "A Market for Ethical Kosher?" *Jewish Weekly,* September 15, 2009.

7. "Bundling Audits," *Supermarket News* (Summer 2012).

8. Steve Lipman, "Good Enough to Eat, Ritually and Ethically, *New York Jewish Week,* February 7, 2012; Morris J. Allen, "A Culture of Kashrut," *Sh'ma* (September 2009).

9. http://chowhound.chow.com/topics/570872.

10. Andy Altman-Ohr, "Urban Adamah Slaughters Chickens in Private," May 22, 2014, http://www.jweekly.com/article/full/71688/urban-adamah-slaughters-chickens -in-private/ and comments December 3, 2014, http://www.jweekly.com/blog/full /71688/urban-adamah-slaughters-chickens-in-private/.

11. *Hazon Food Guide and Food Audit Toolkit* (New York: Hazon, 2011), 7, 11.

EPILOGUE

1. E. P. Thompson, *The Making of the English Working Class* (New York: Random House, 1963), 12.

INDEX

ARTS AND TRADITIONS OF THE TABLE
PERSPECTIVES ON CULINARY HISTORY

....

ALBERT SONNENFELD, SERIES EDITOR